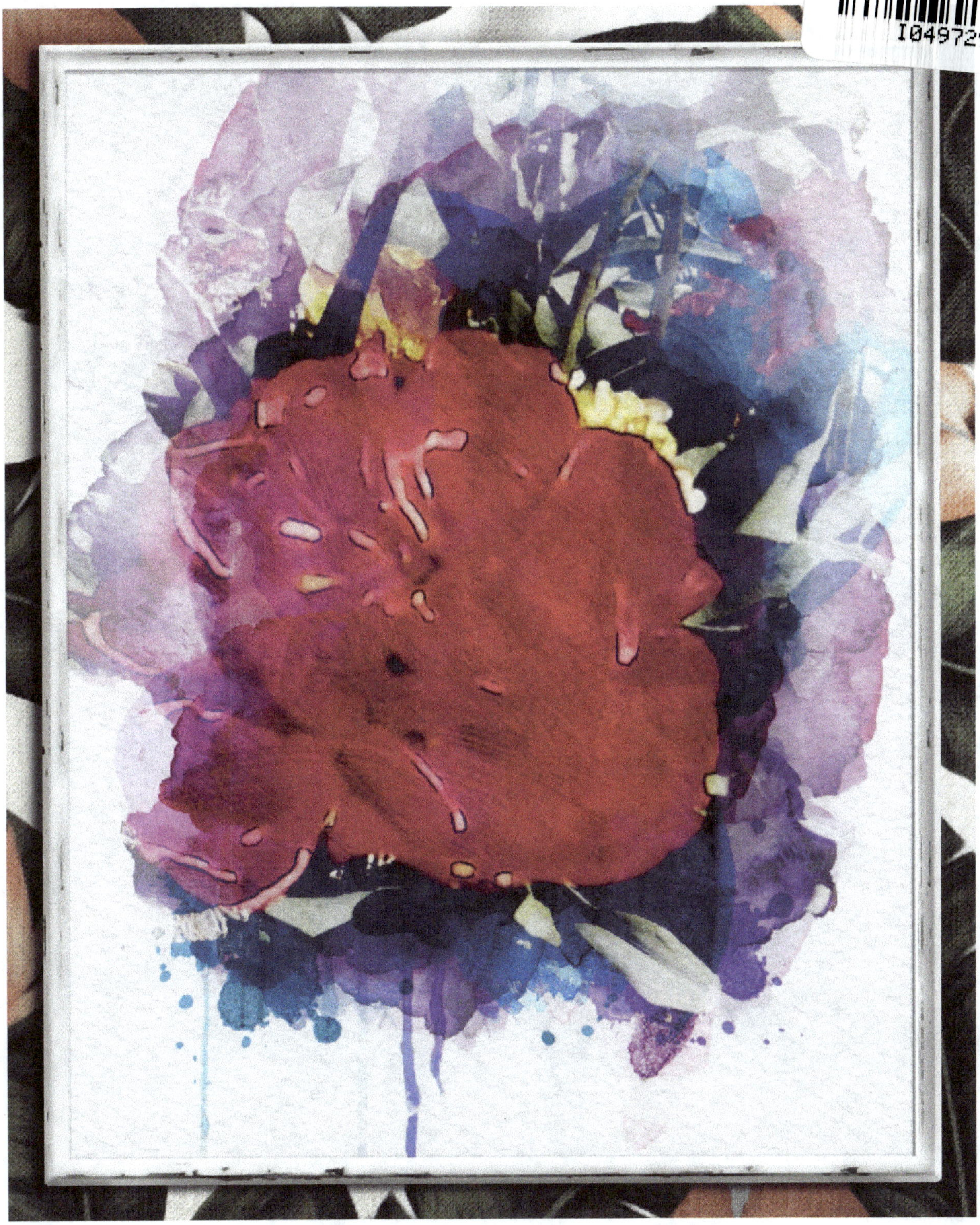

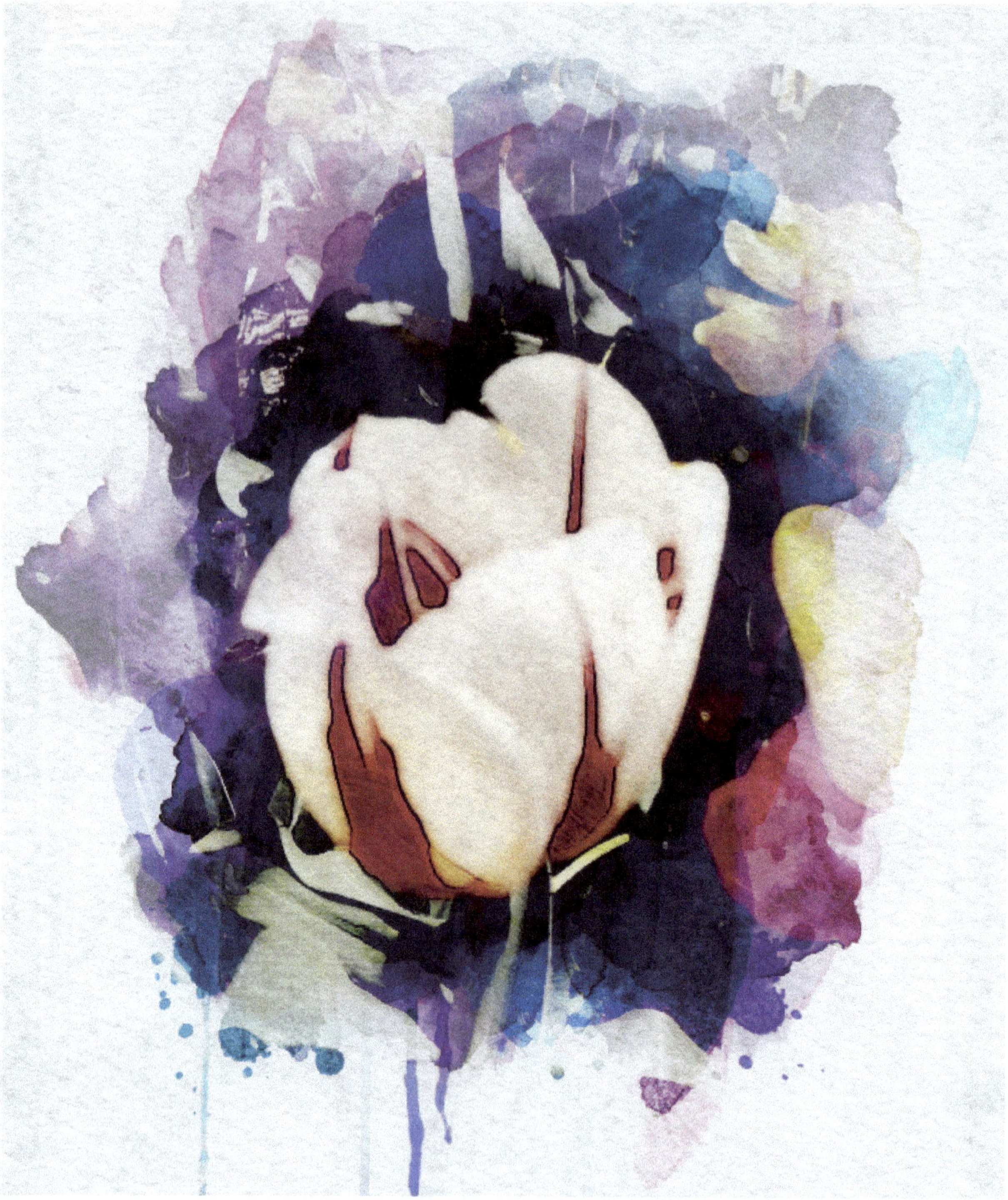

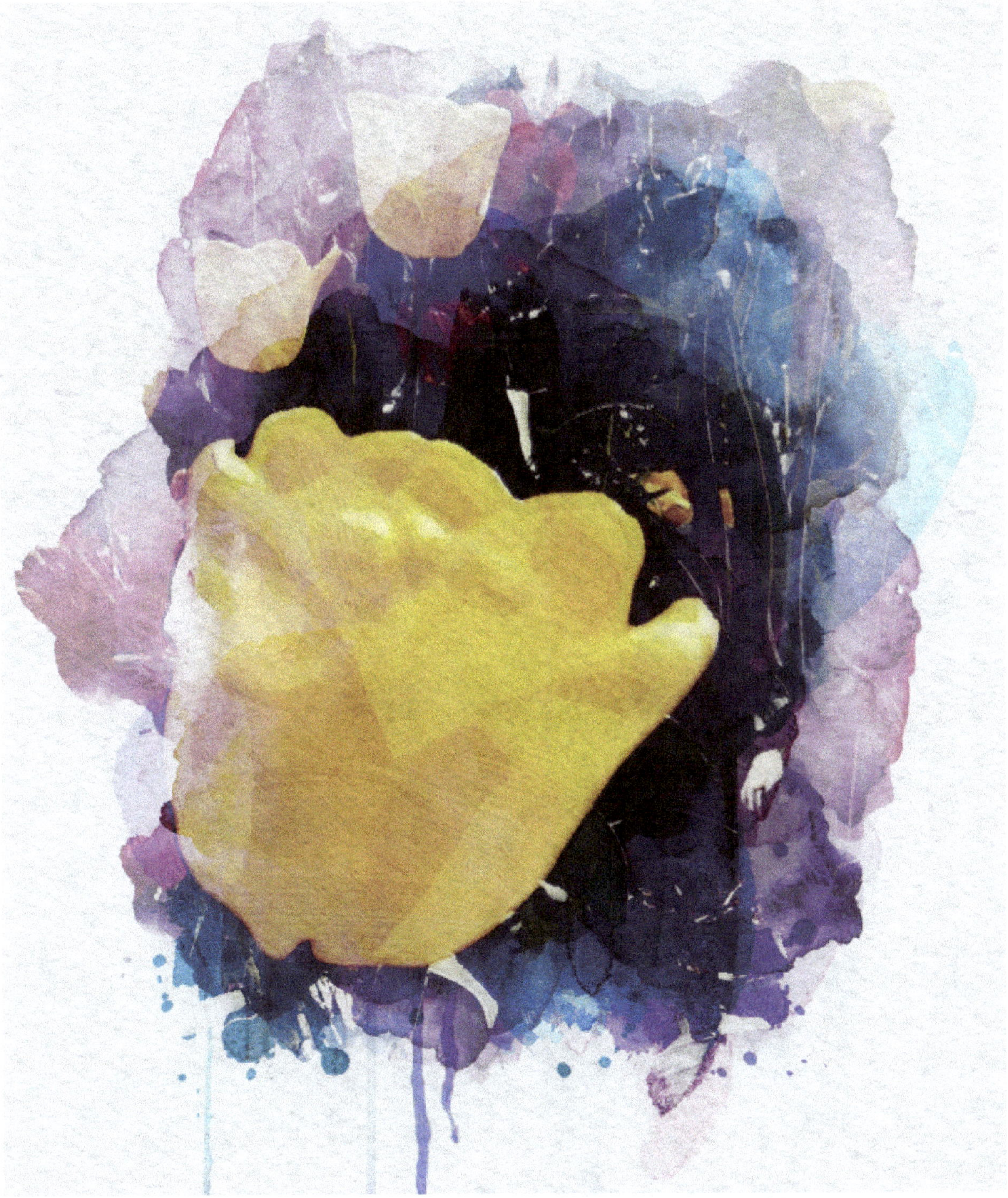

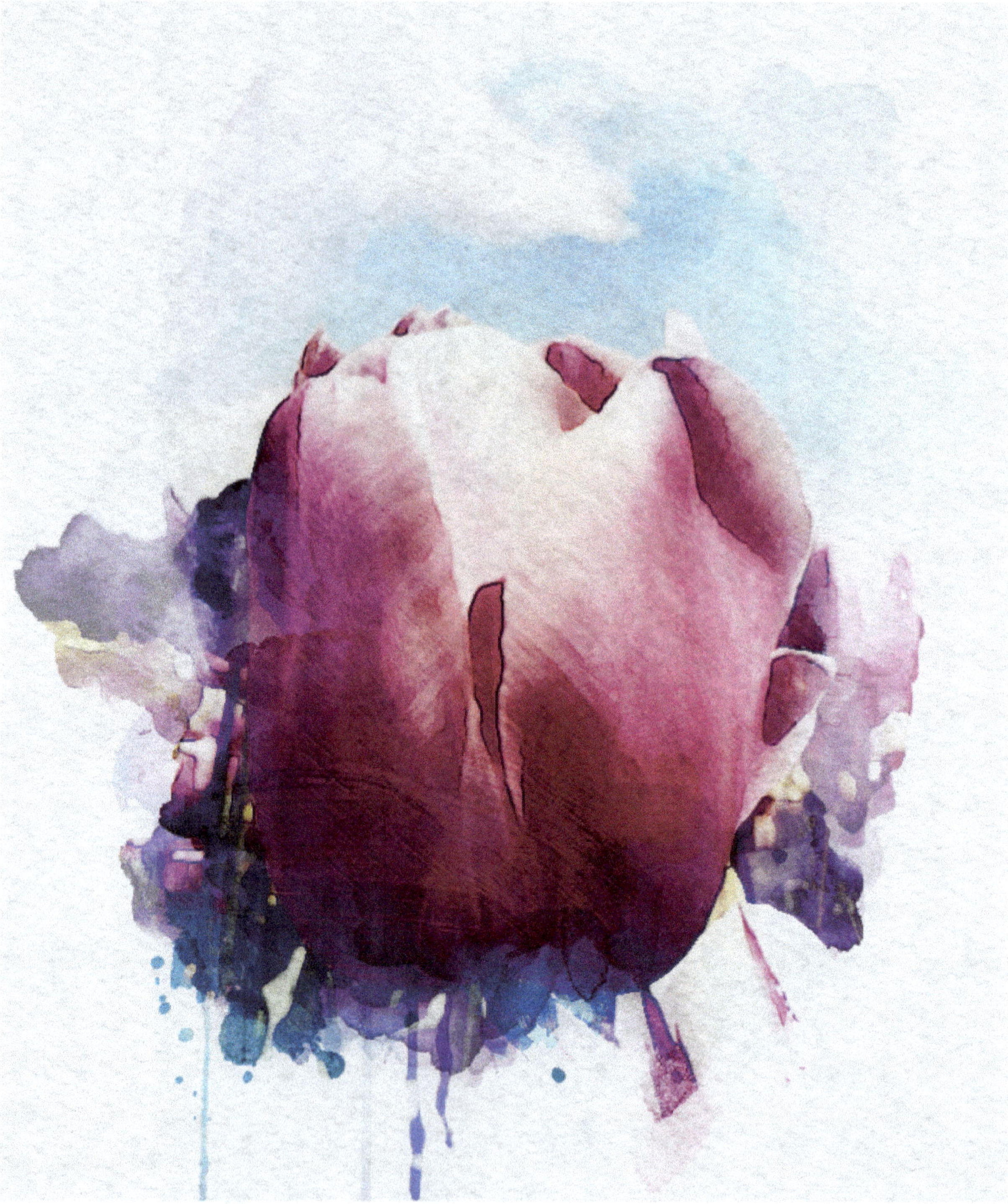

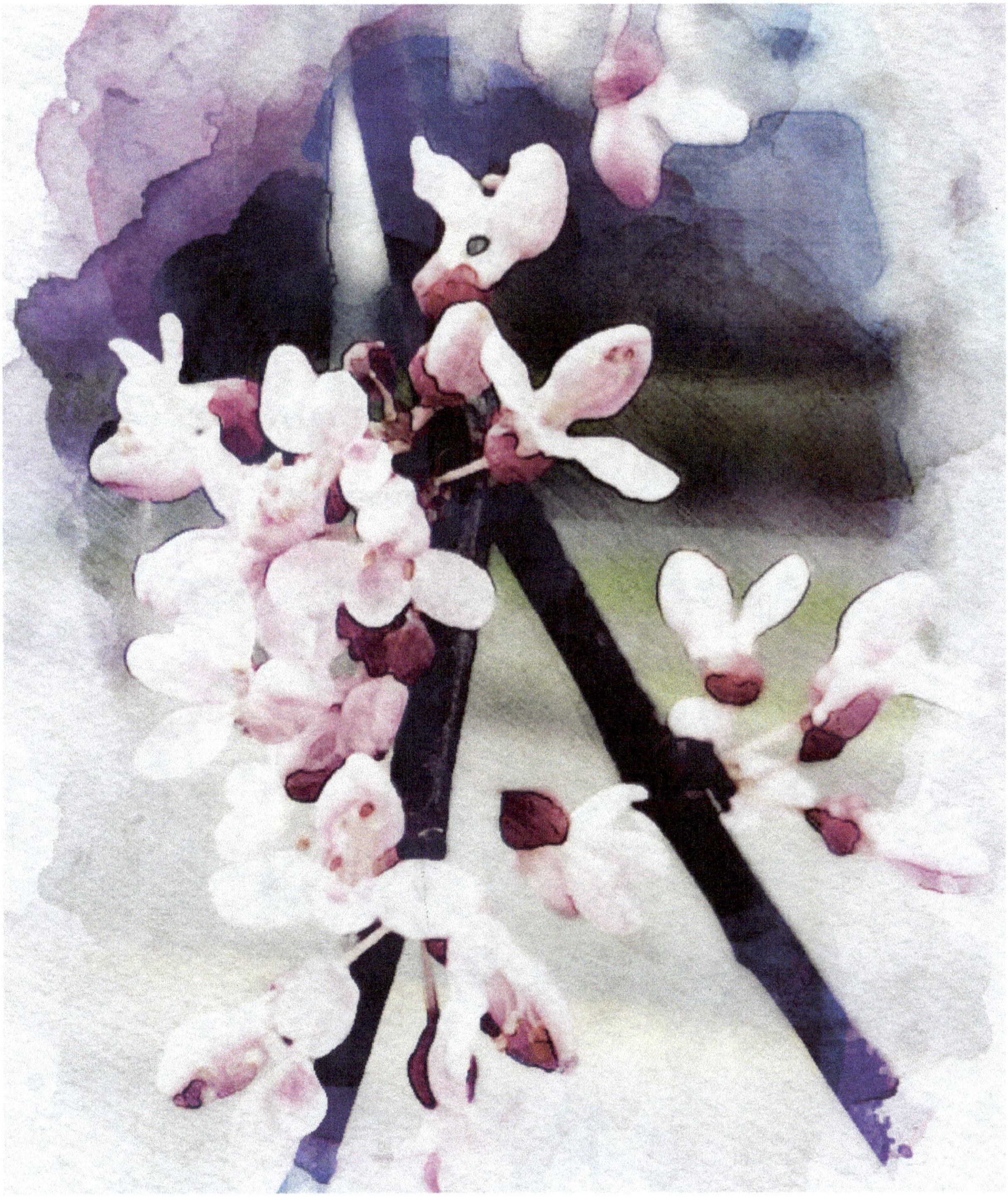

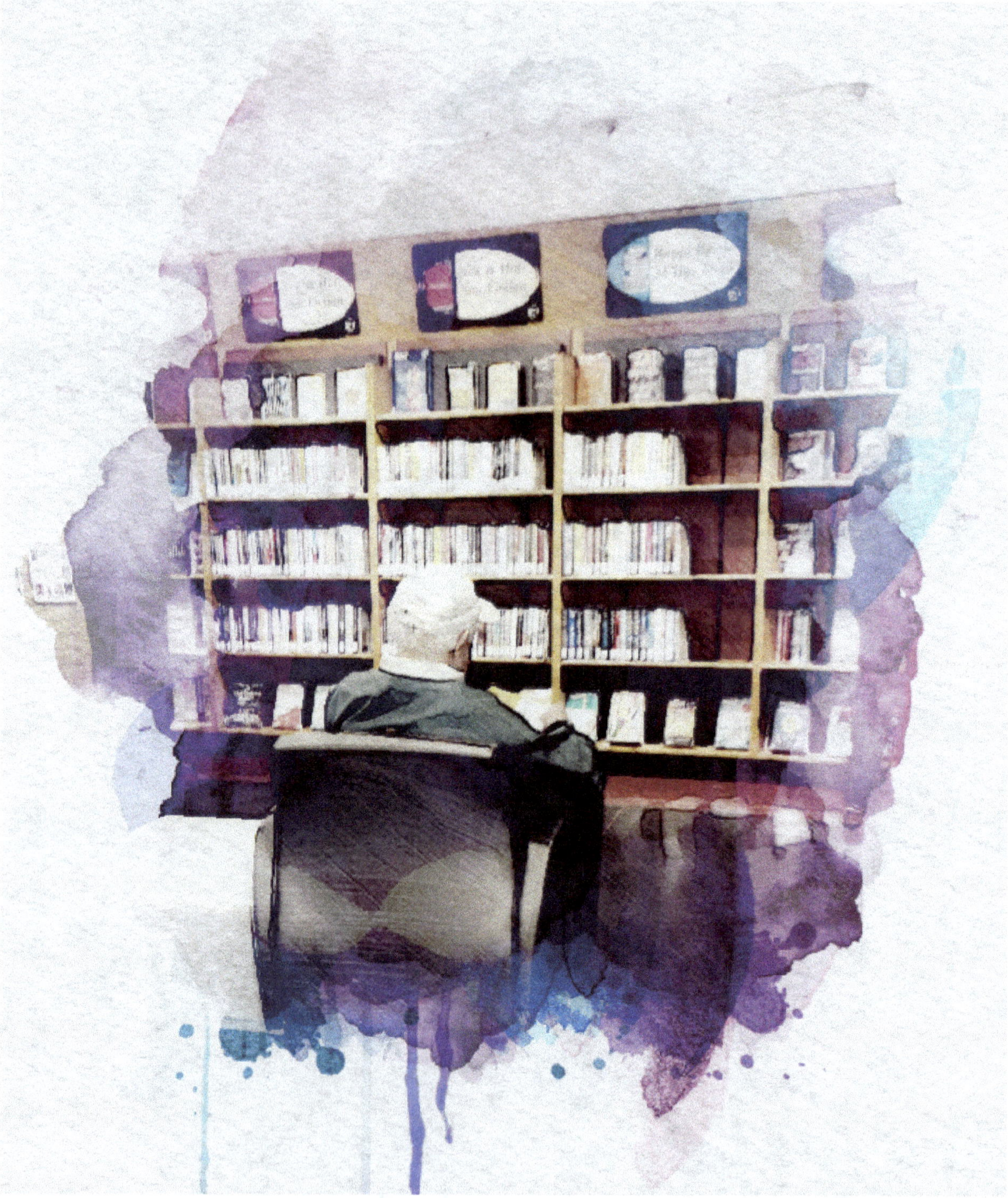

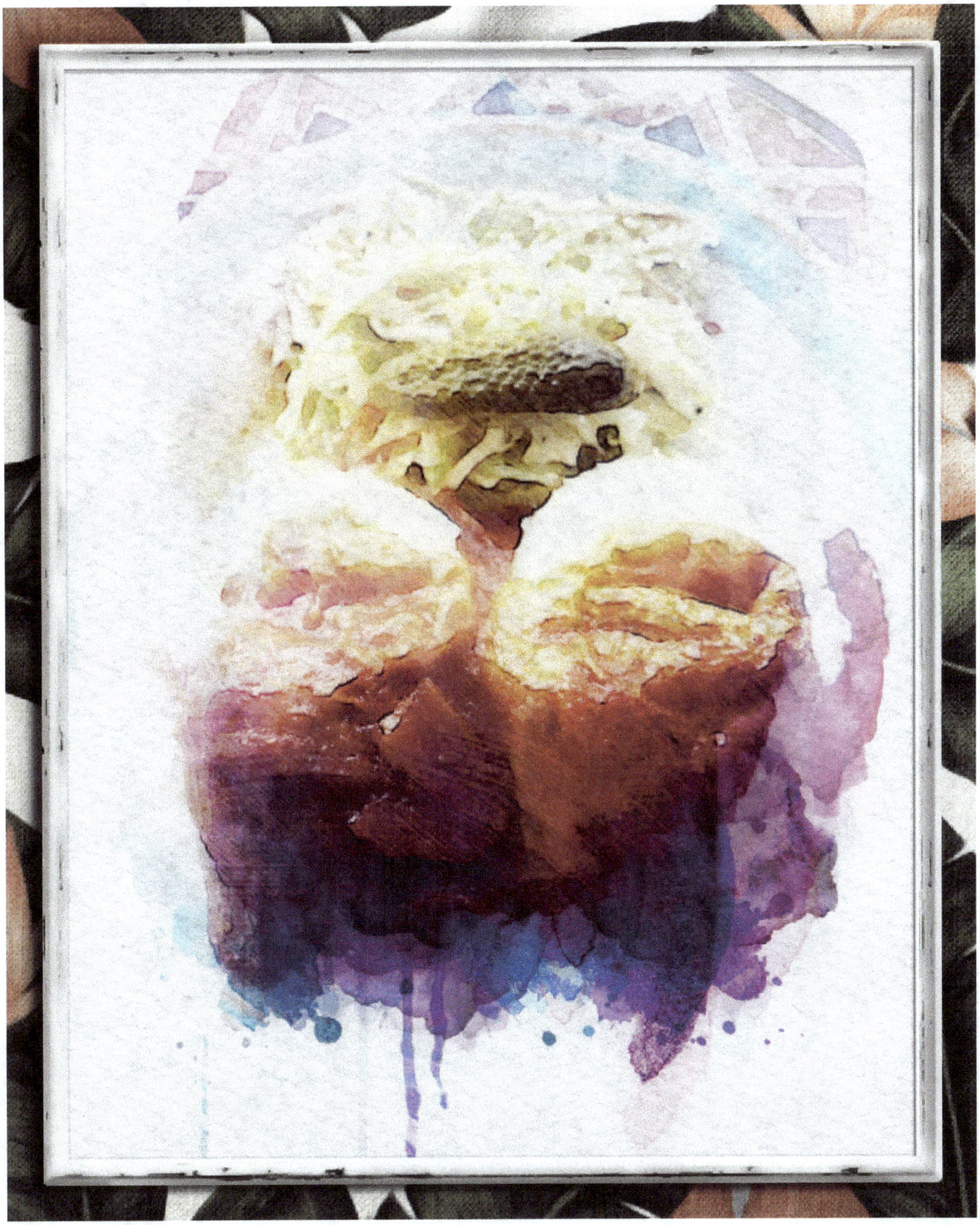

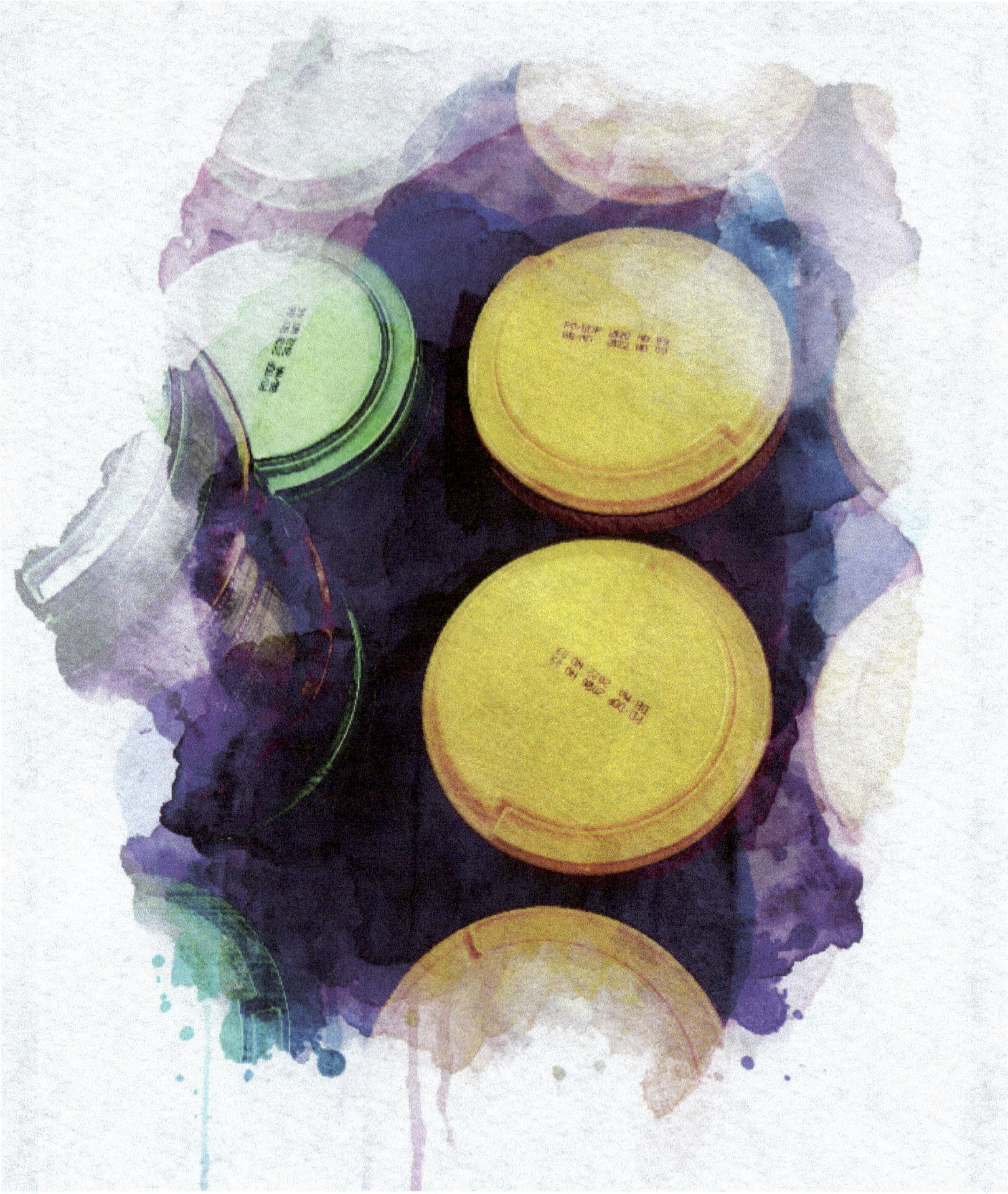

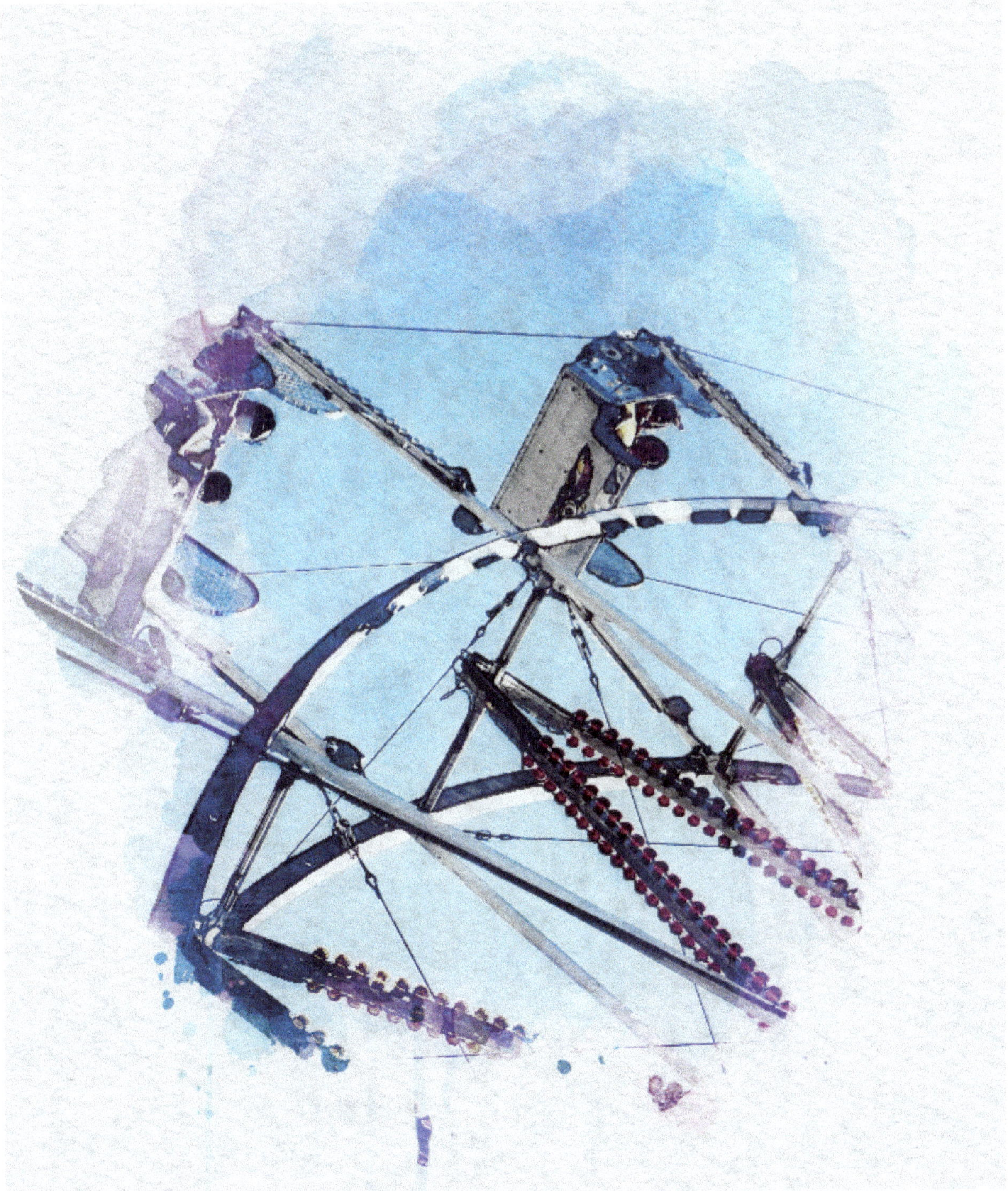

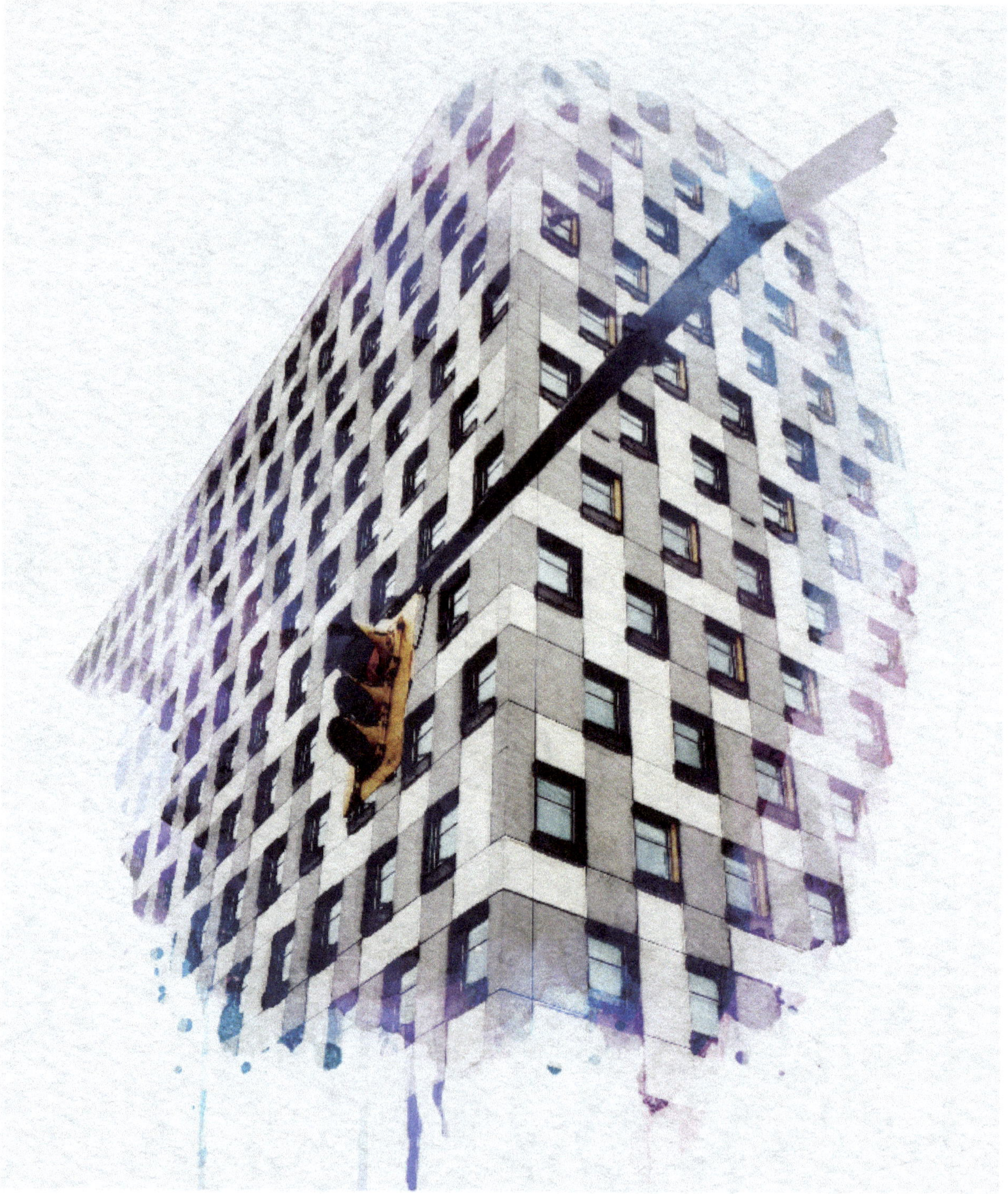

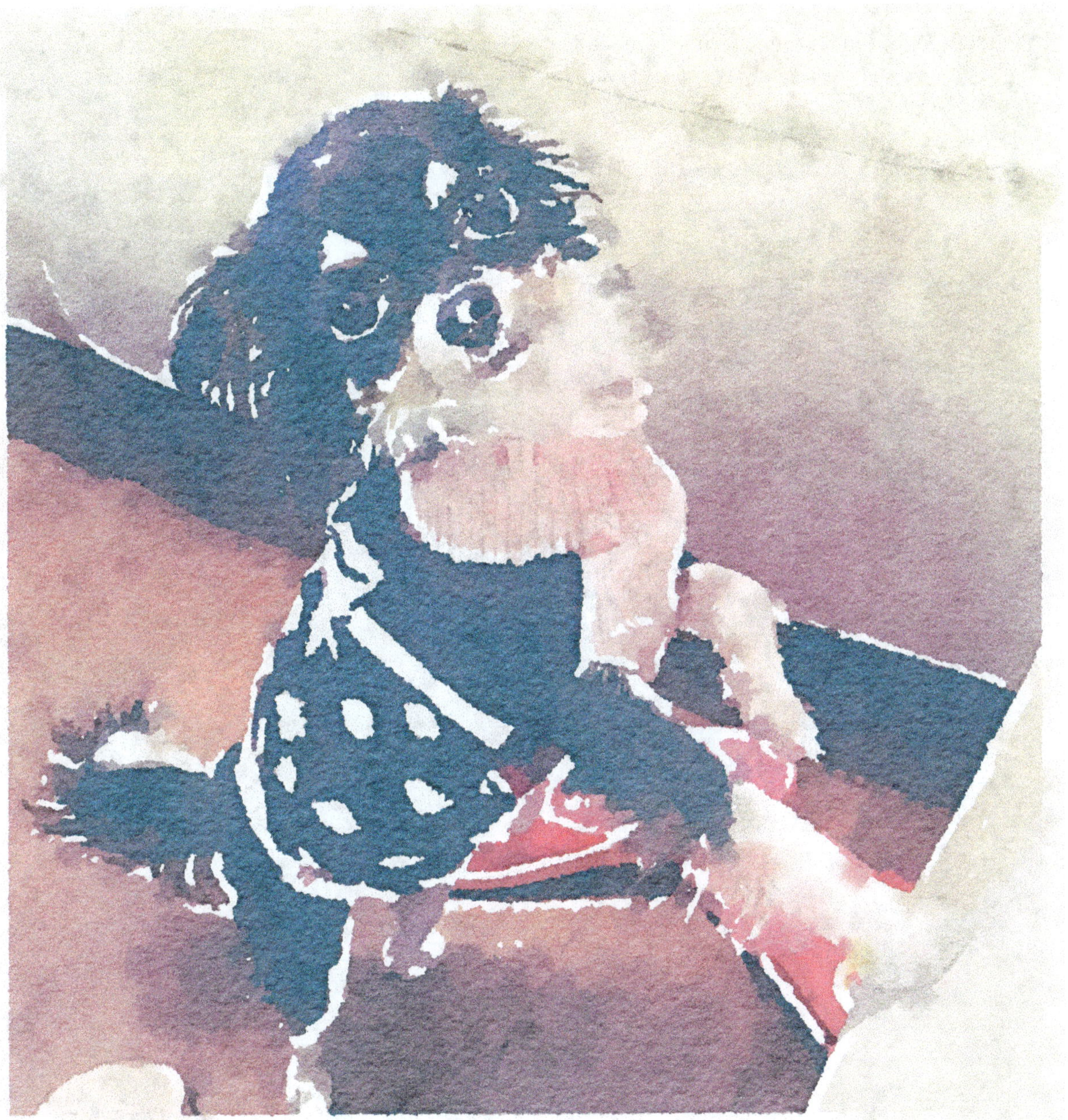

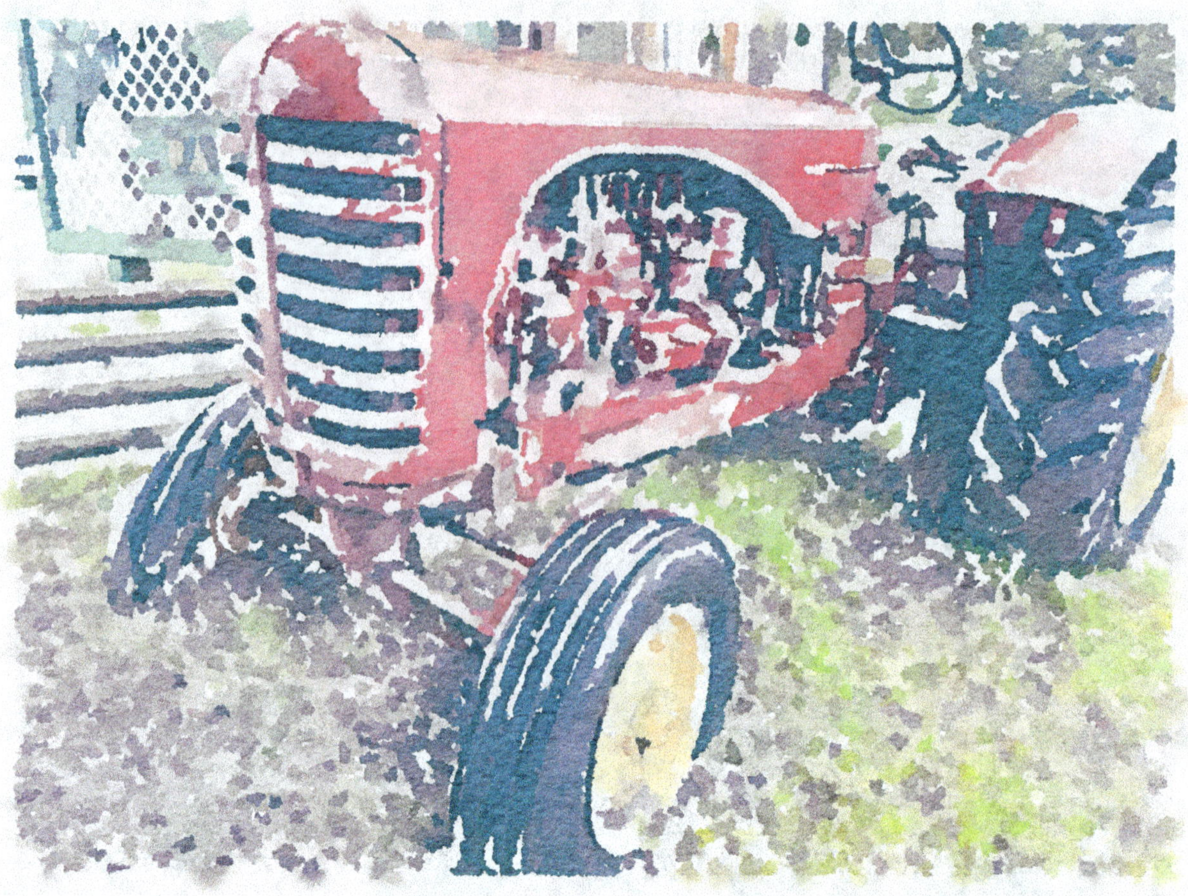

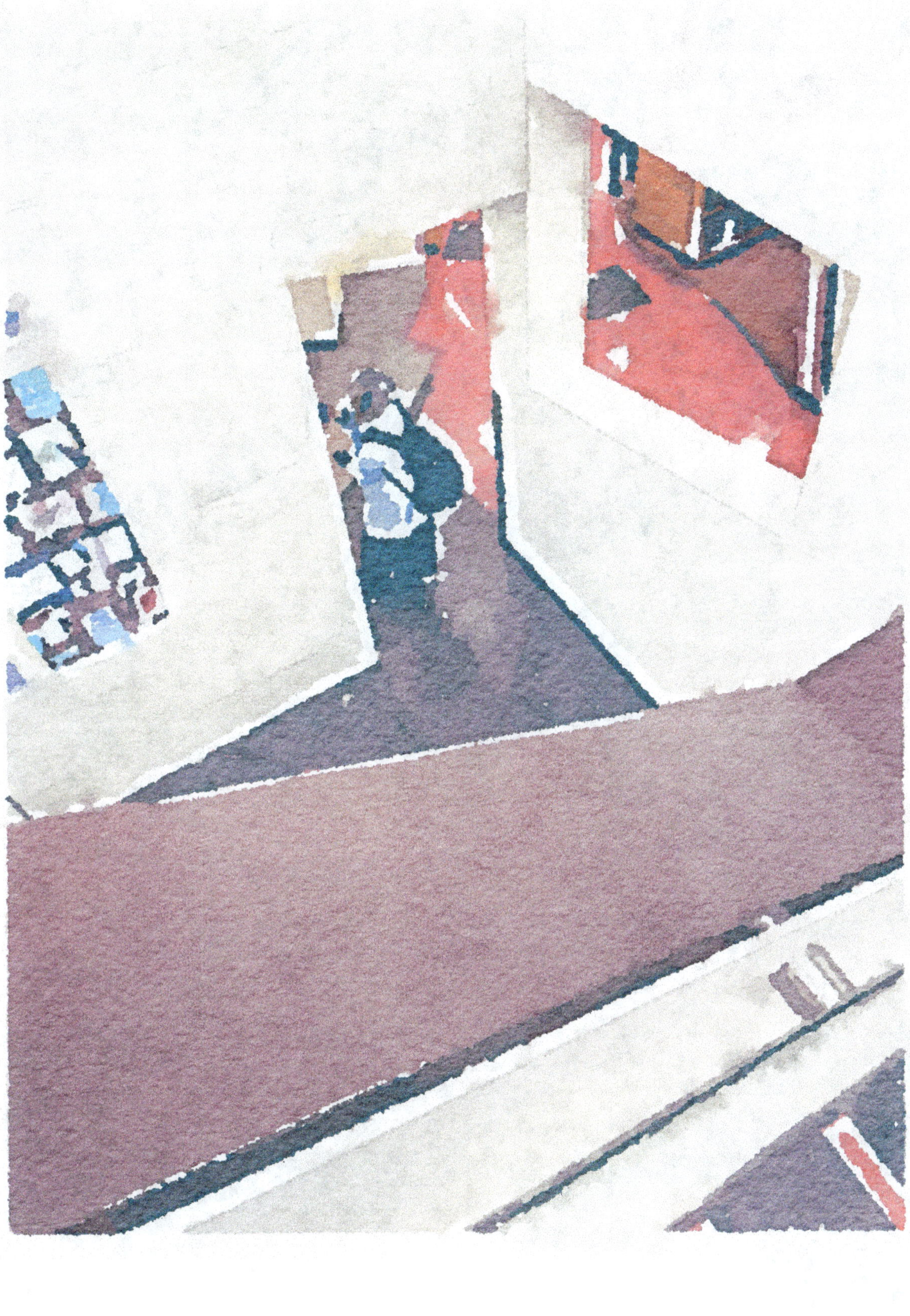

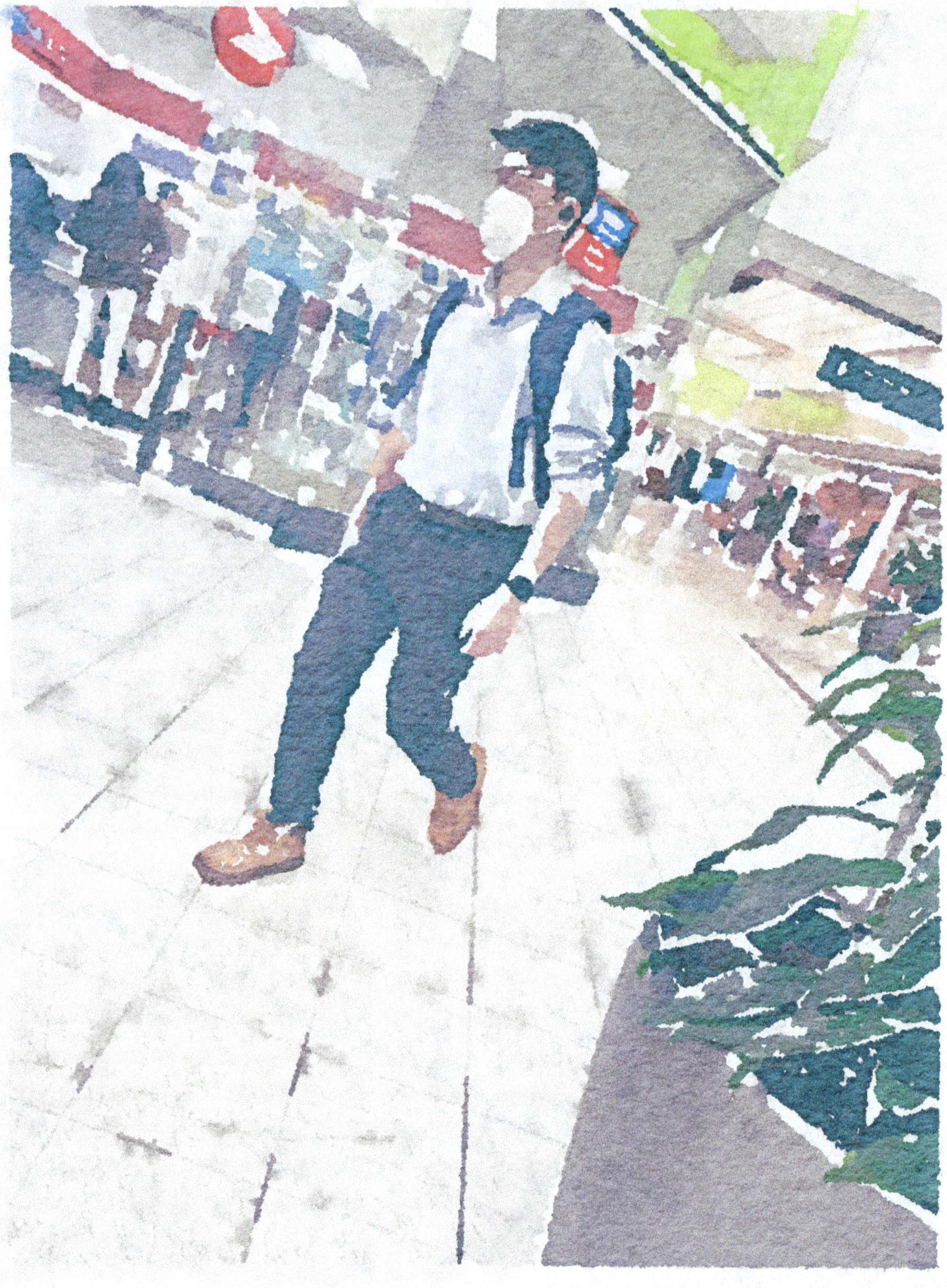

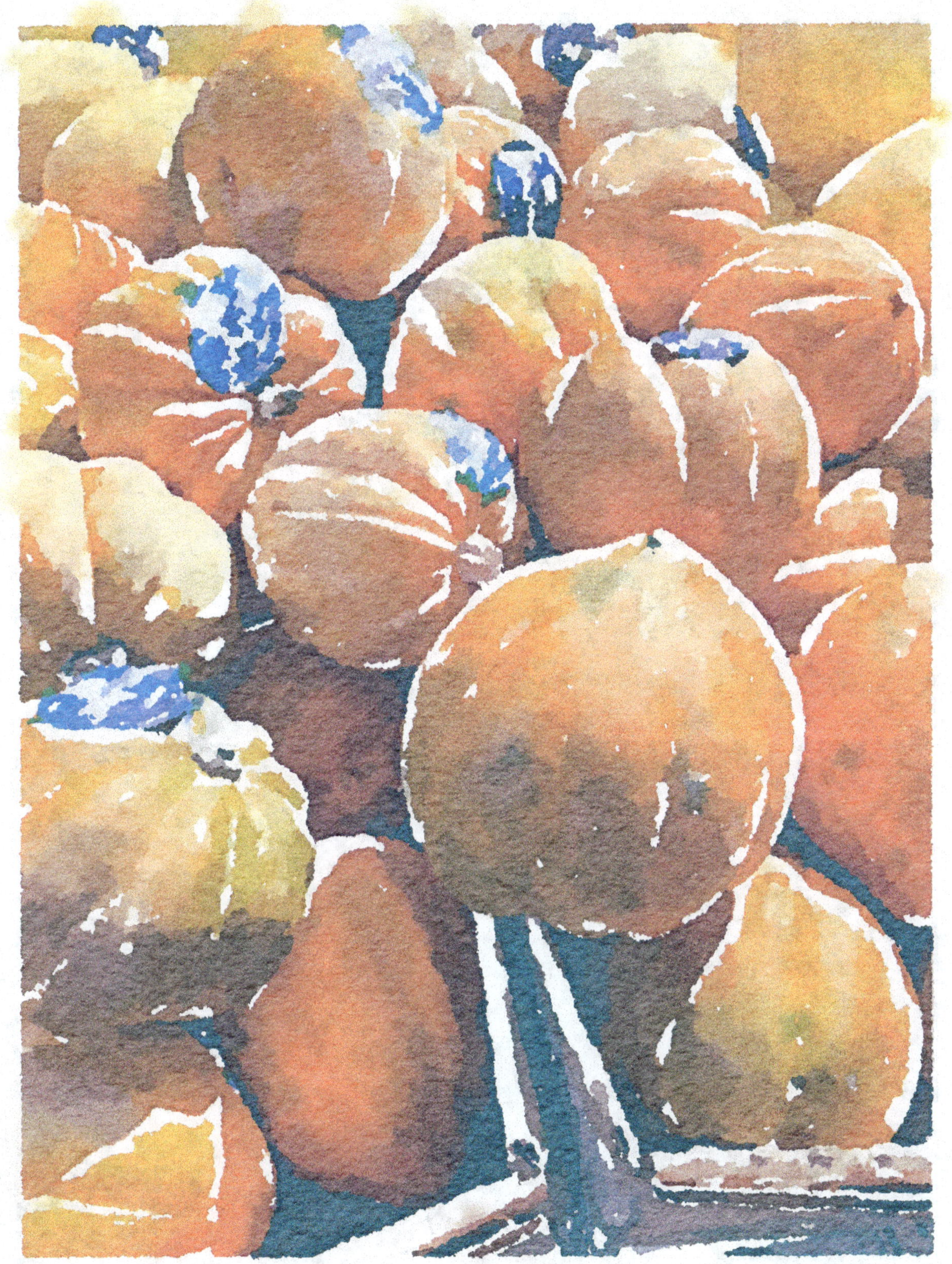

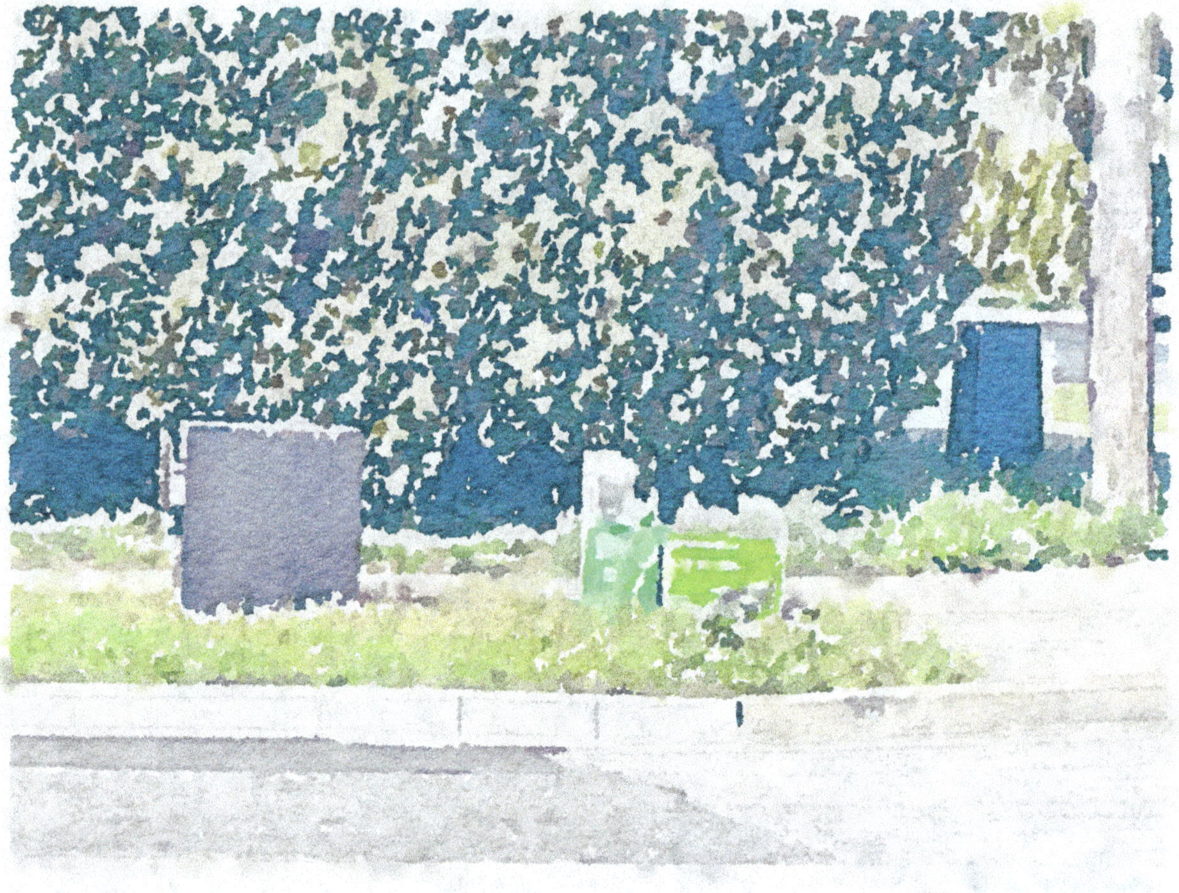

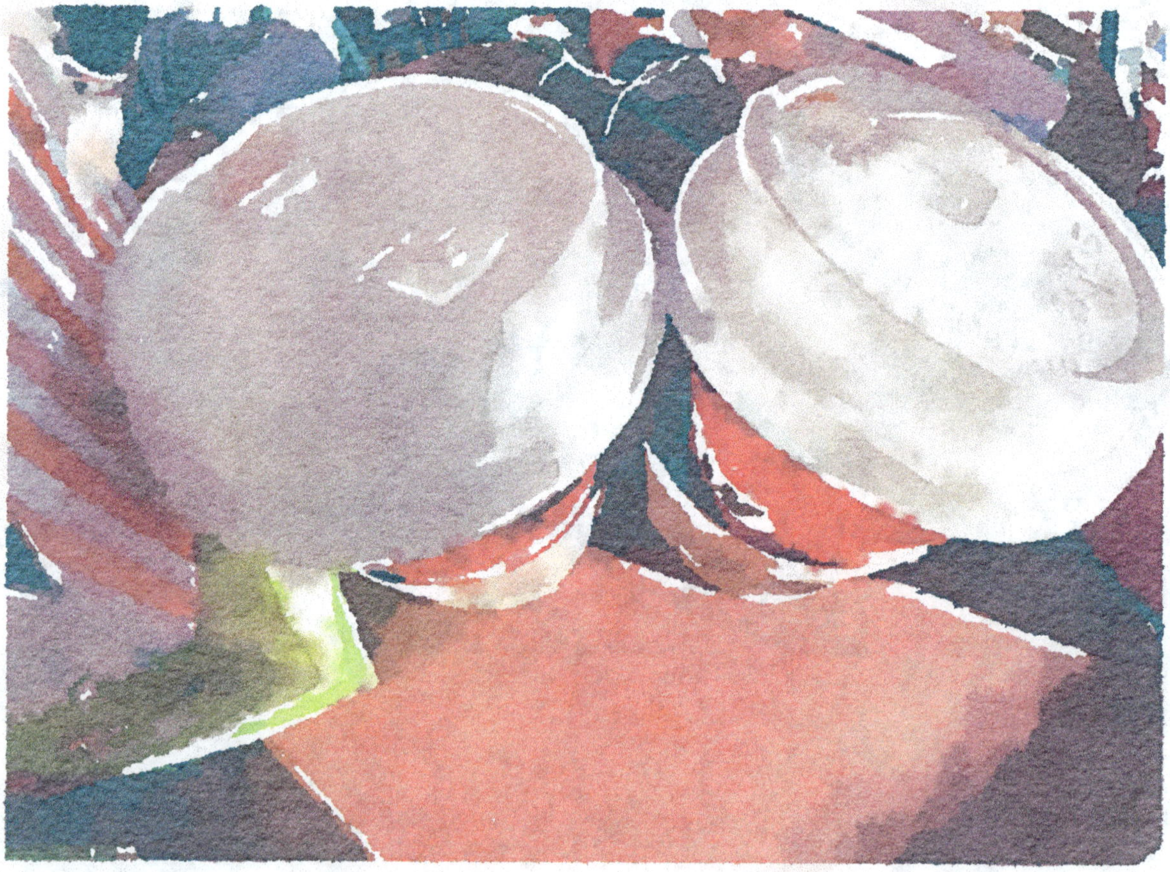

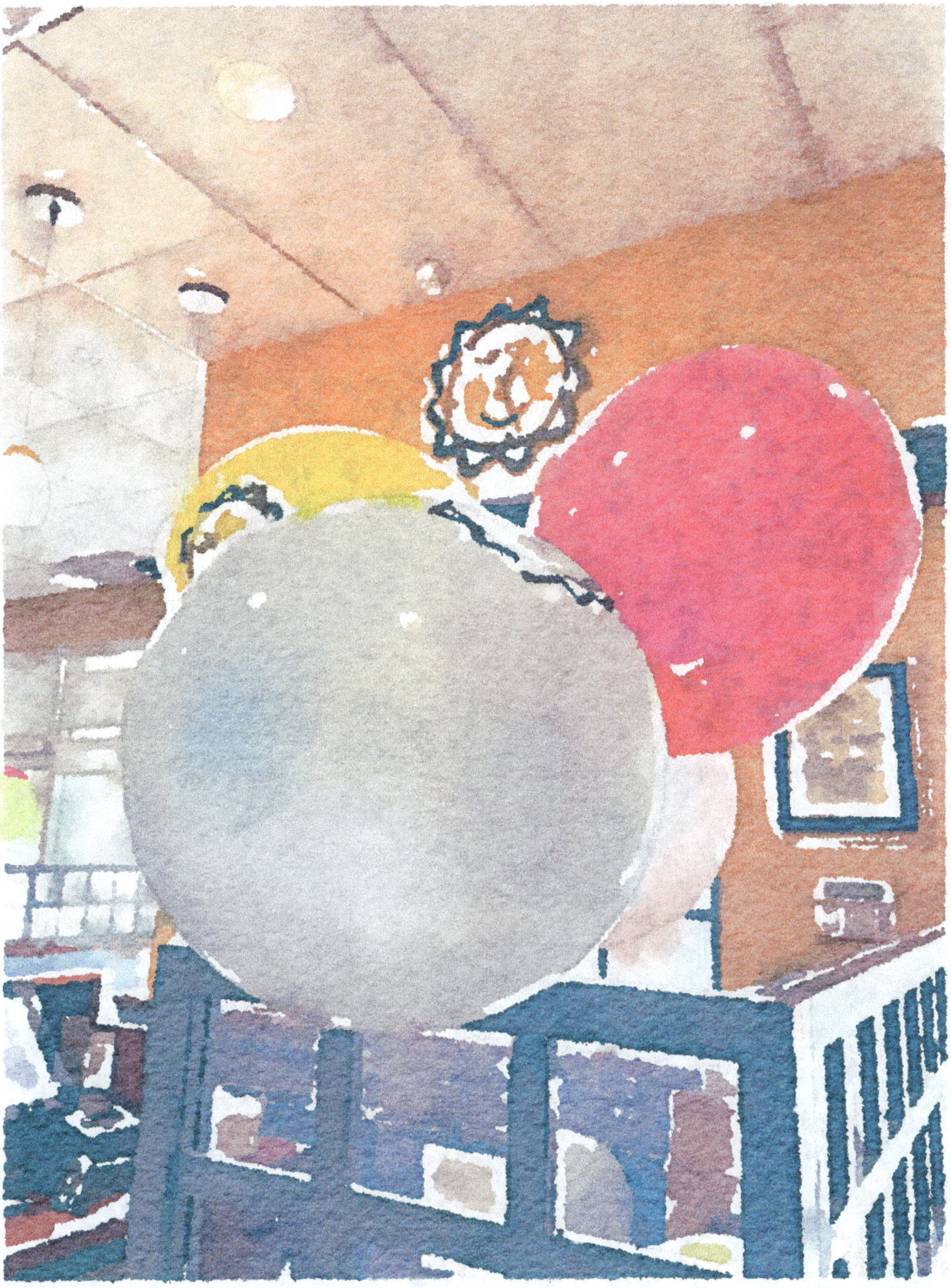

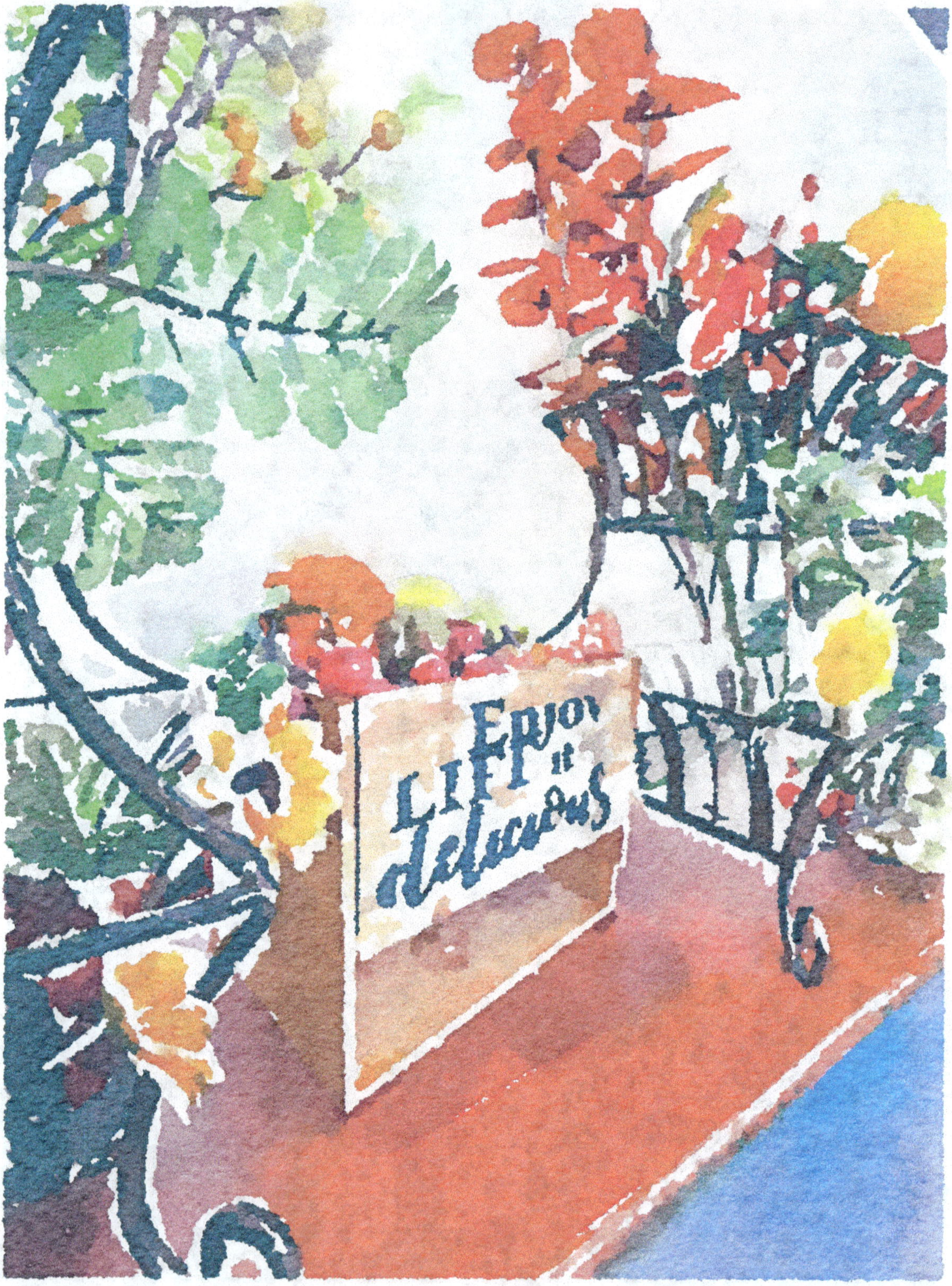

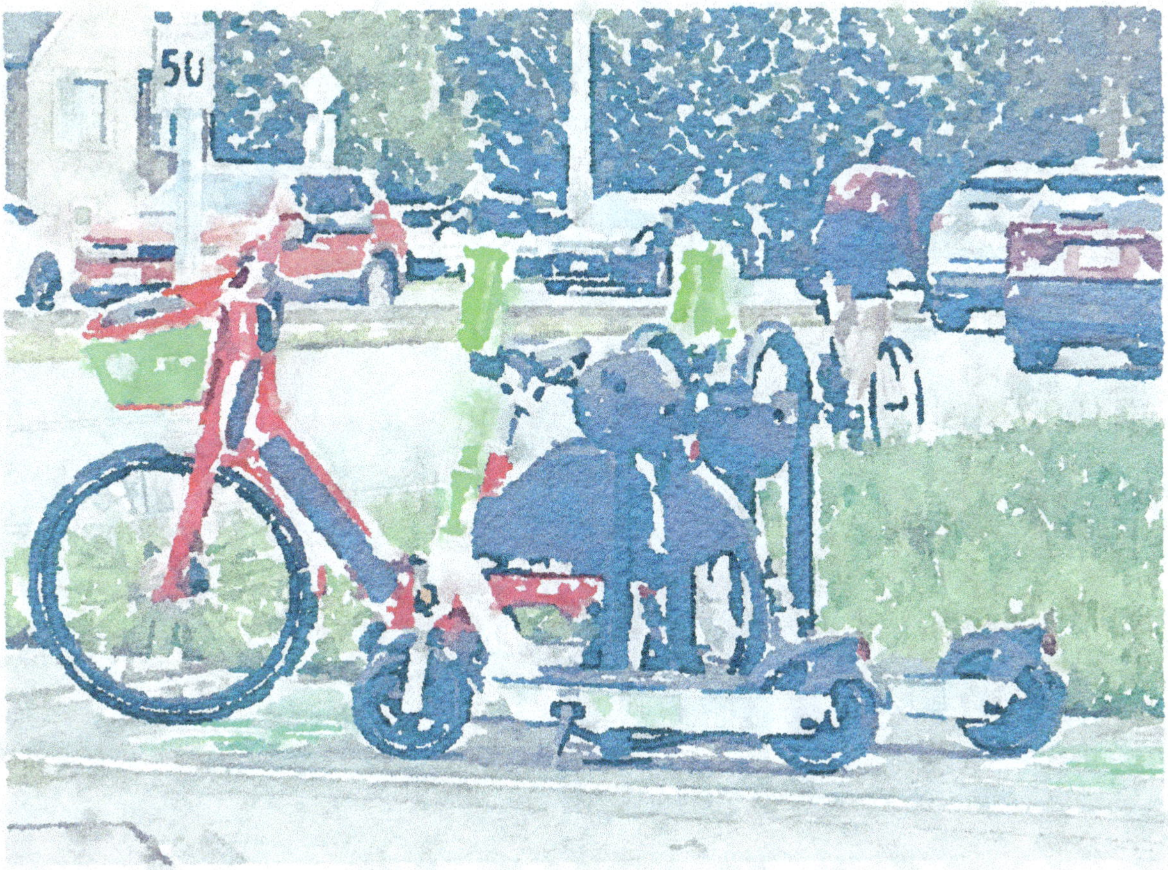
50

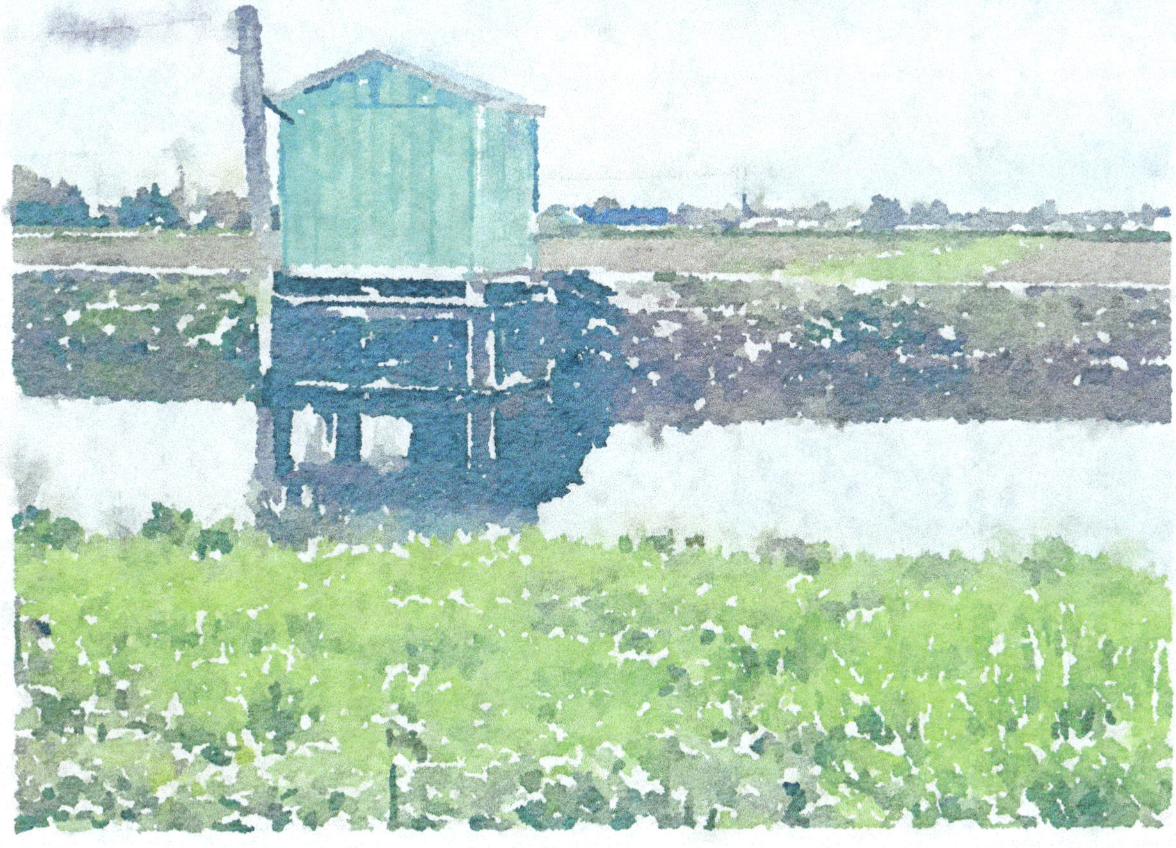

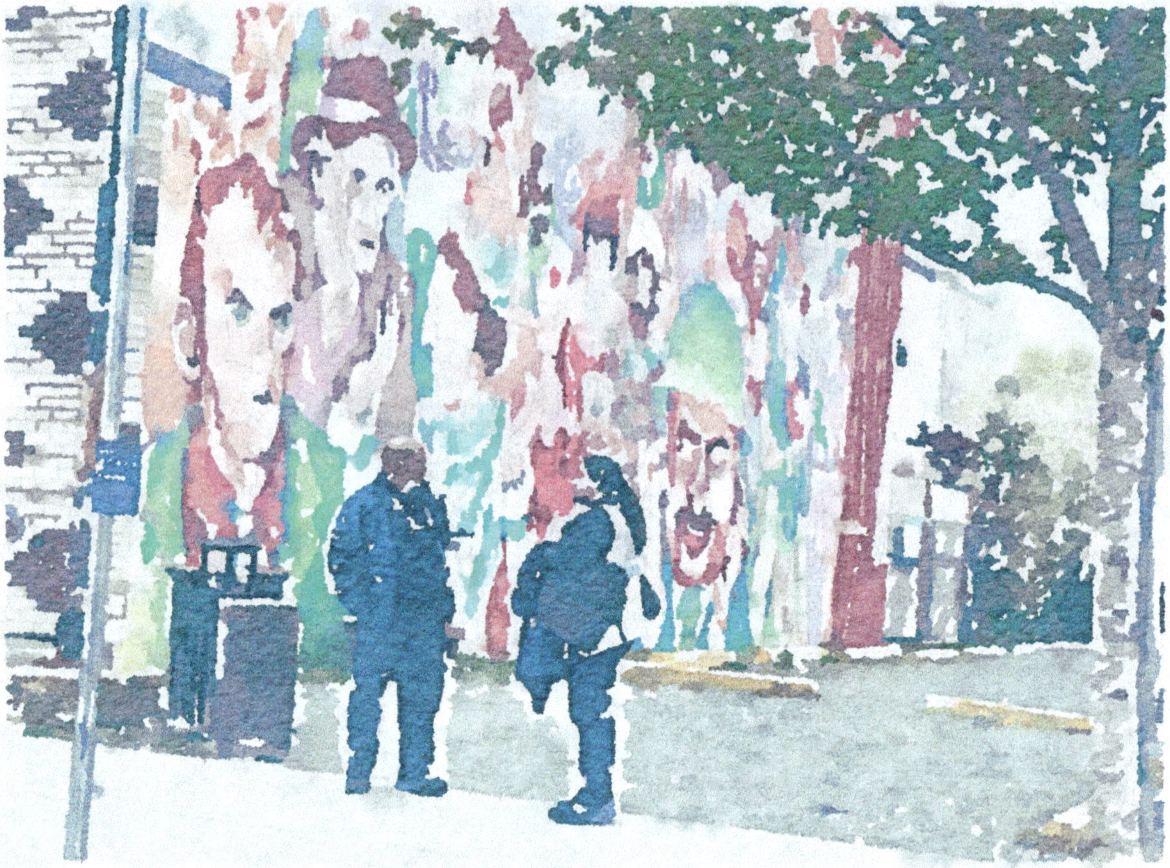

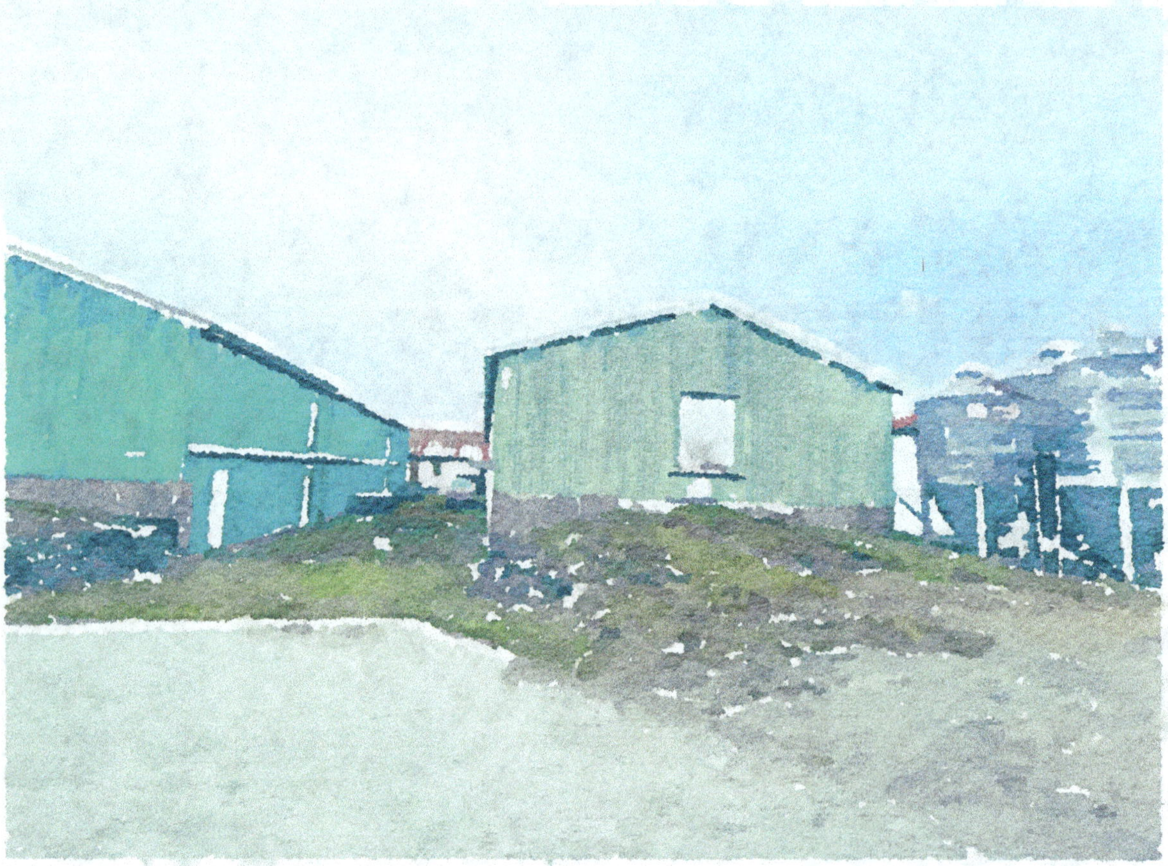

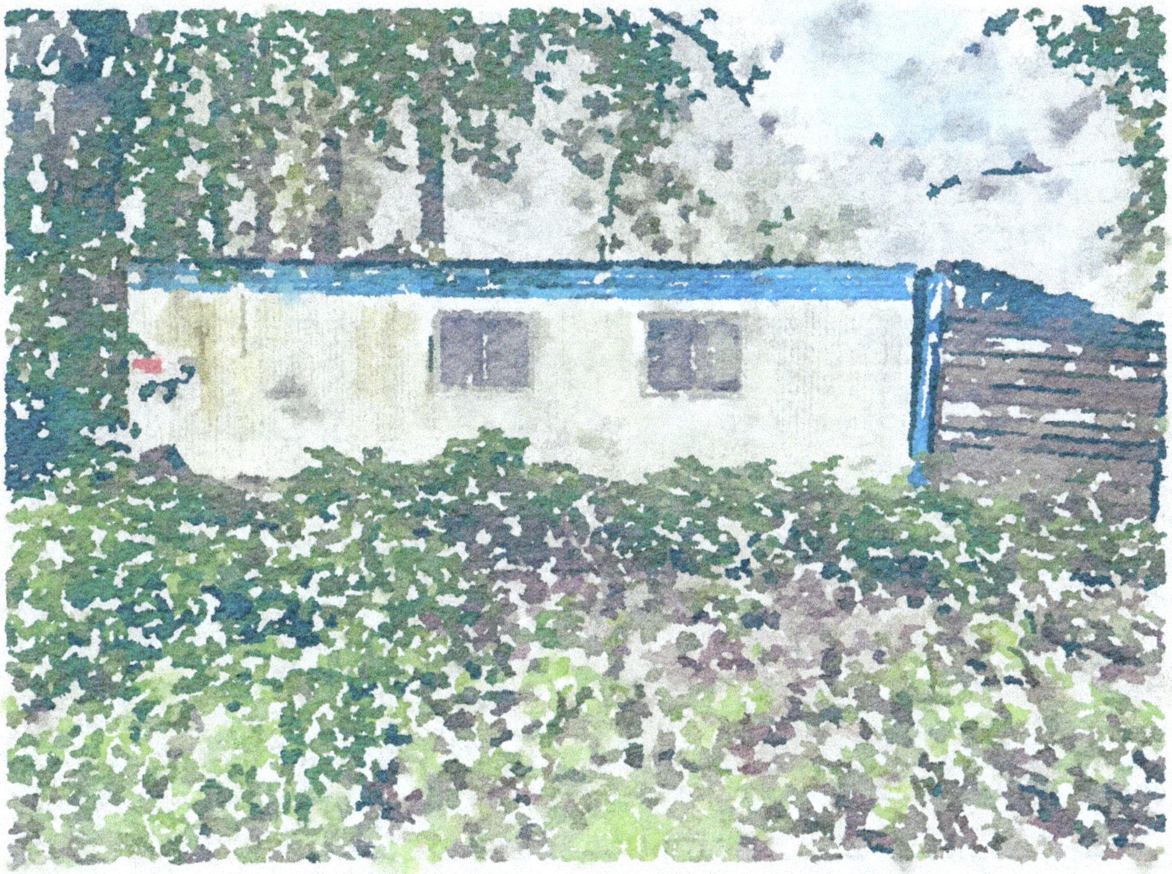

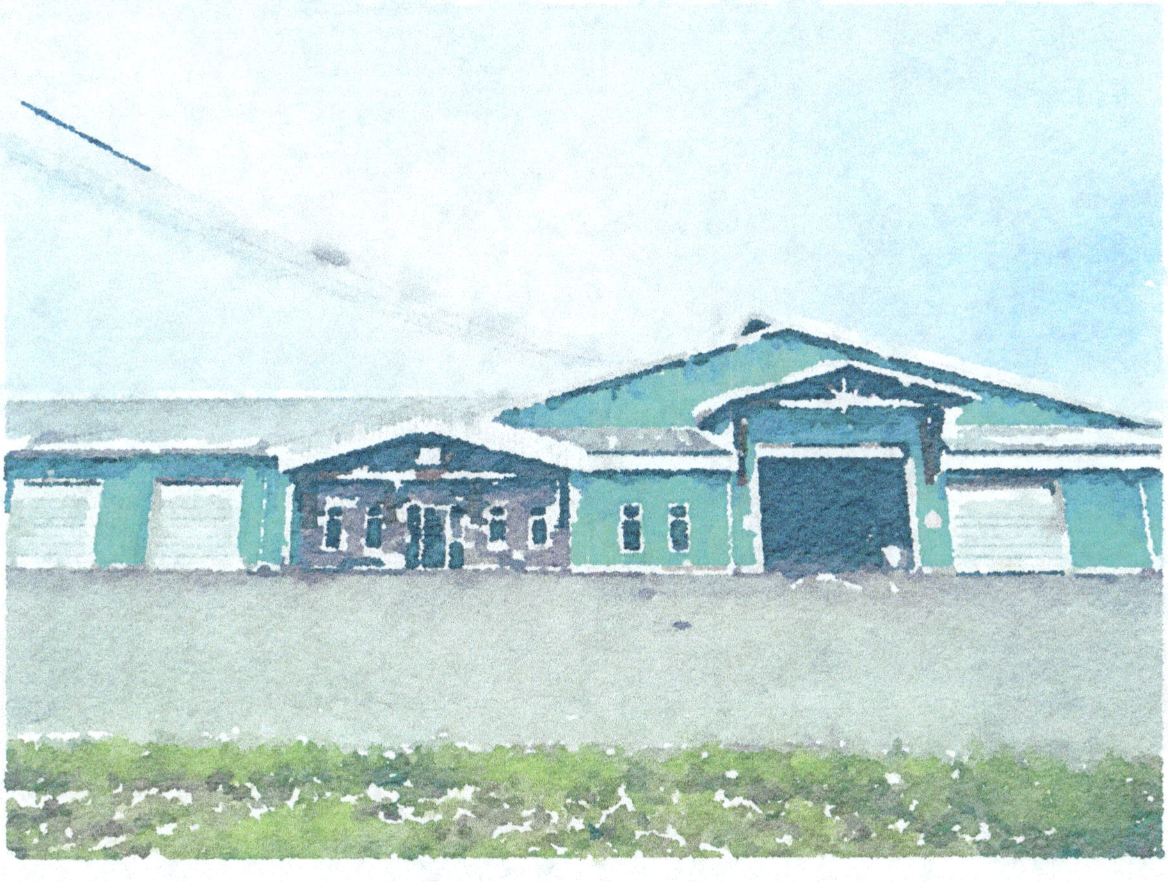

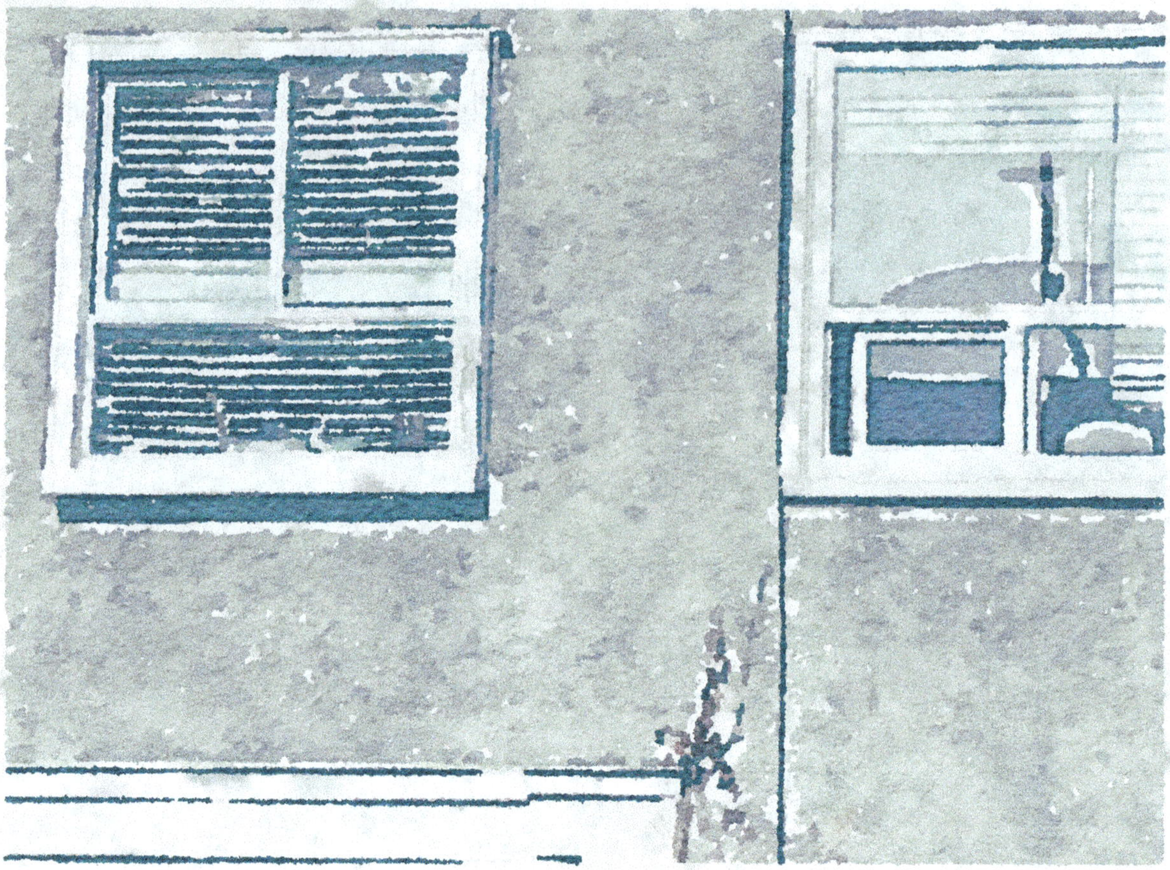

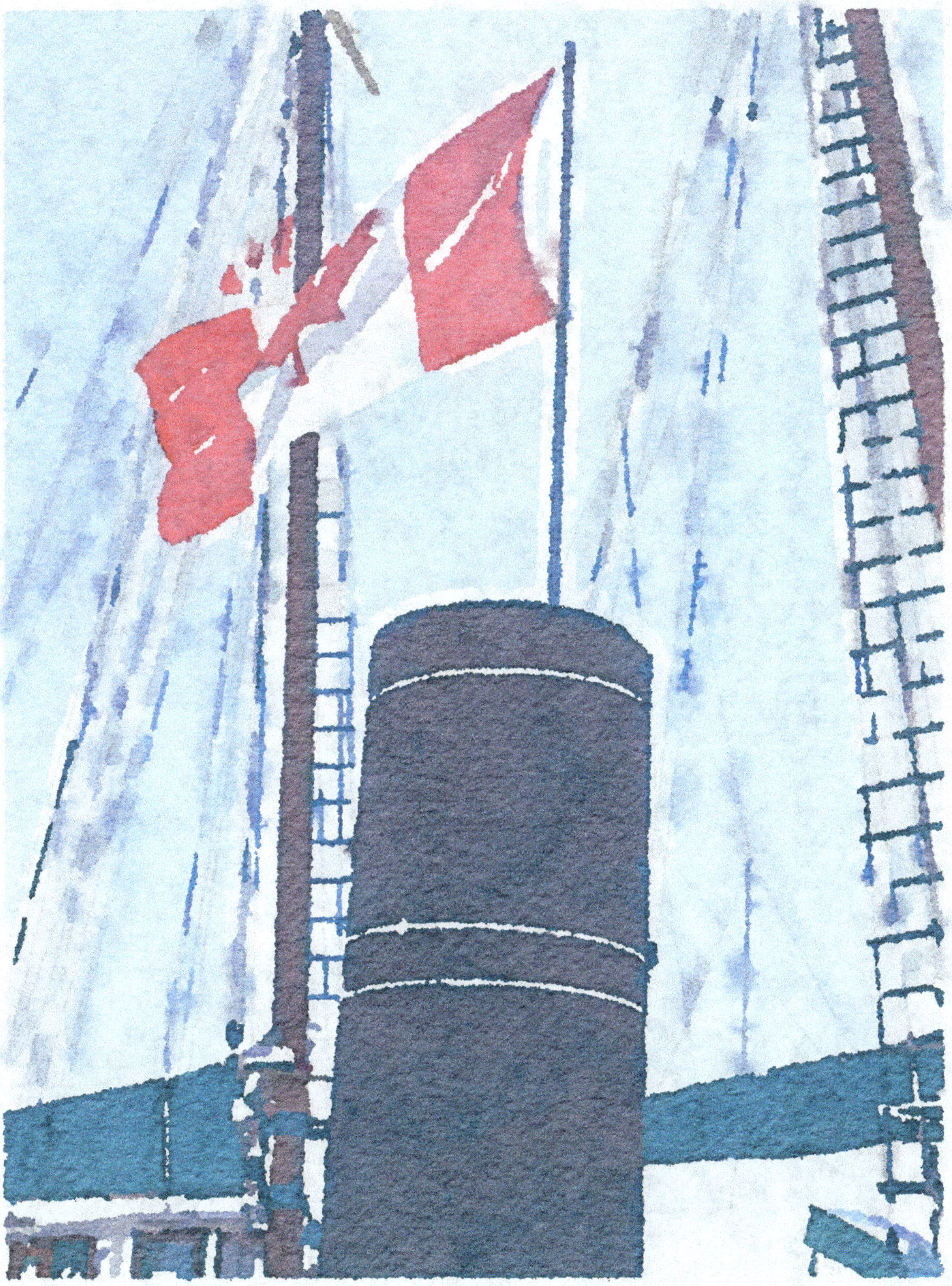

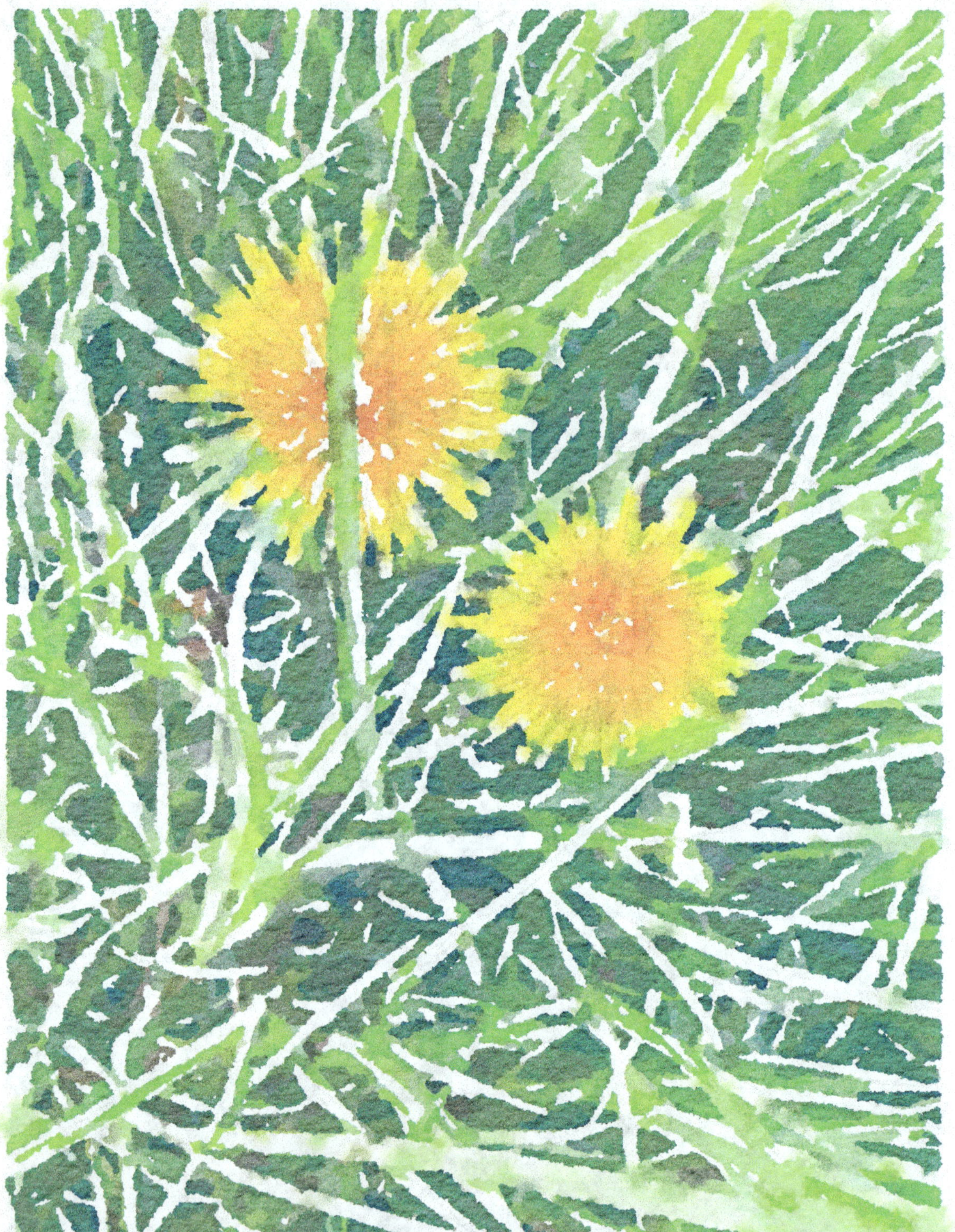

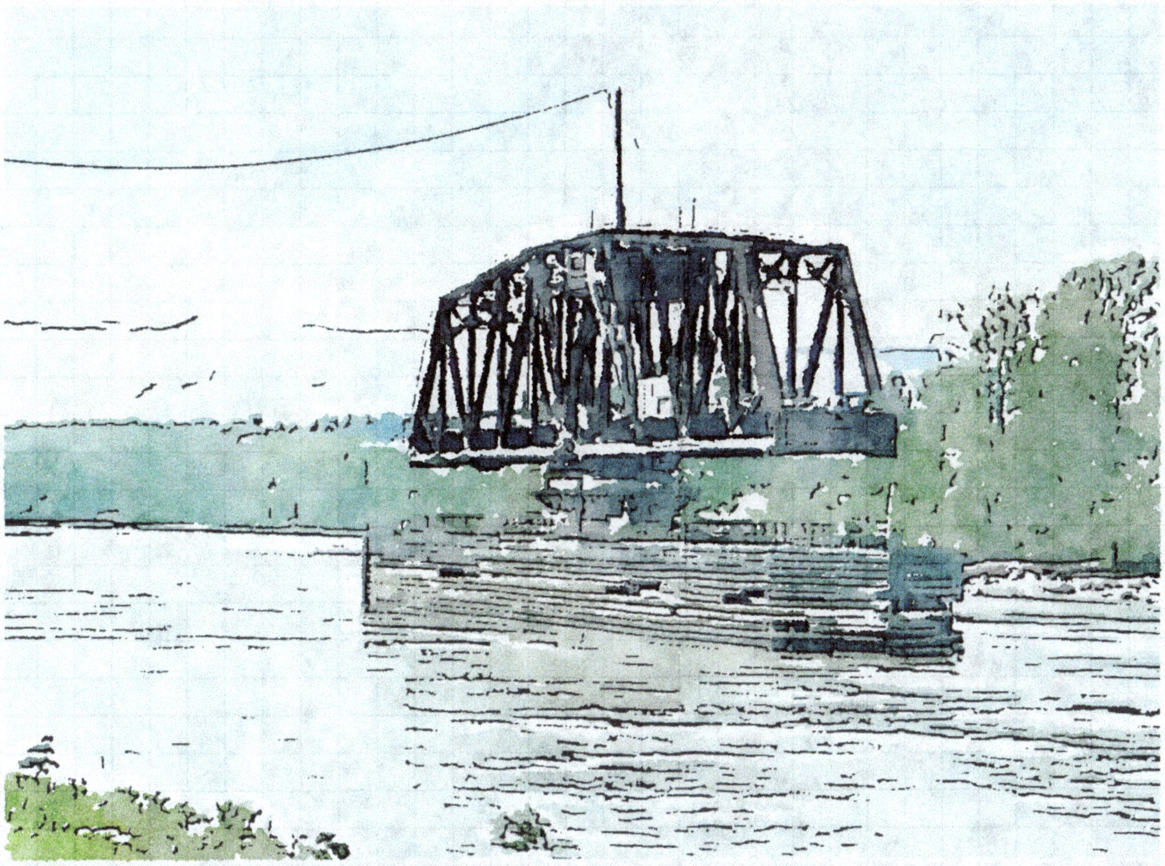

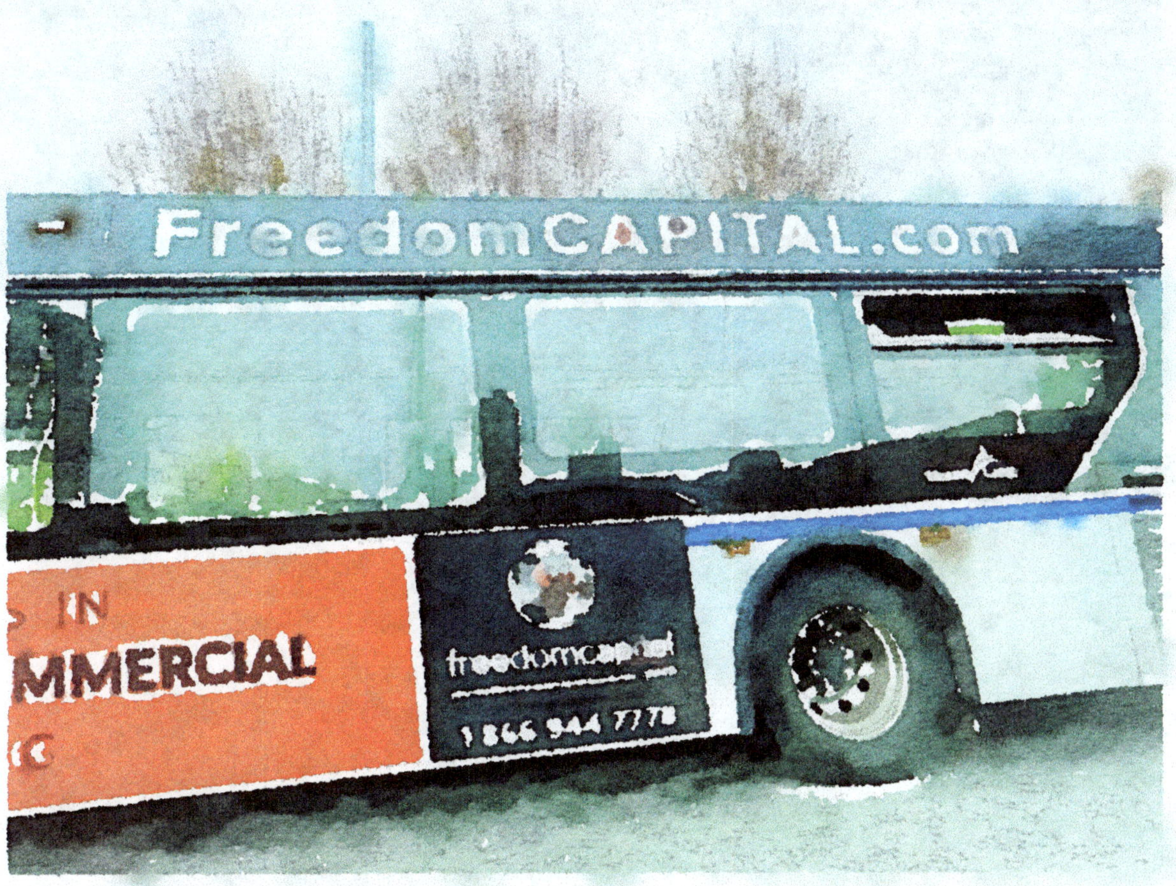
FreedomCAPITAL.com
IN
MMERCIAL
1 866 944 7778

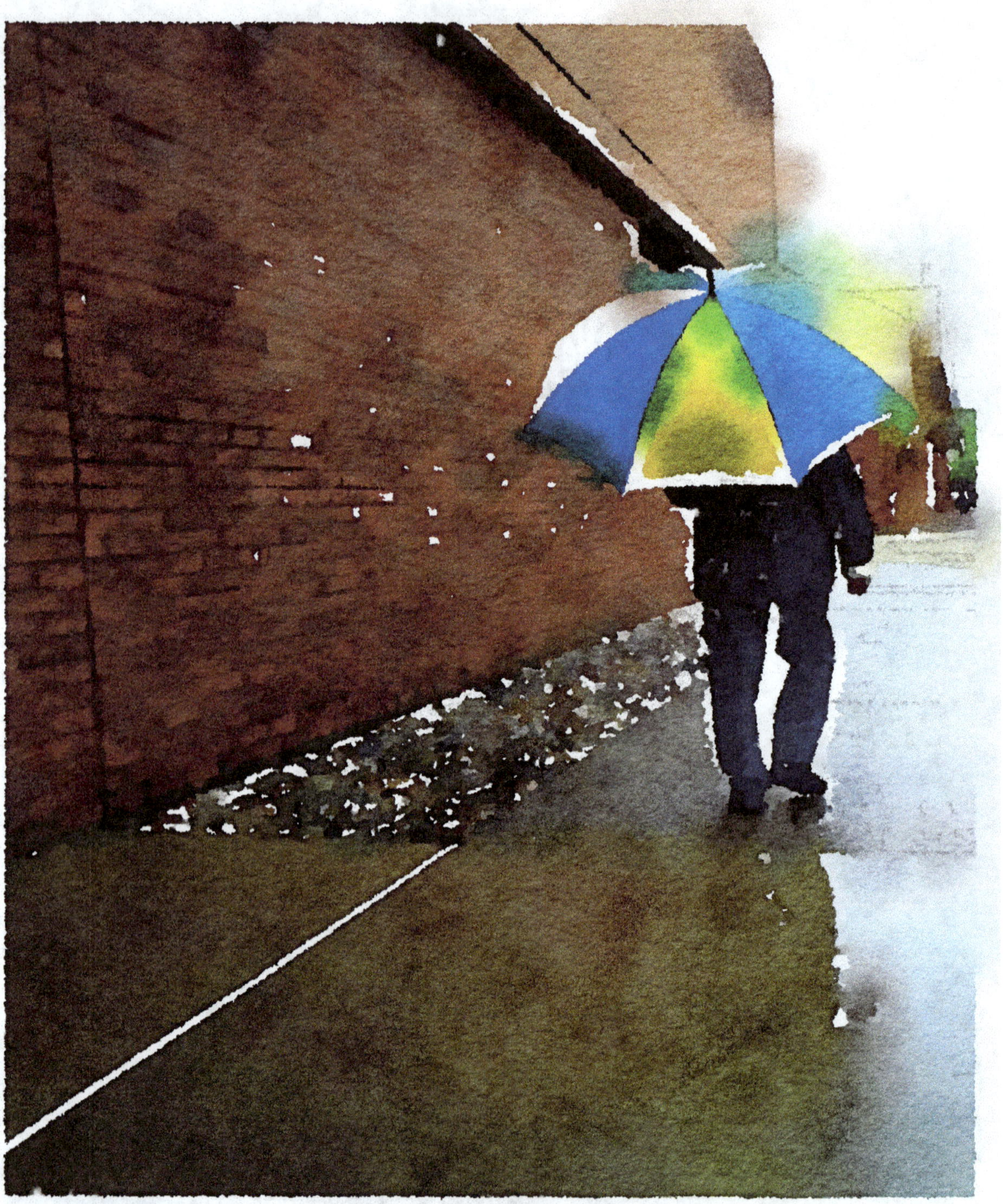

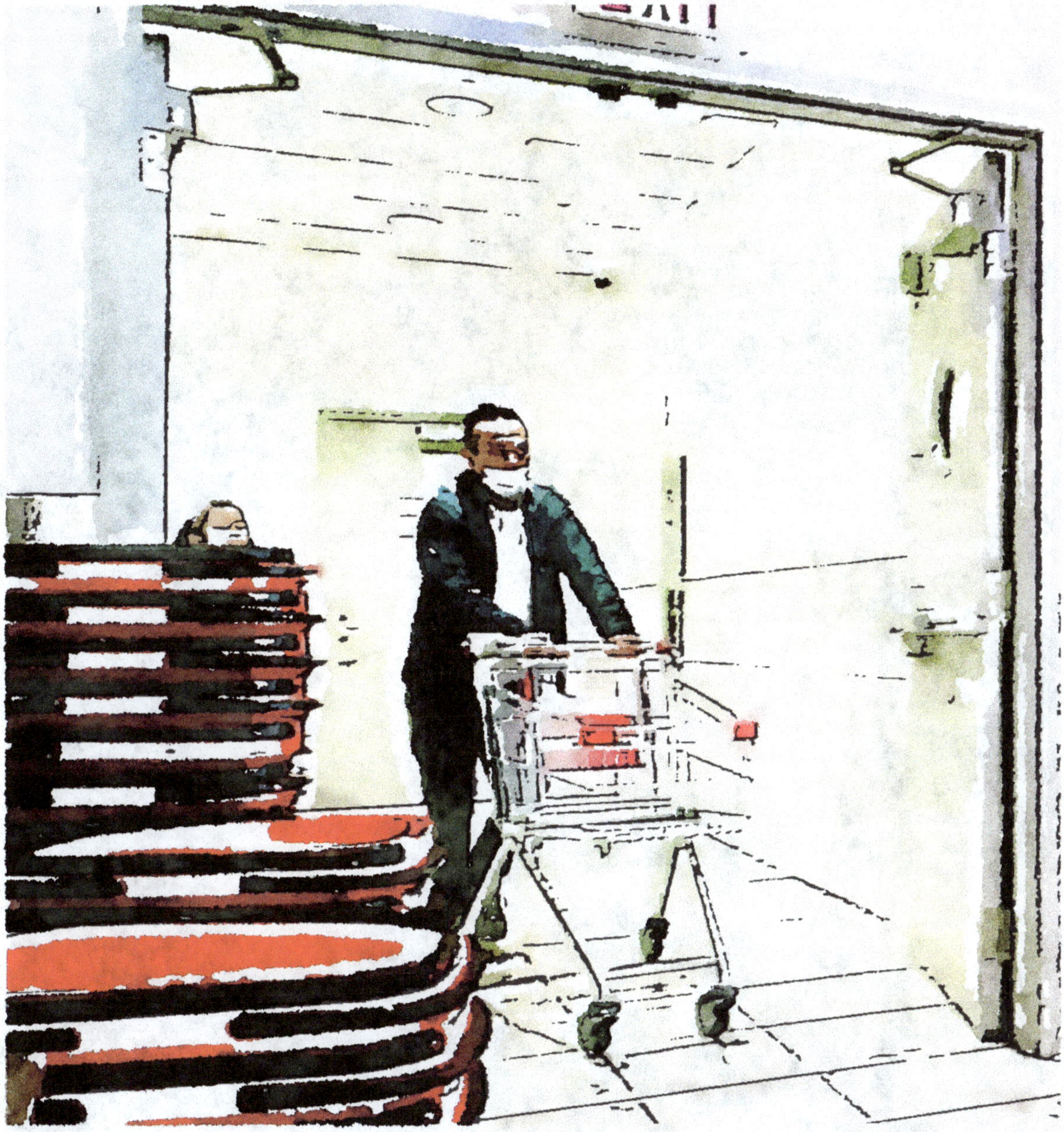

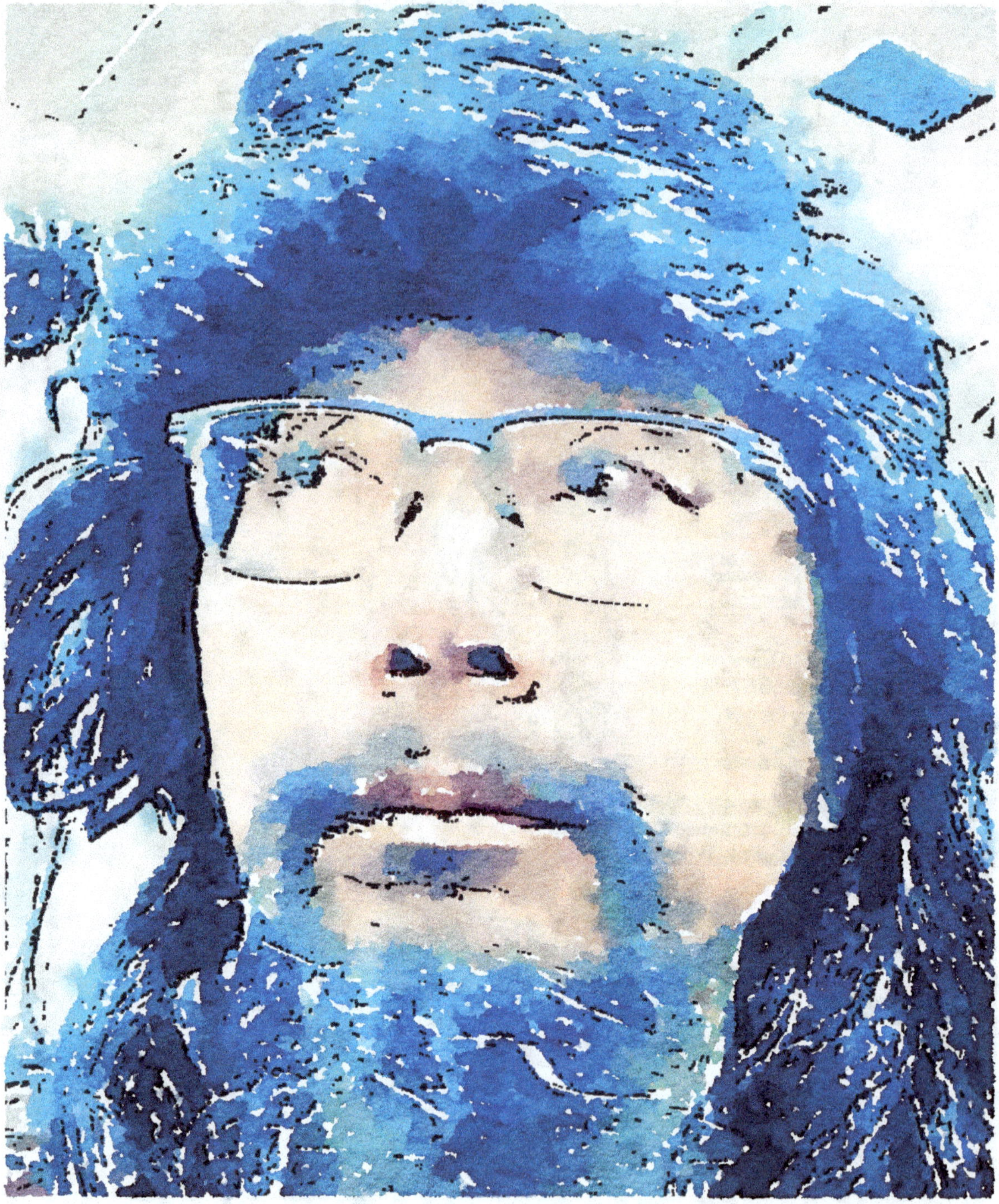

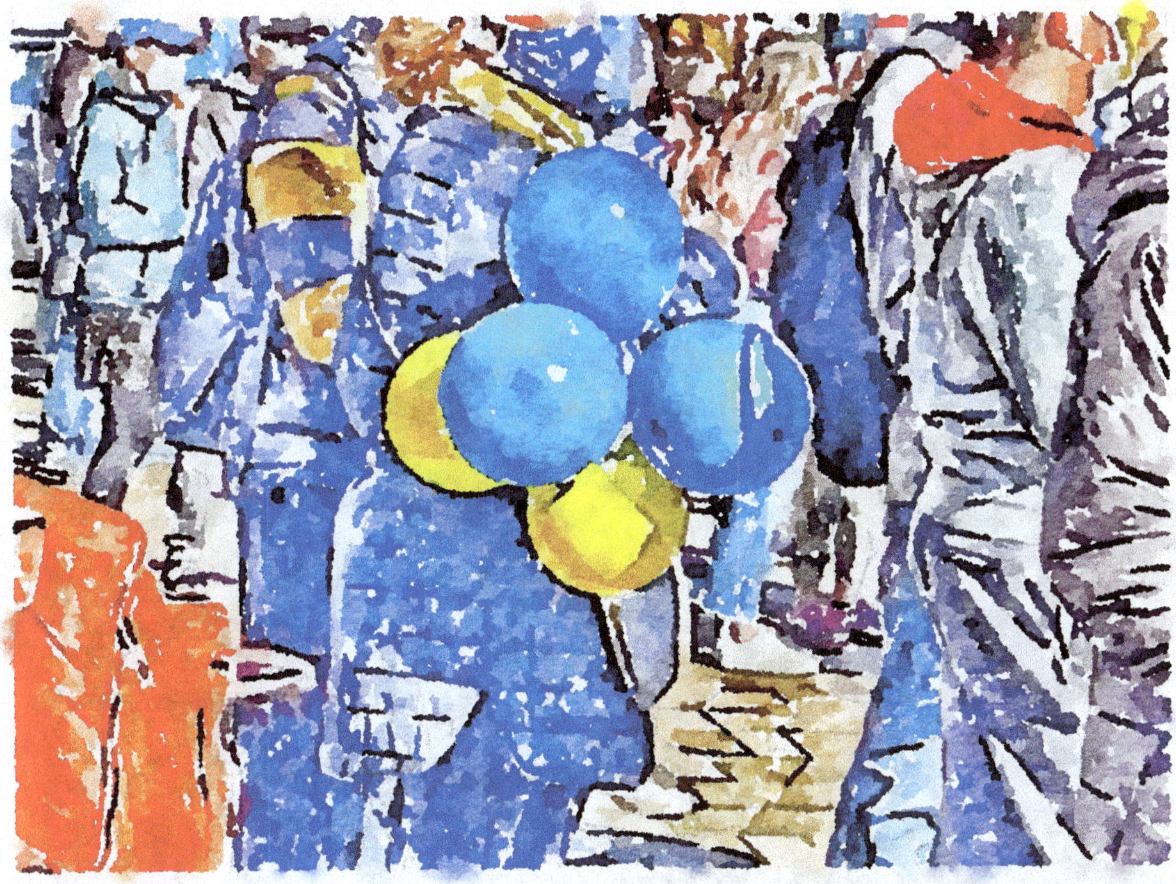

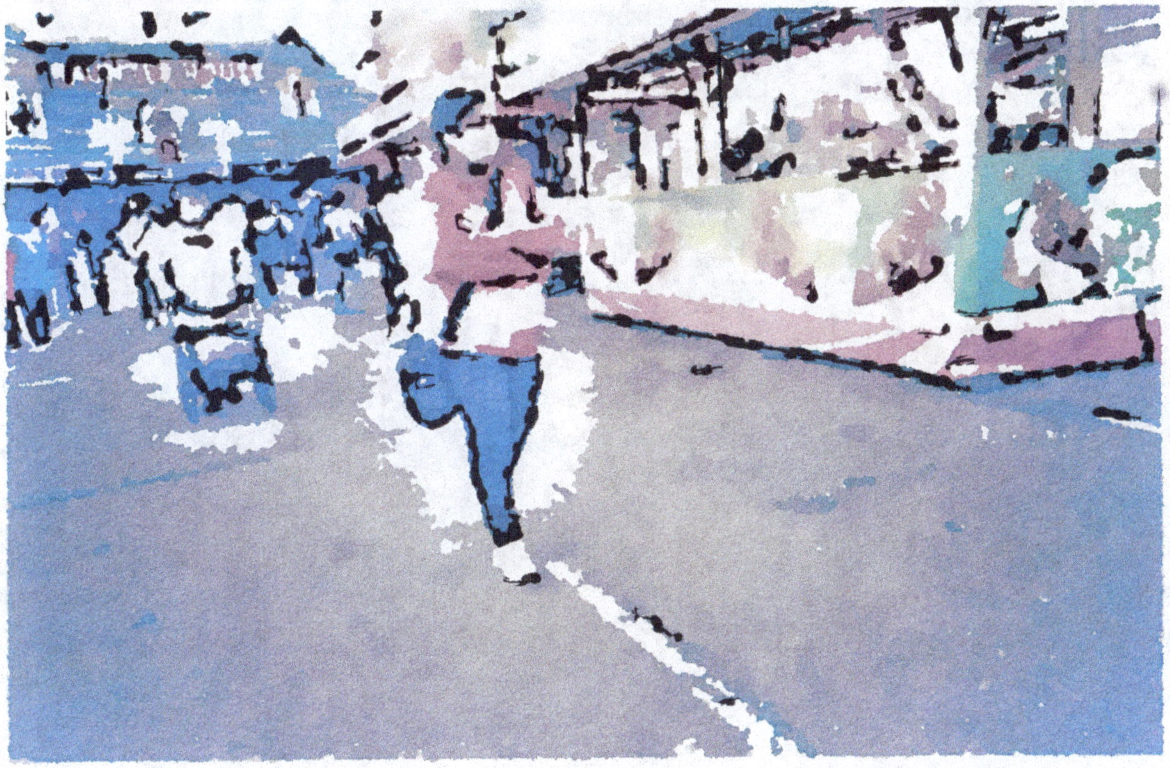

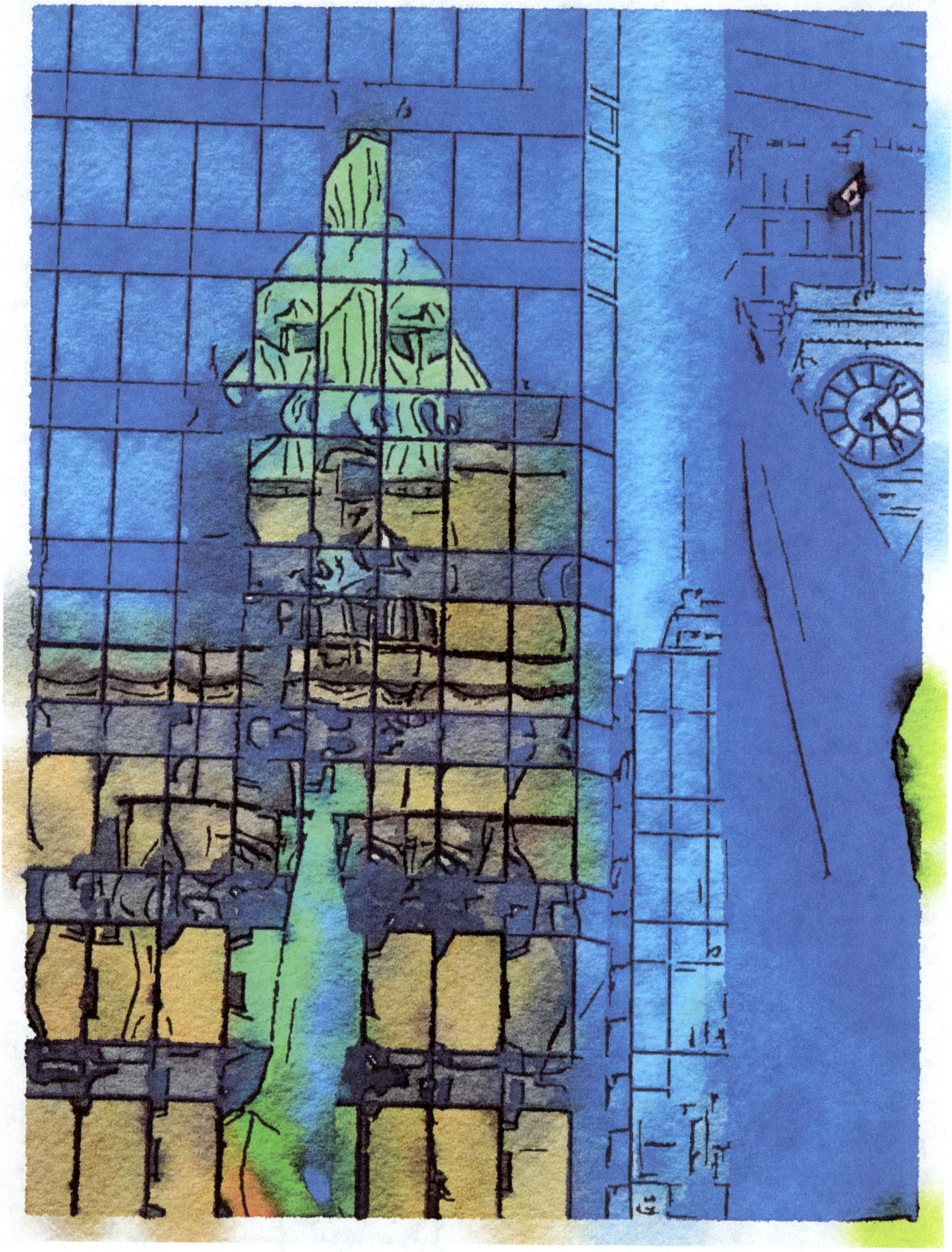

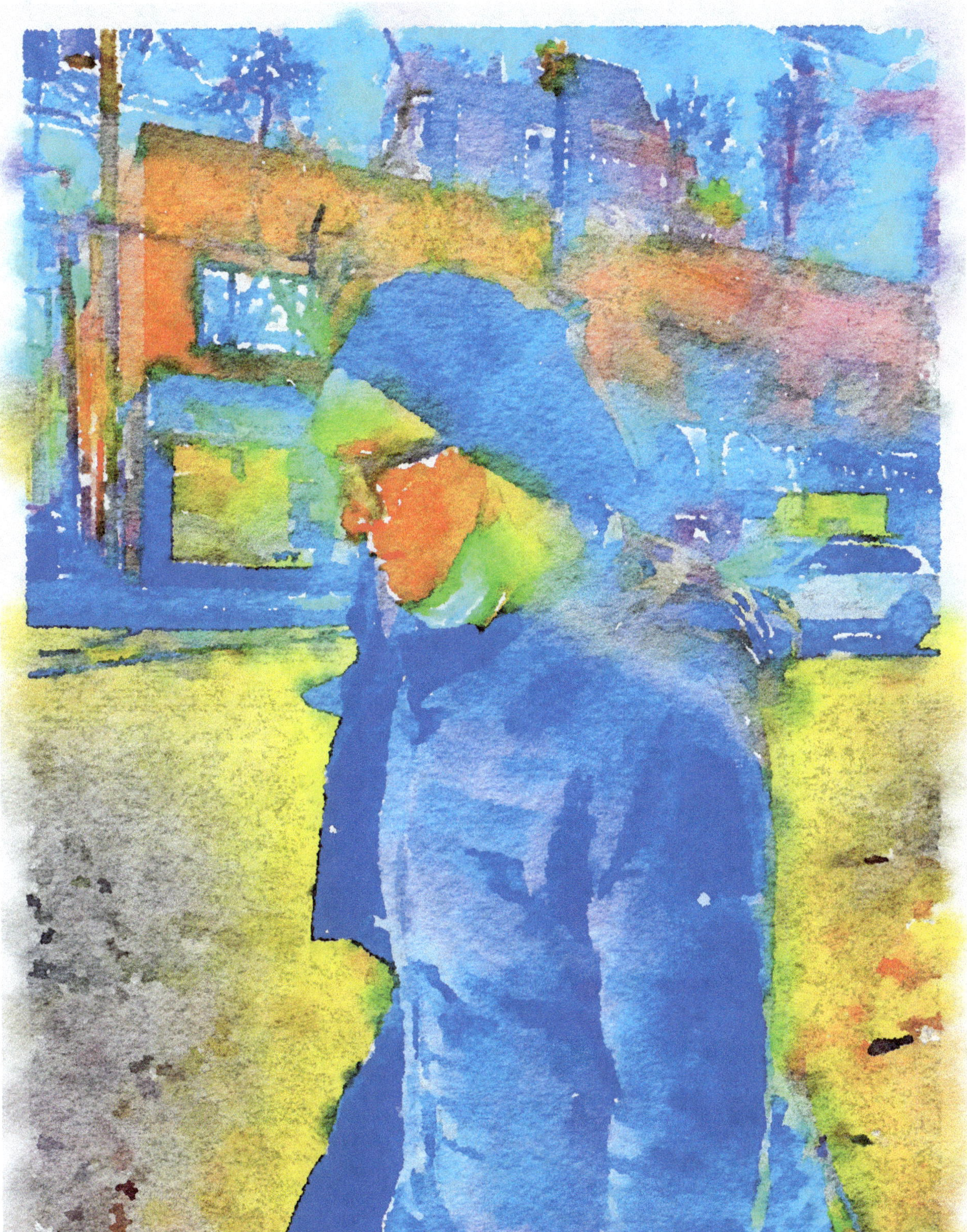

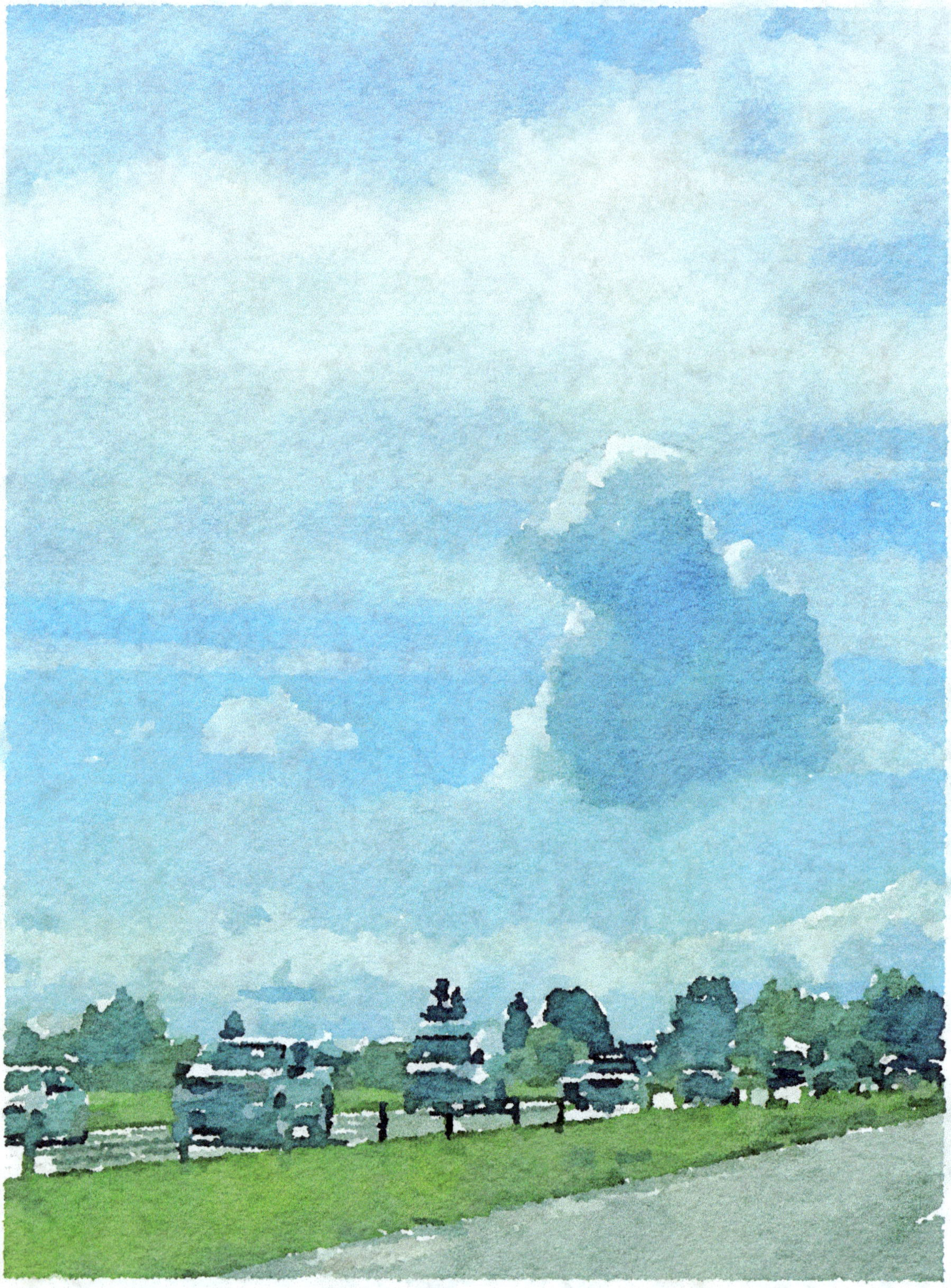

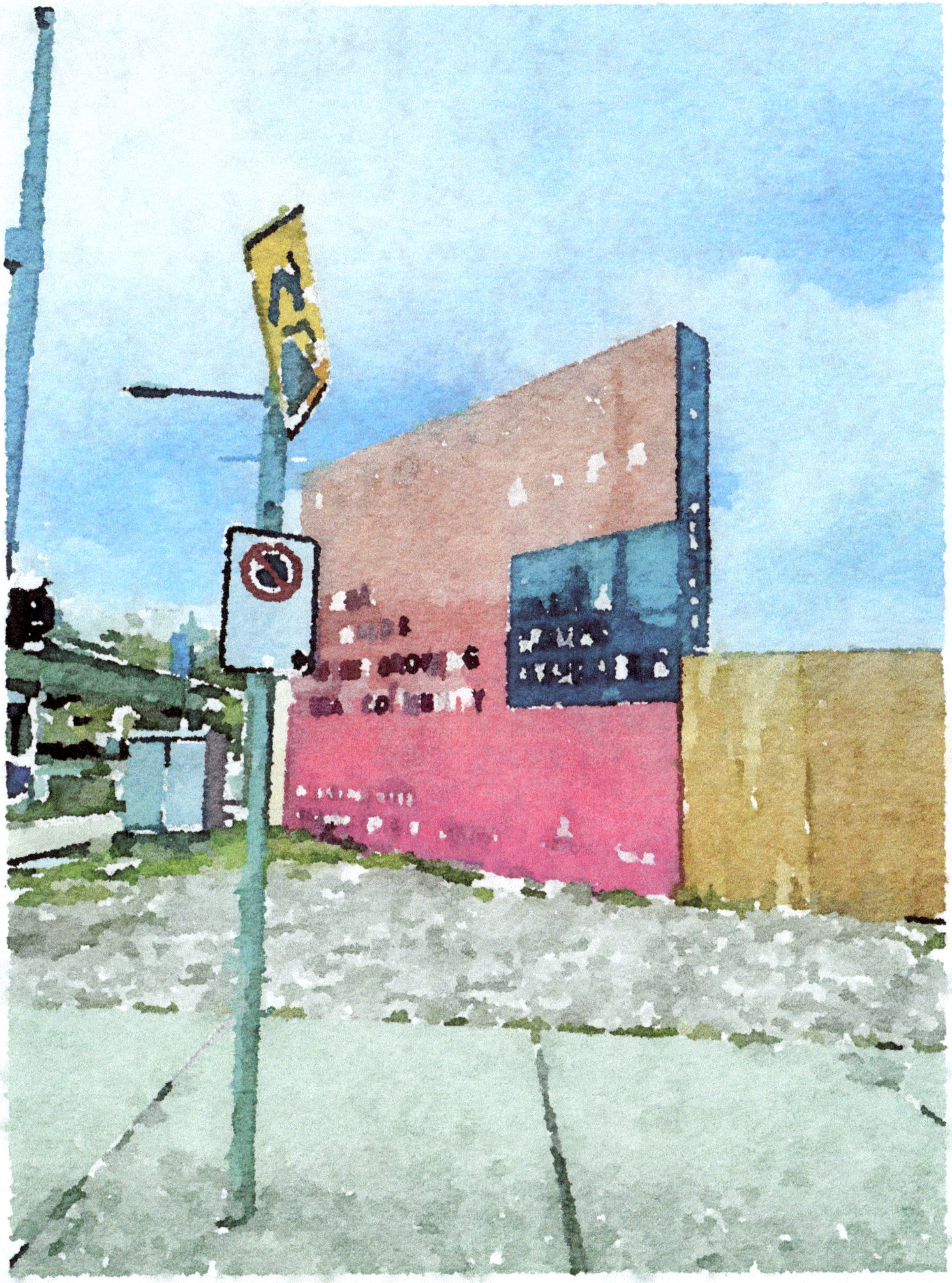

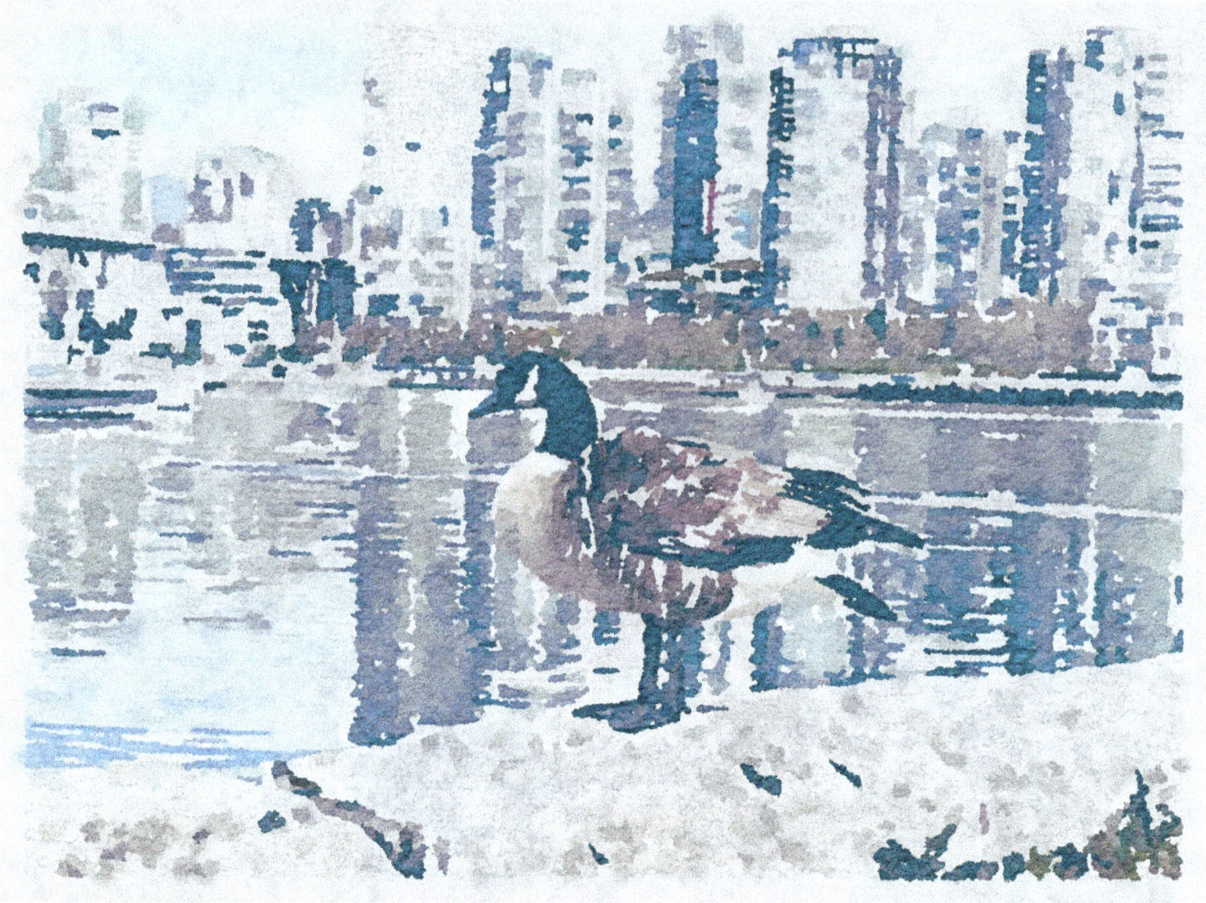

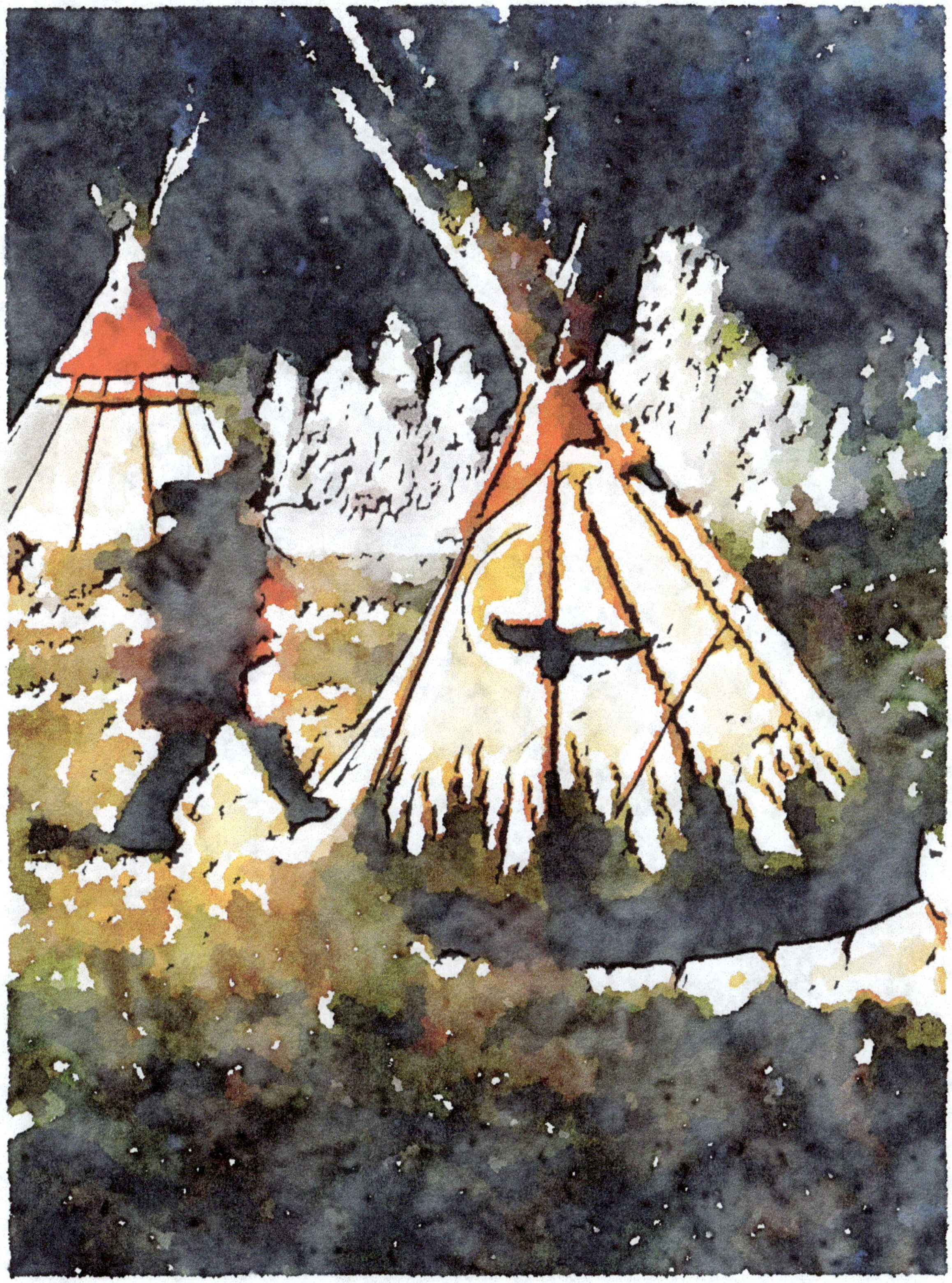

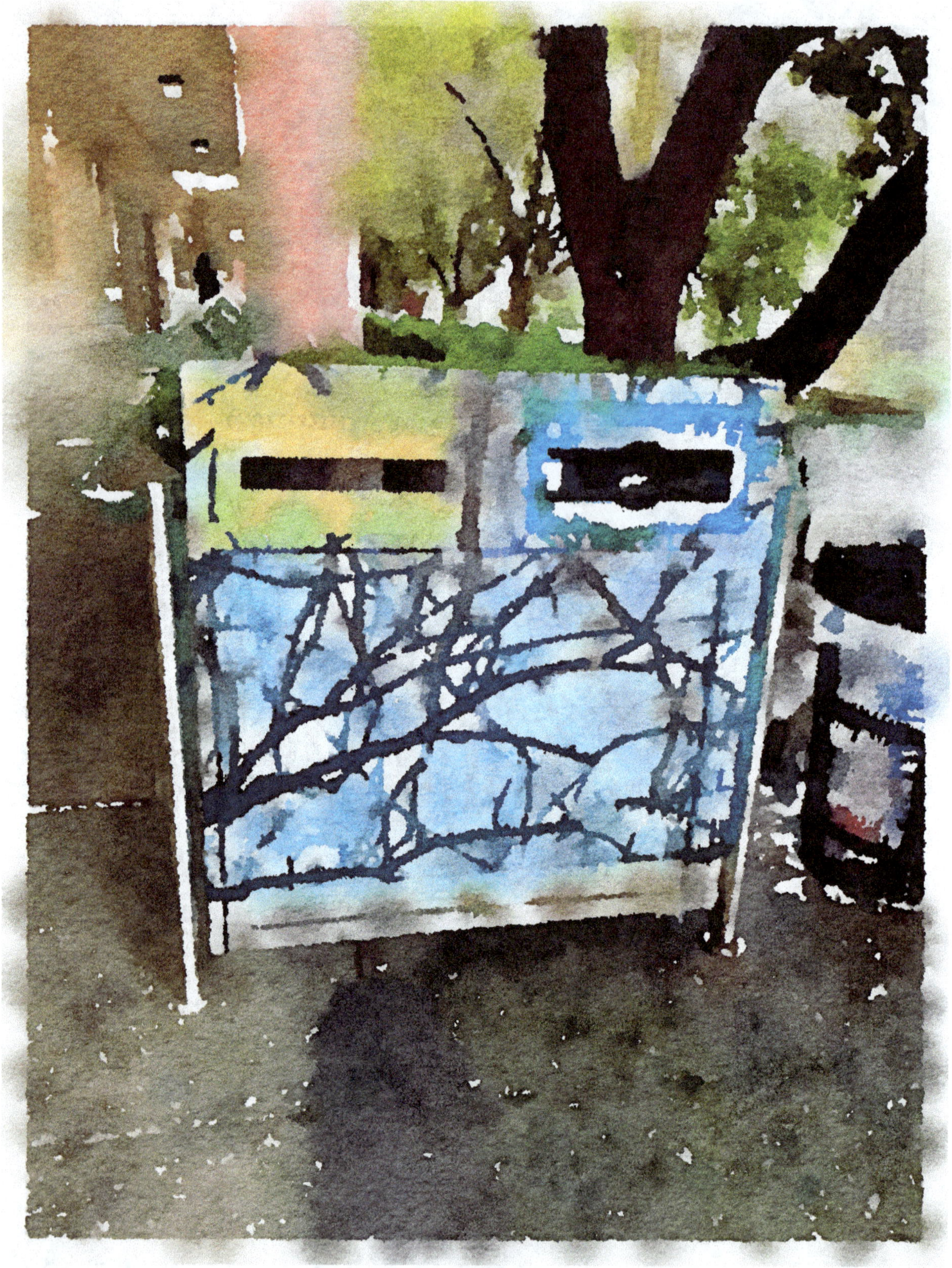

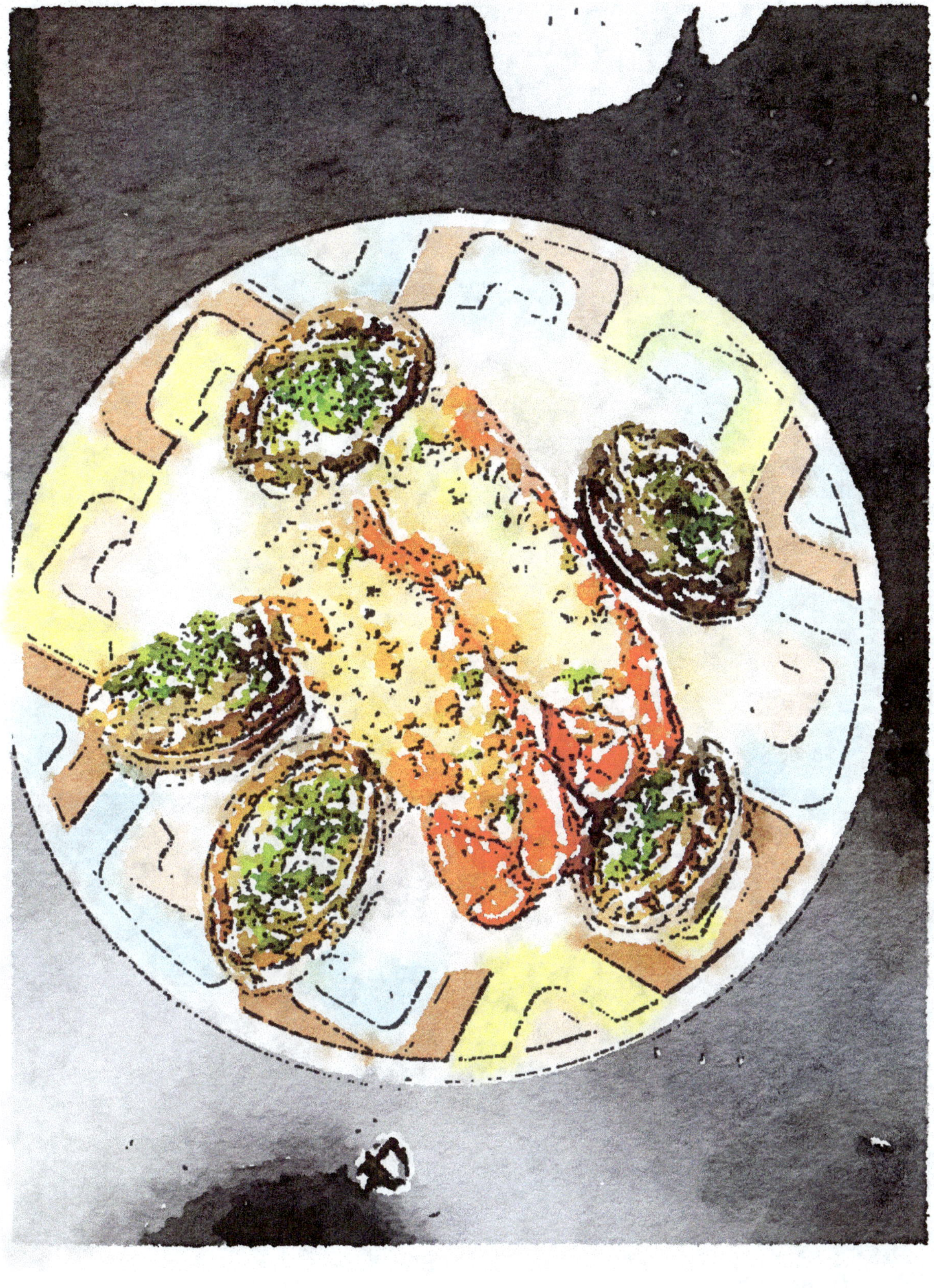

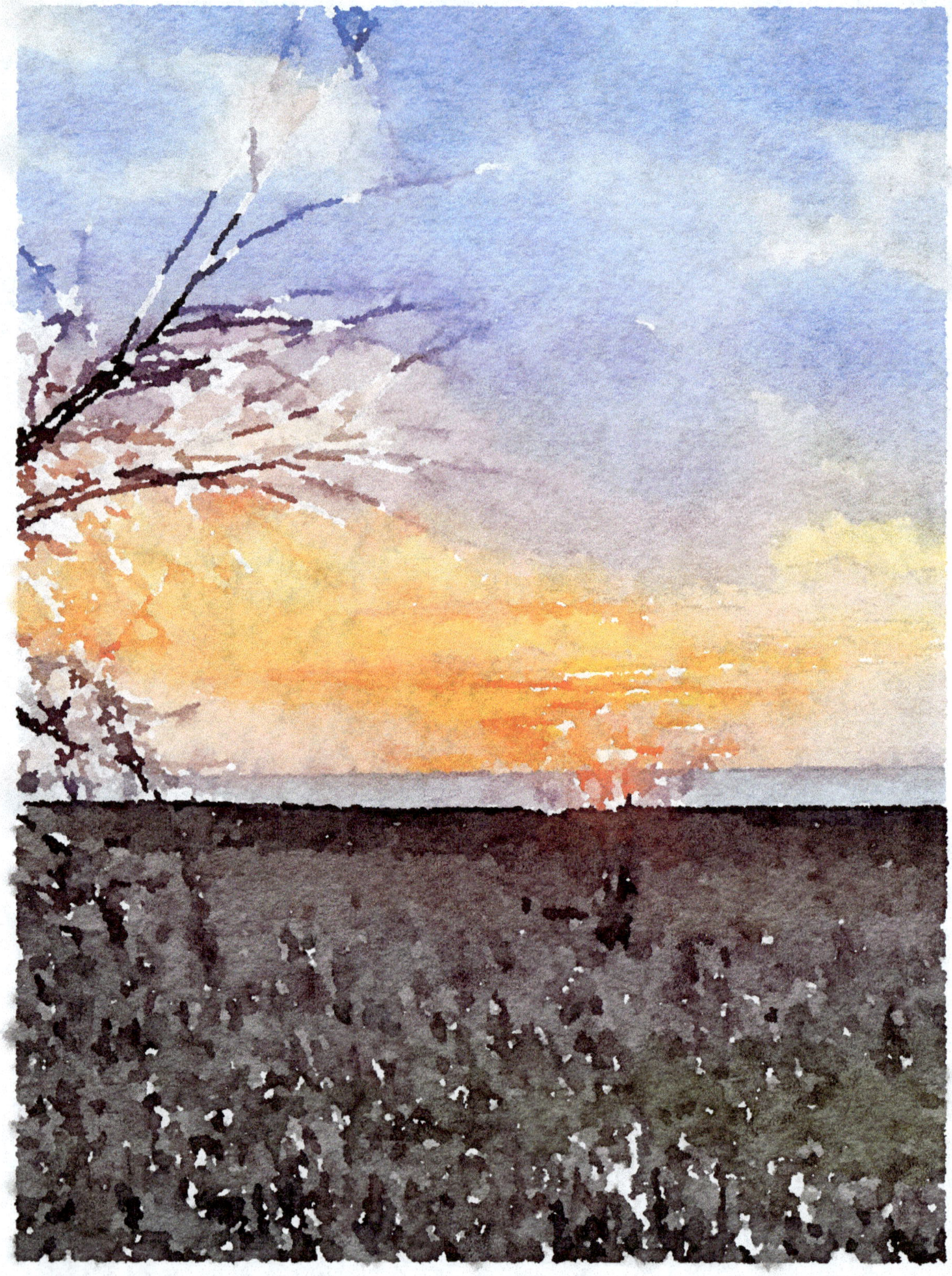

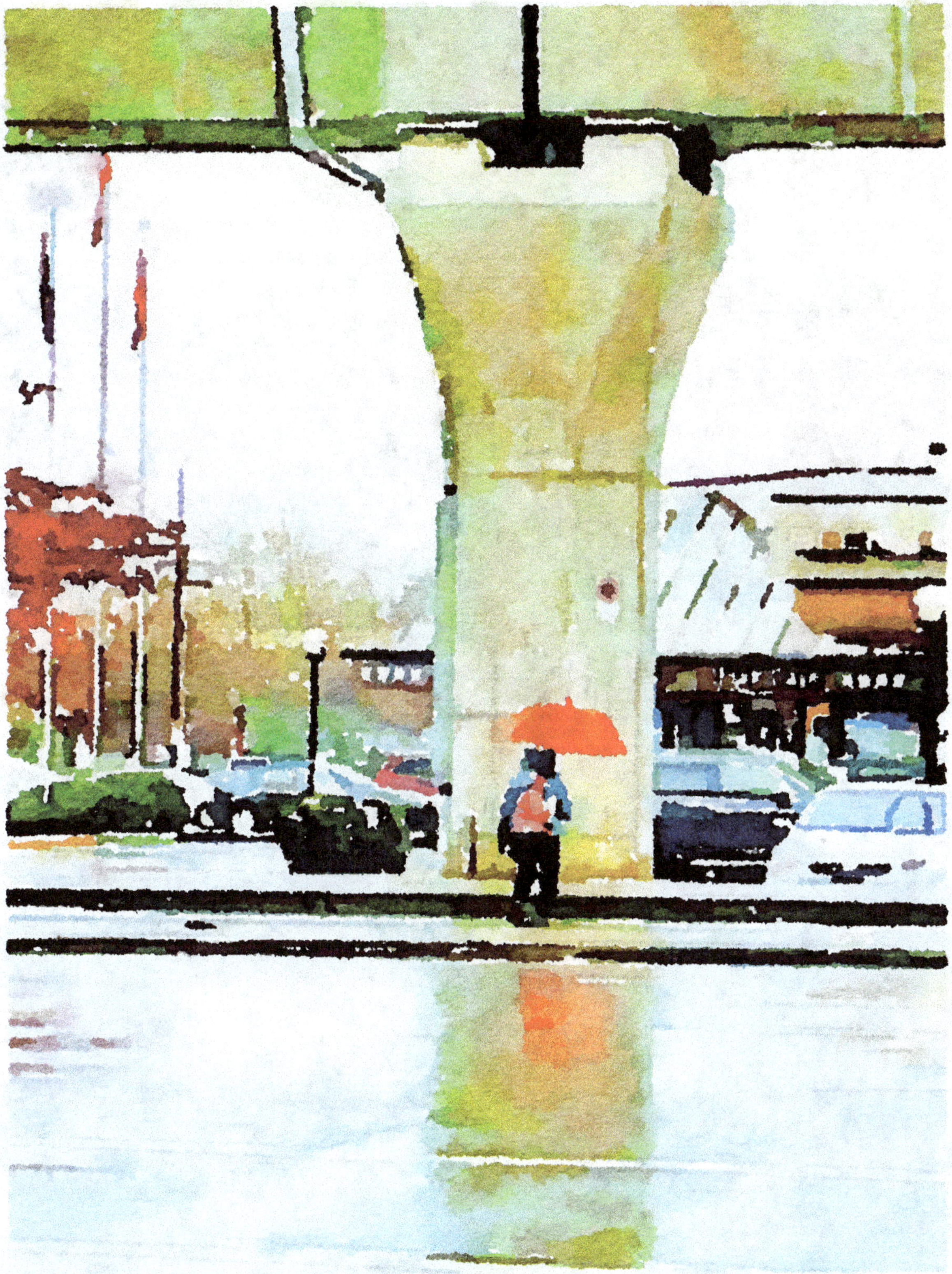

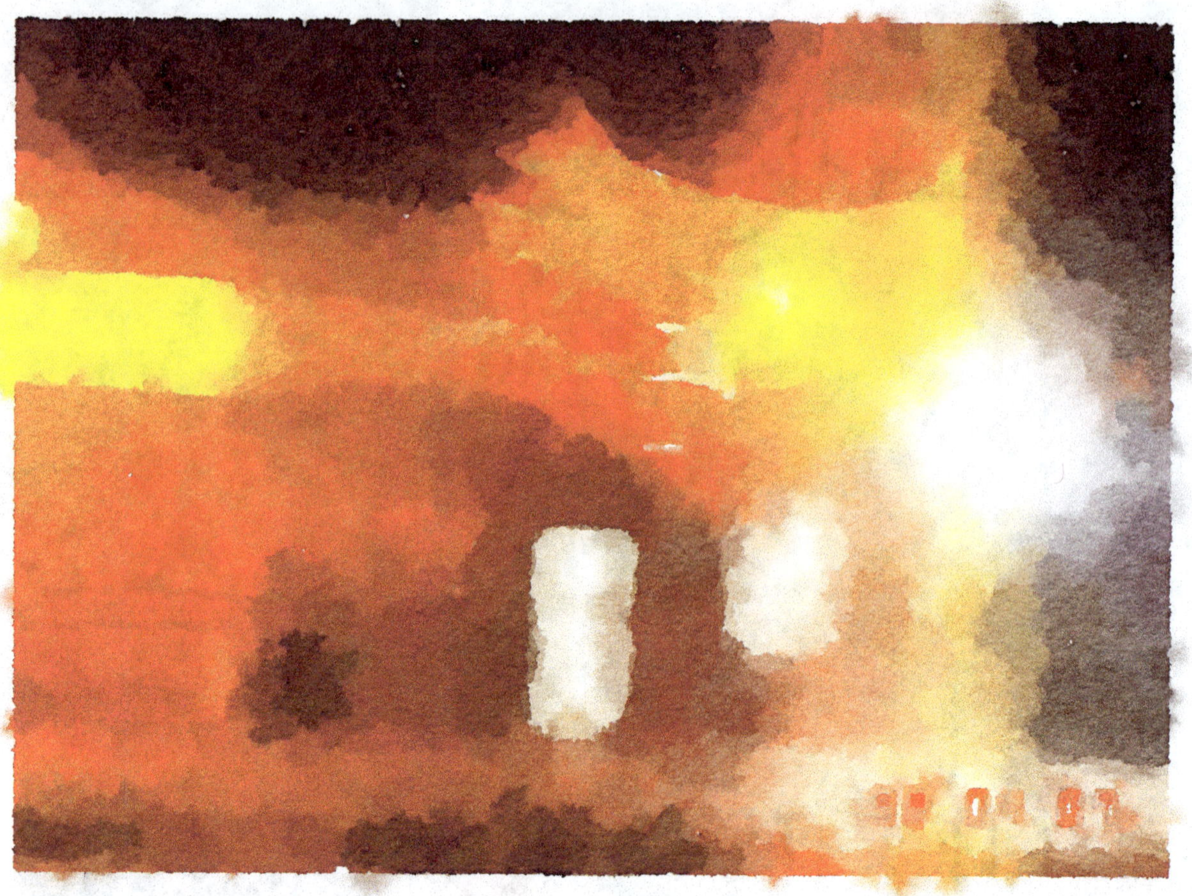

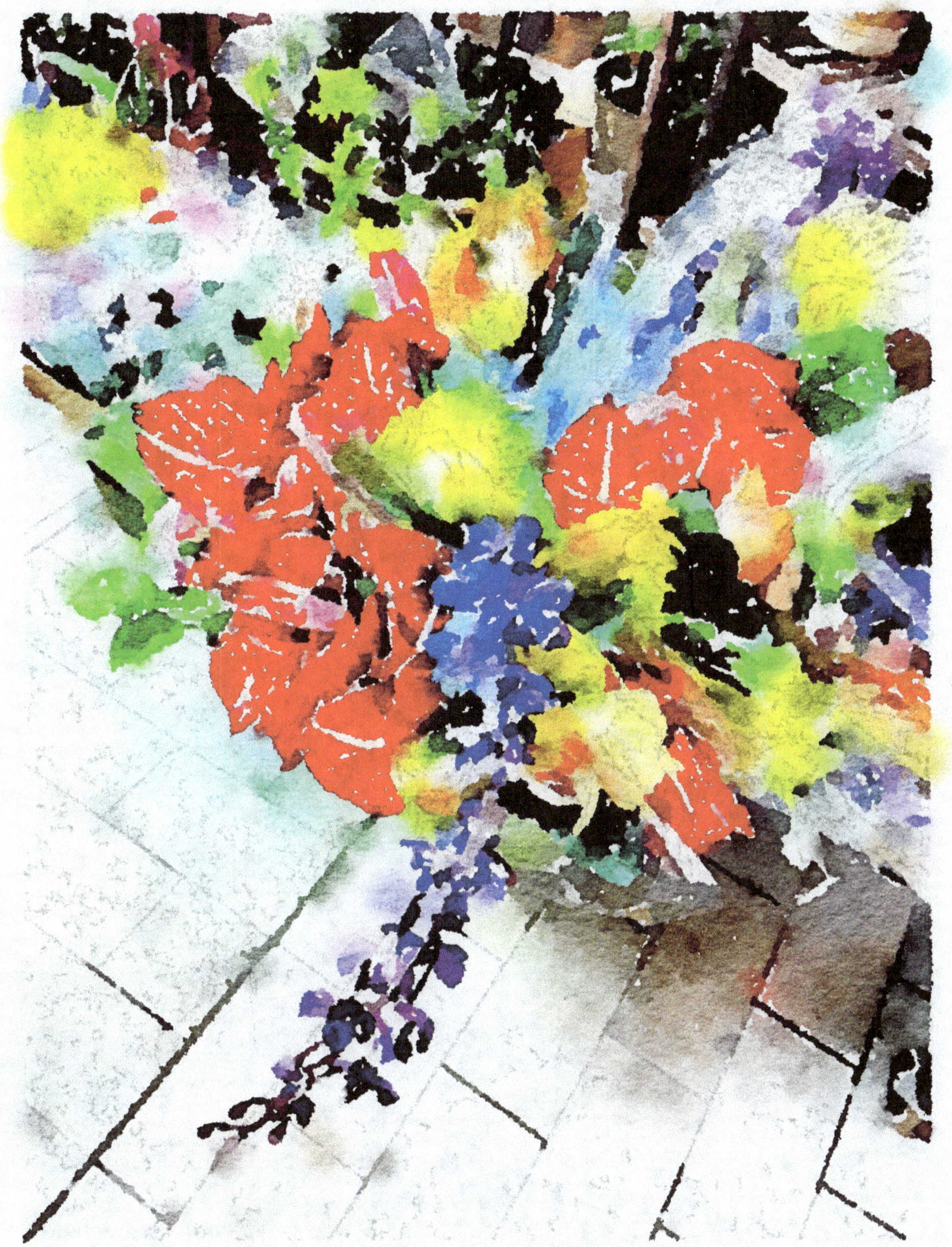

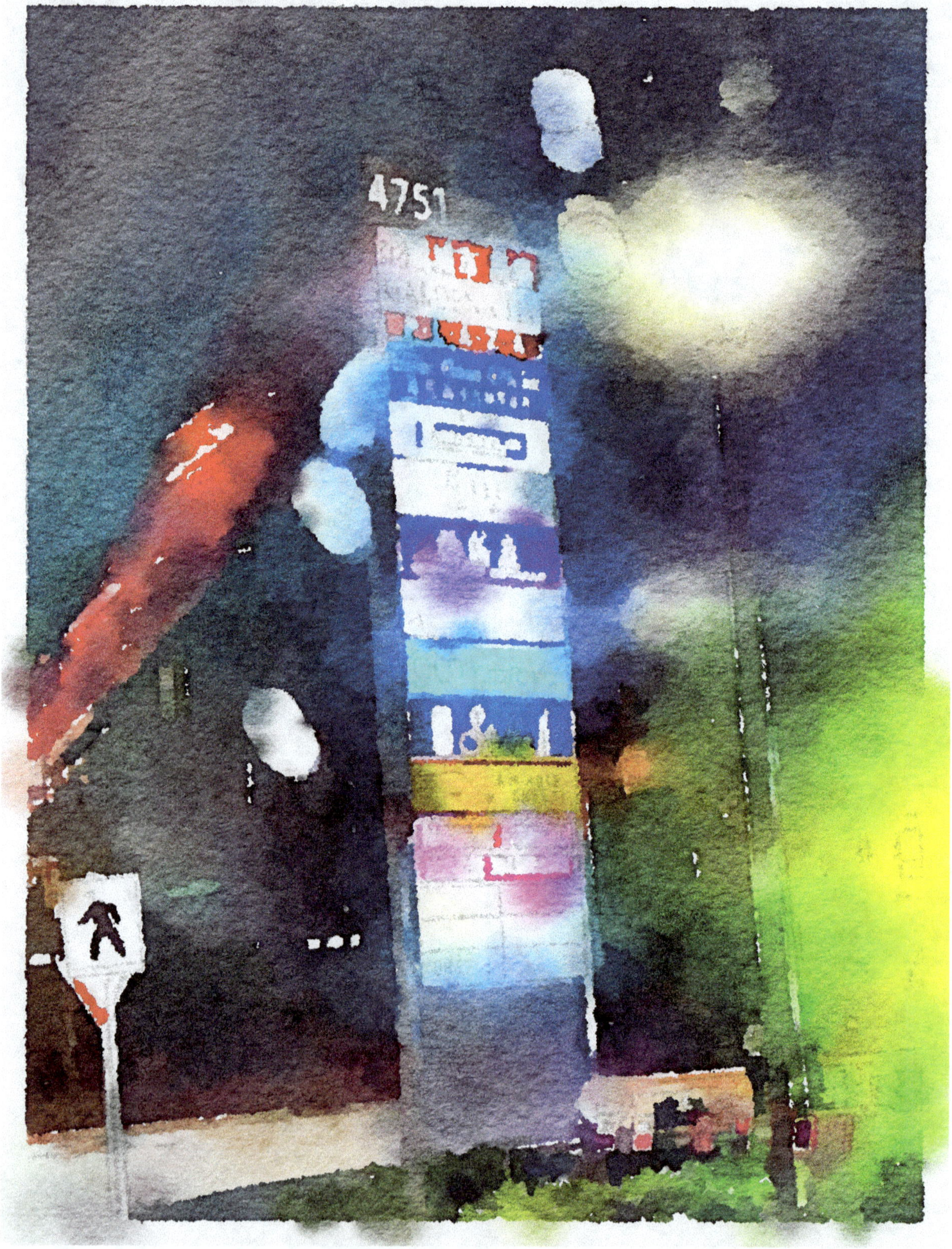
4751

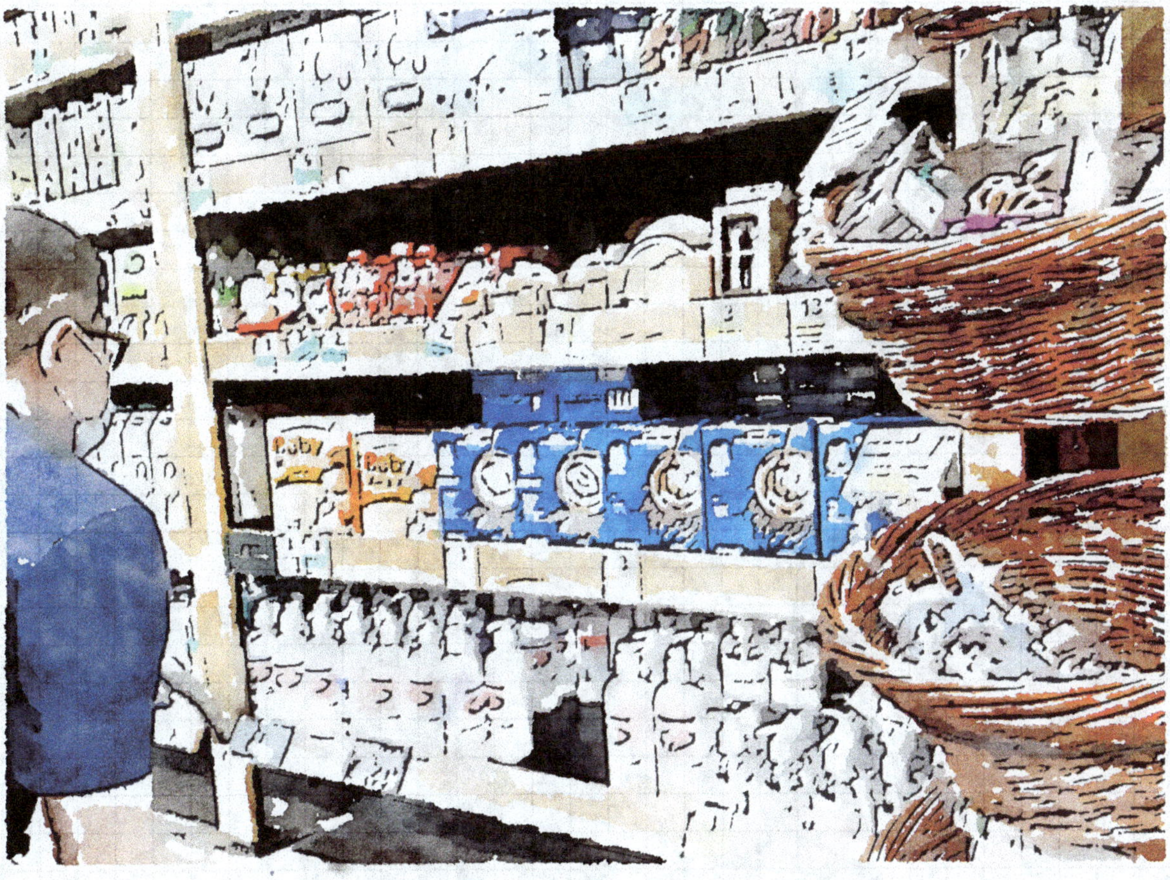

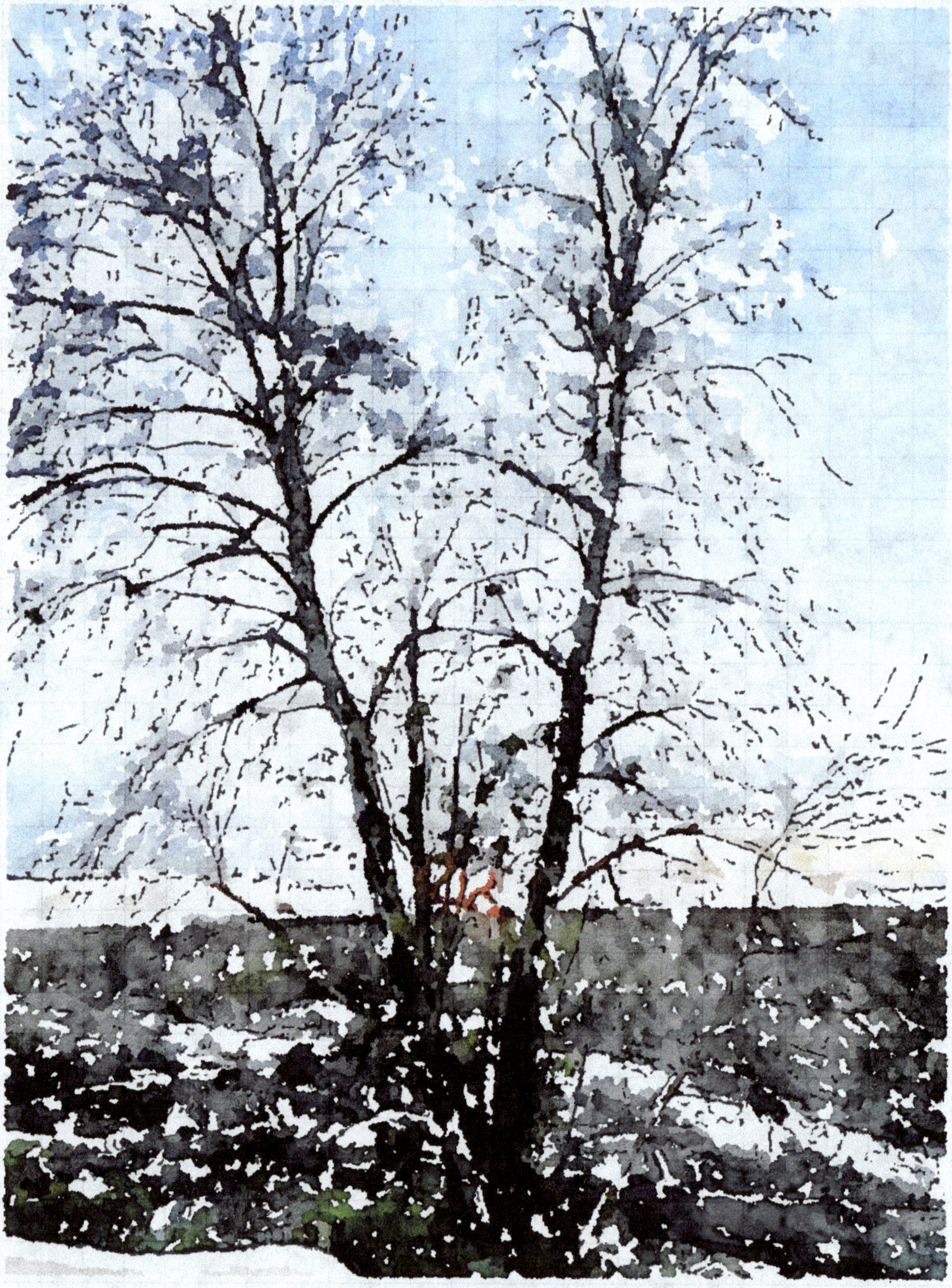

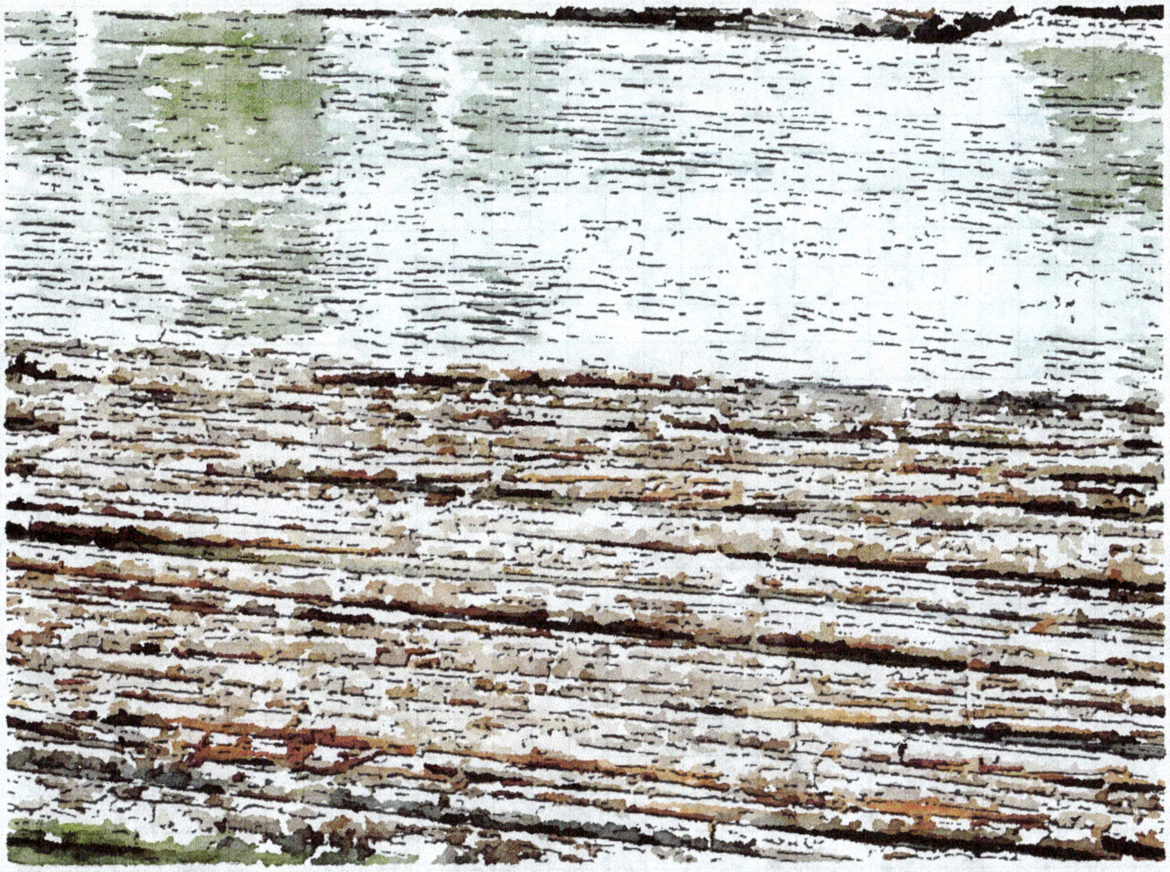

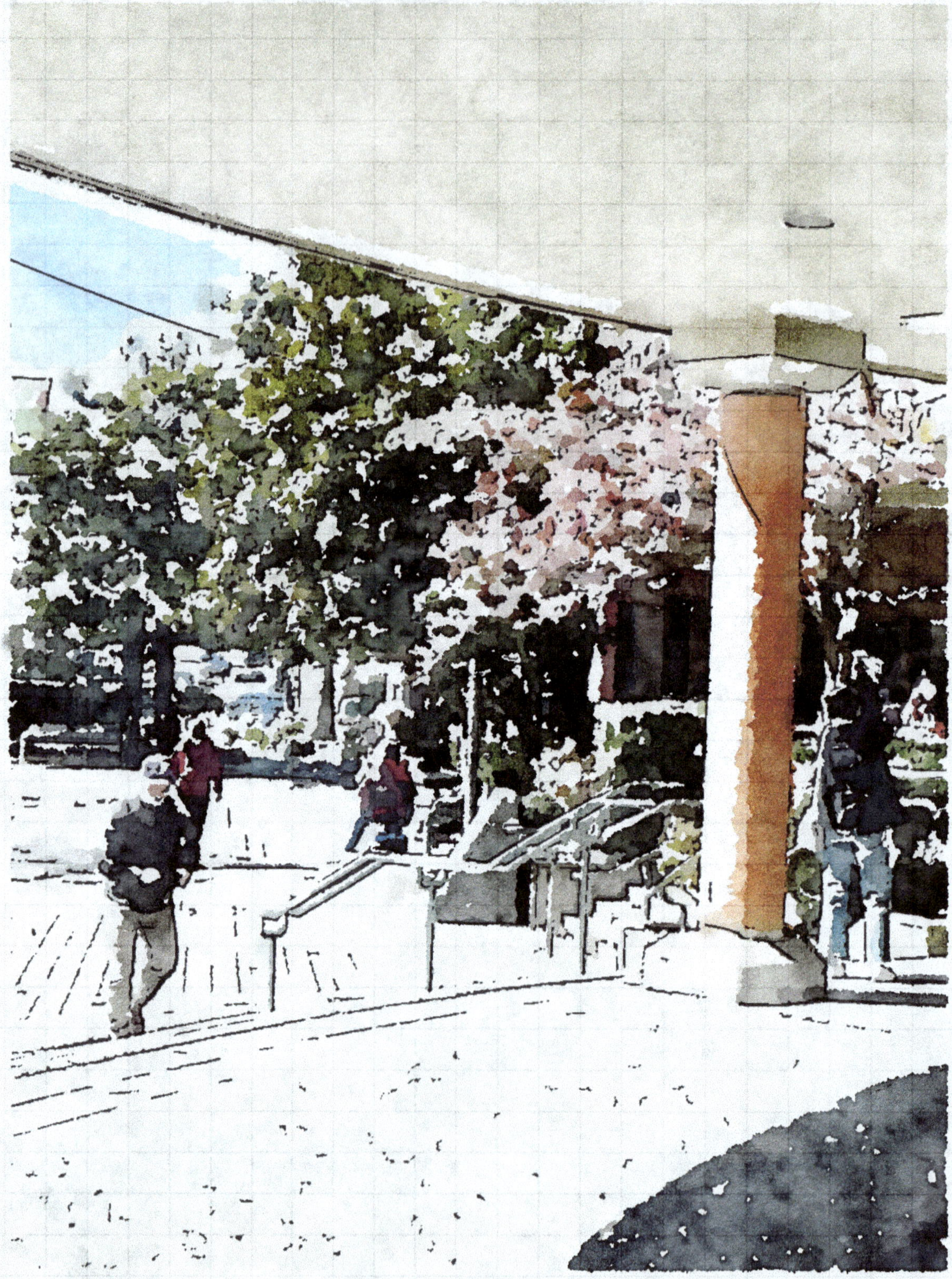

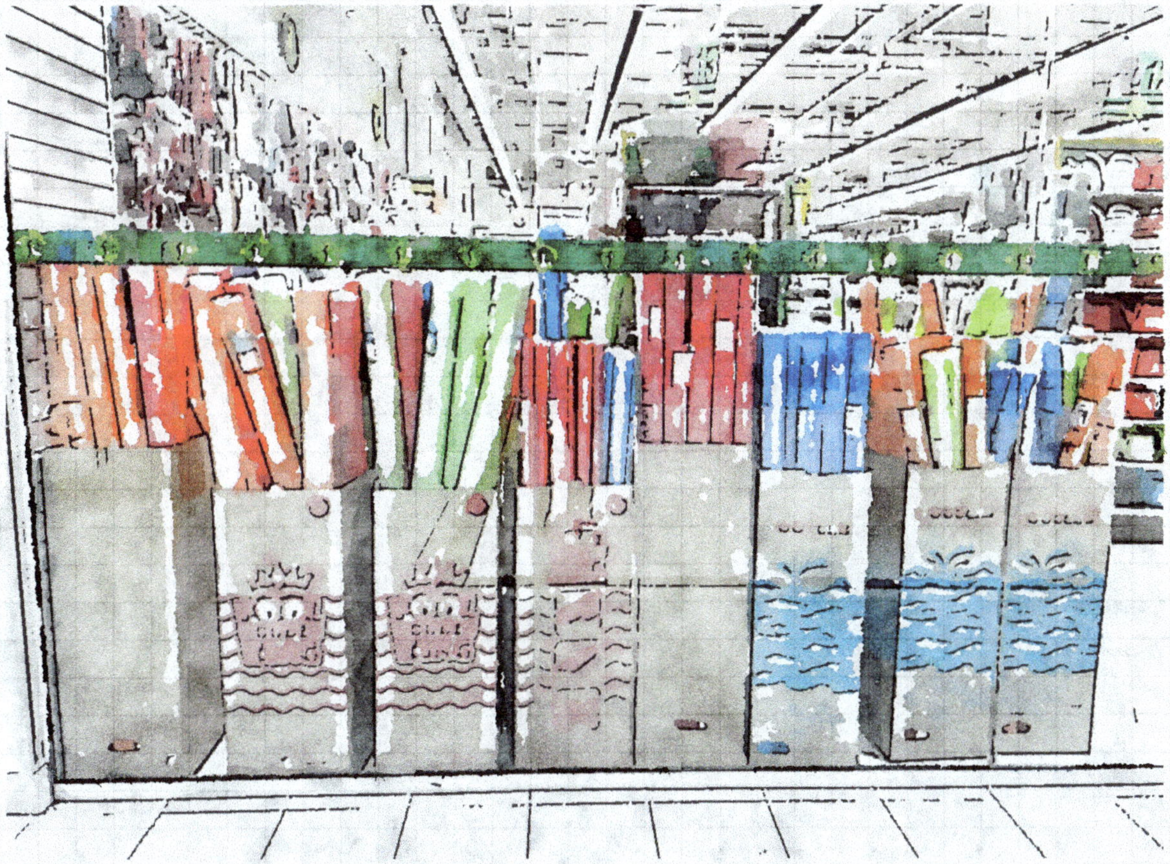

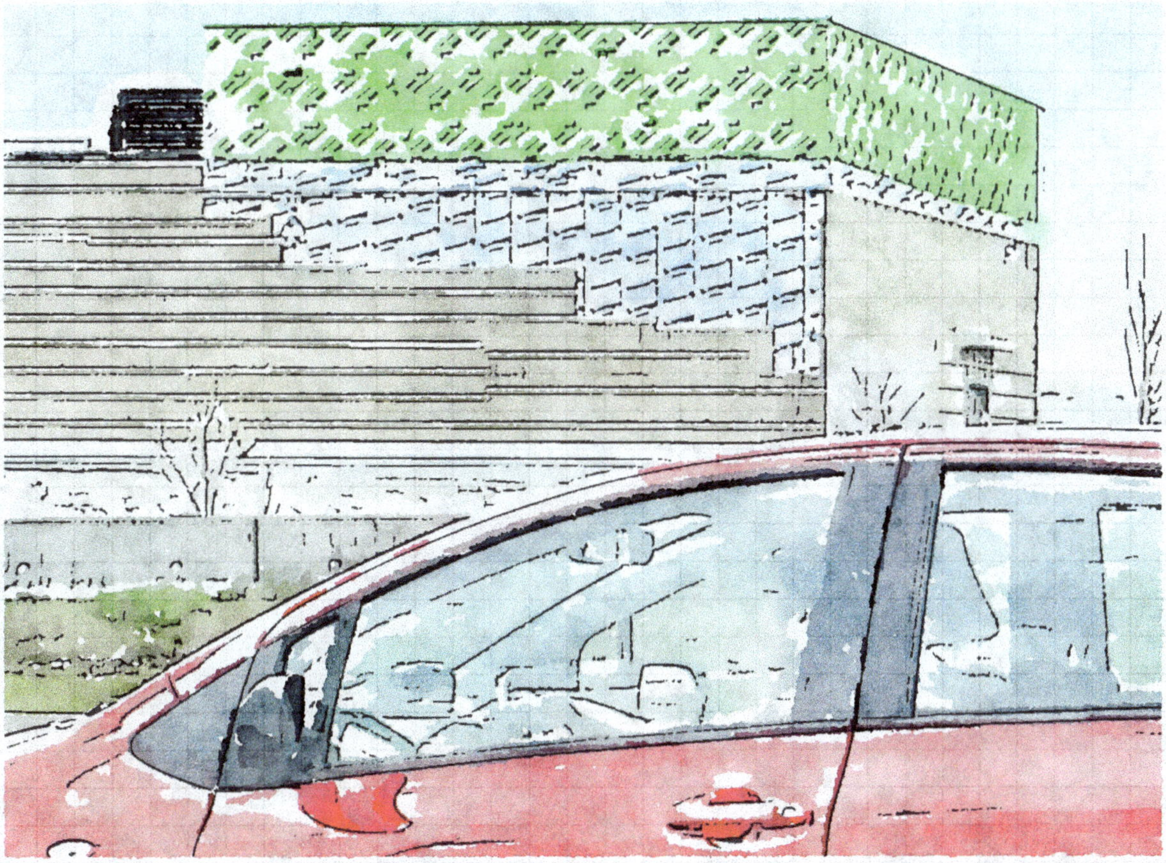

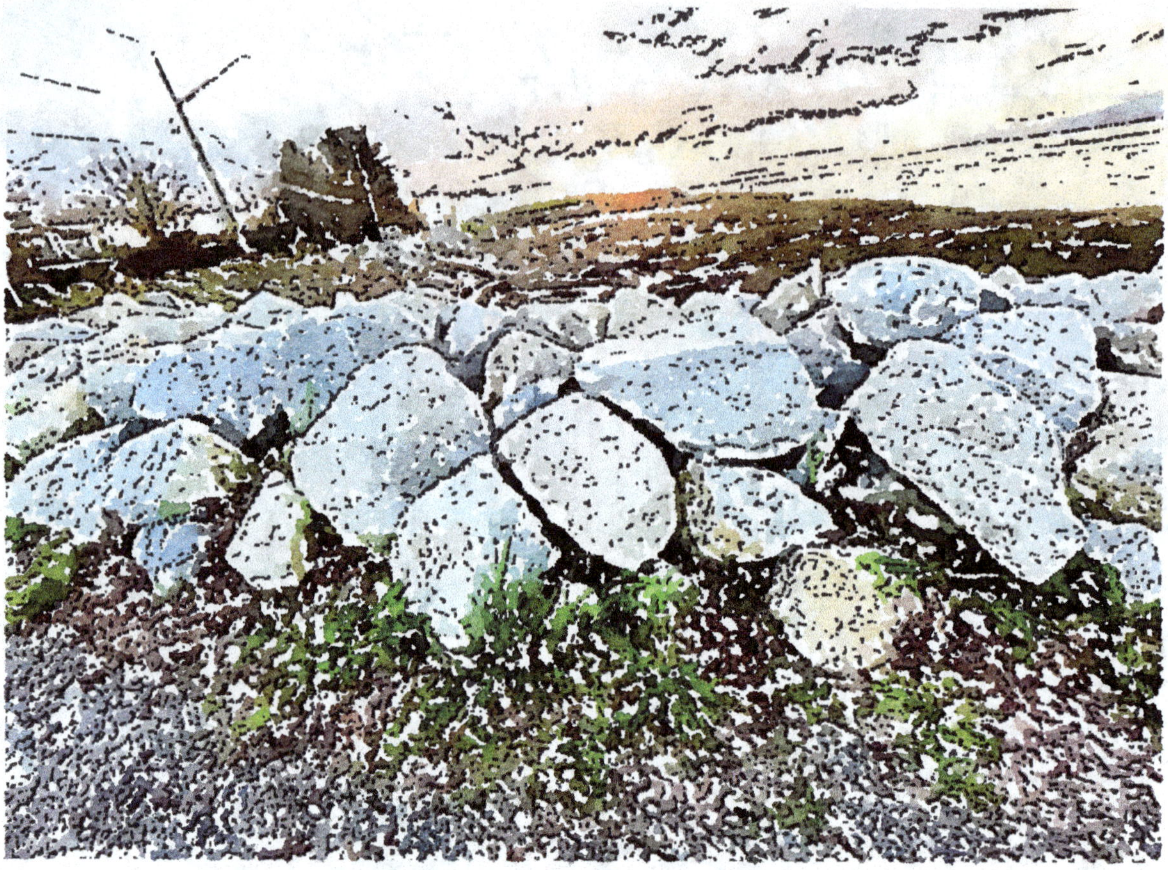

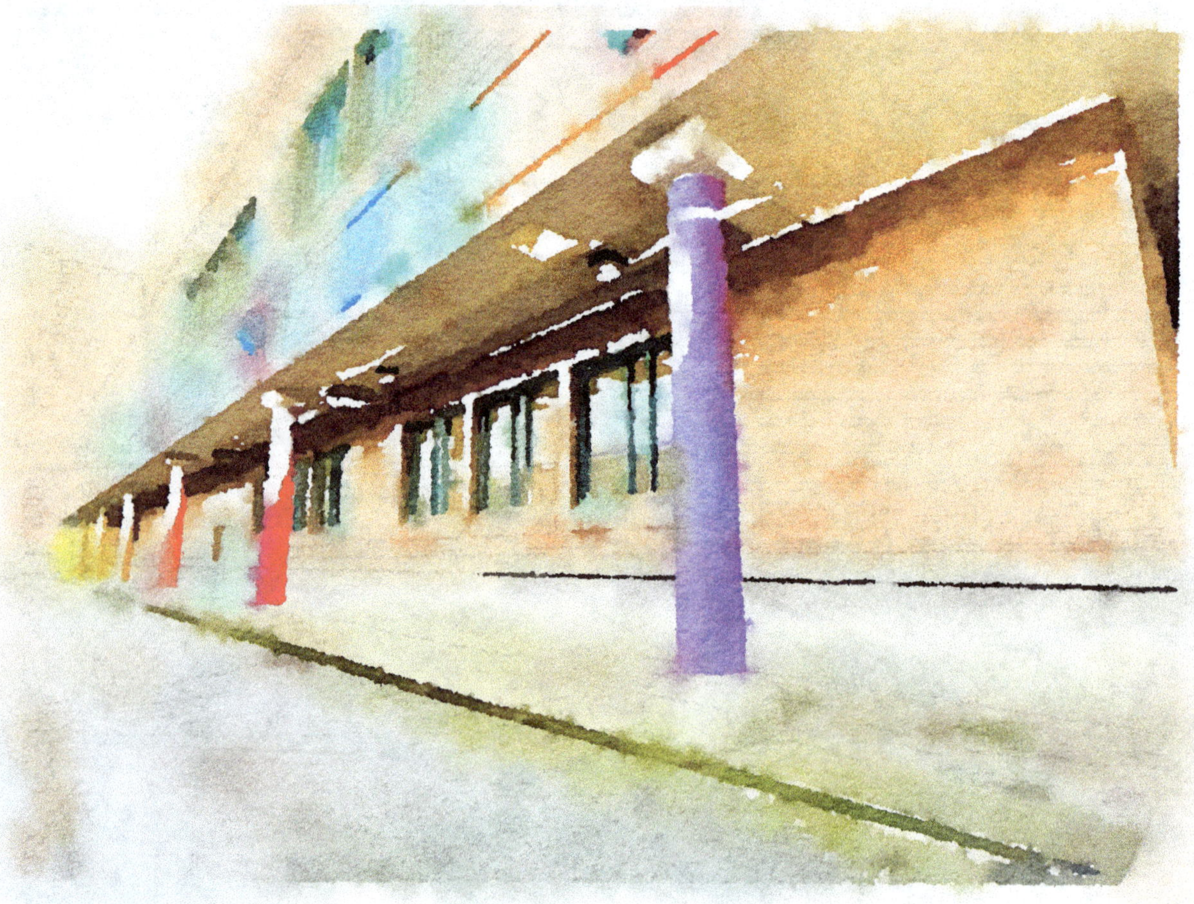

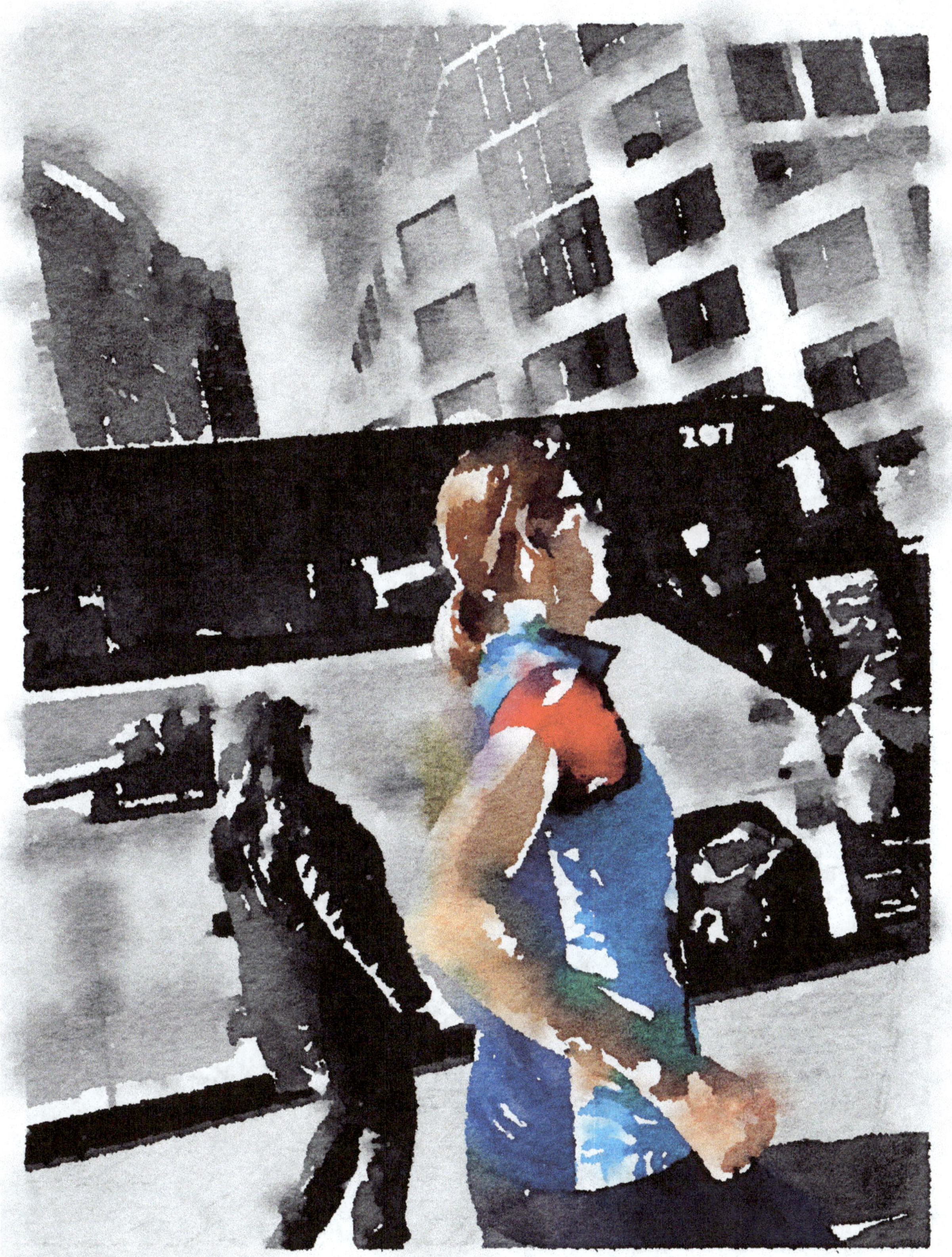
207

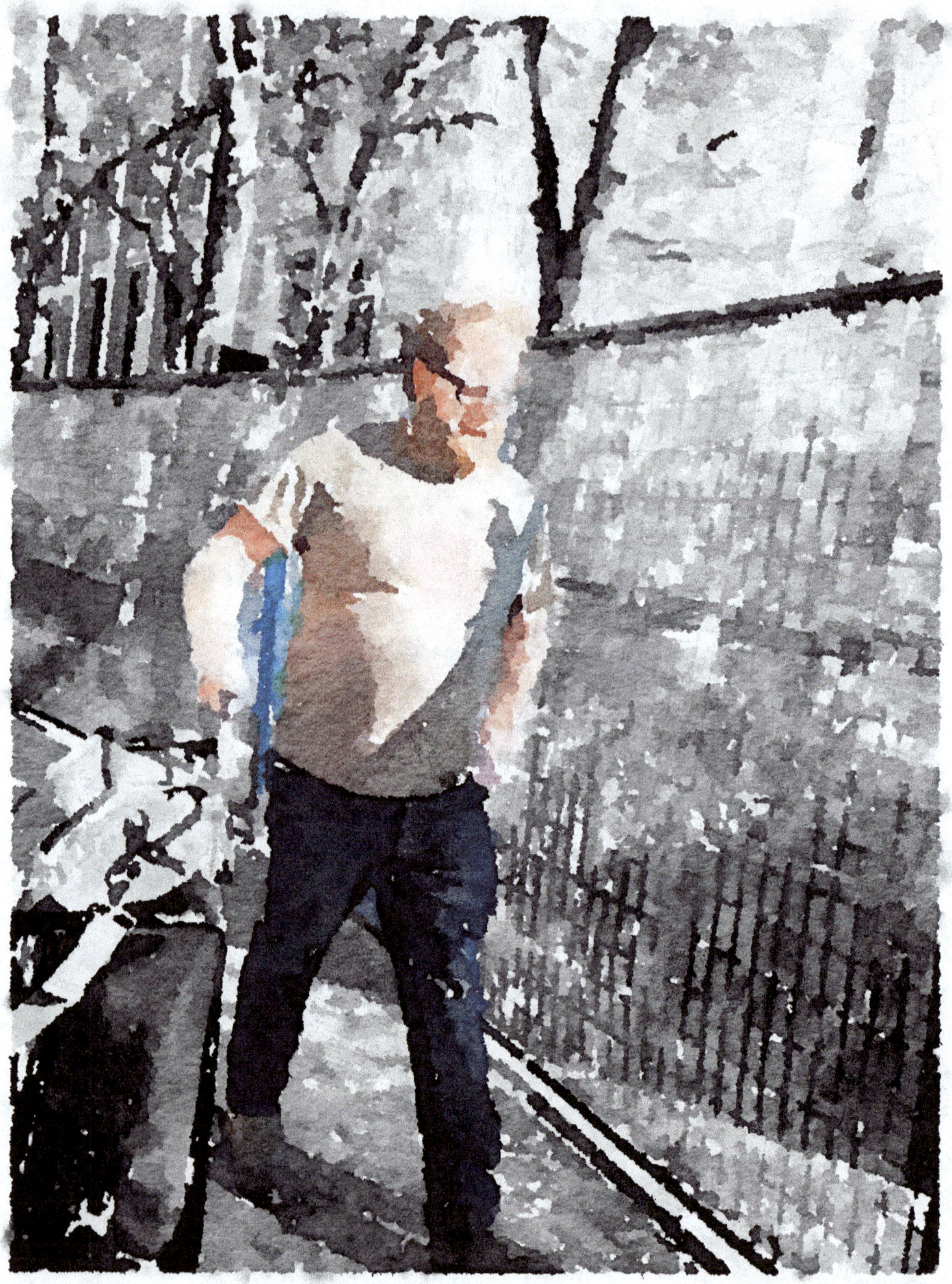

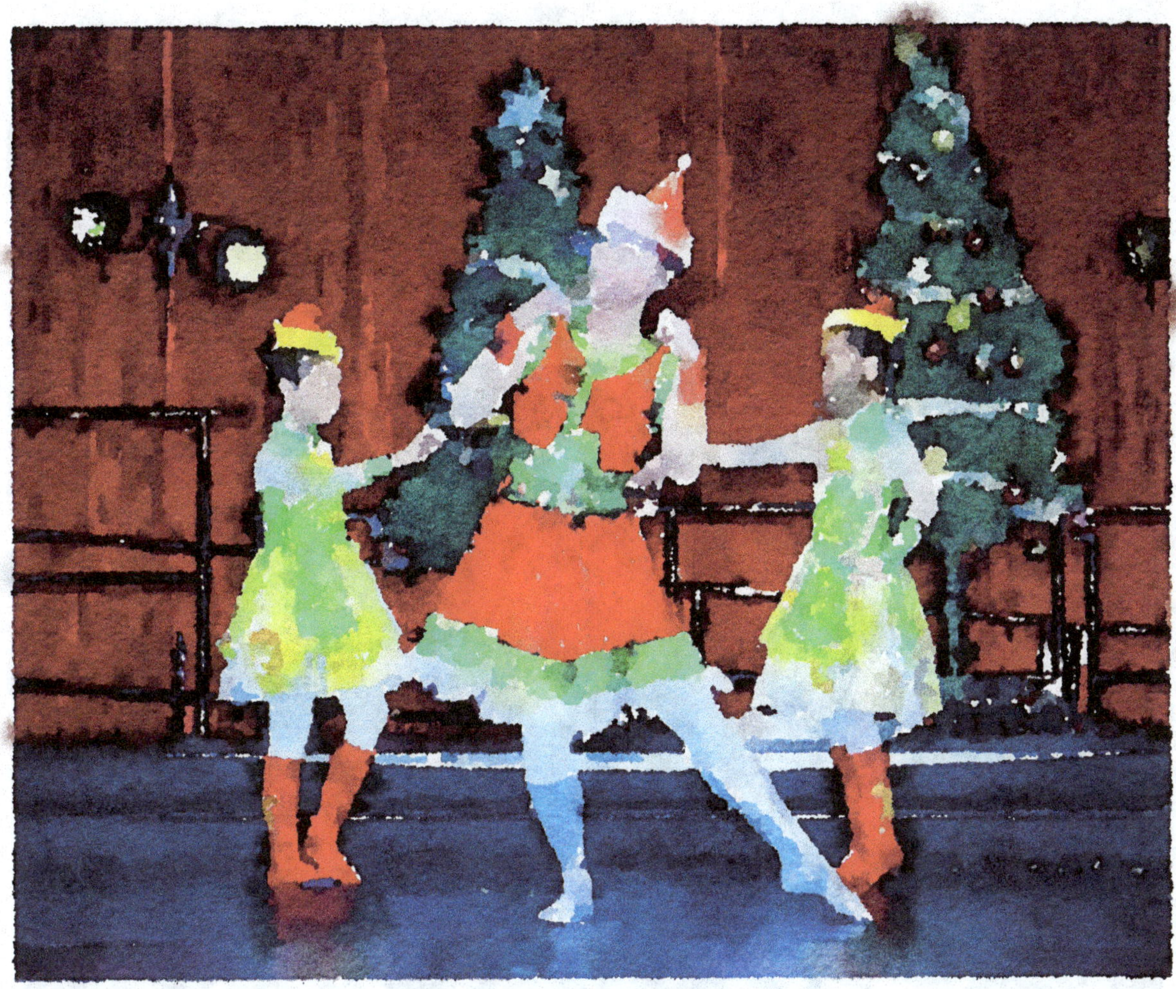

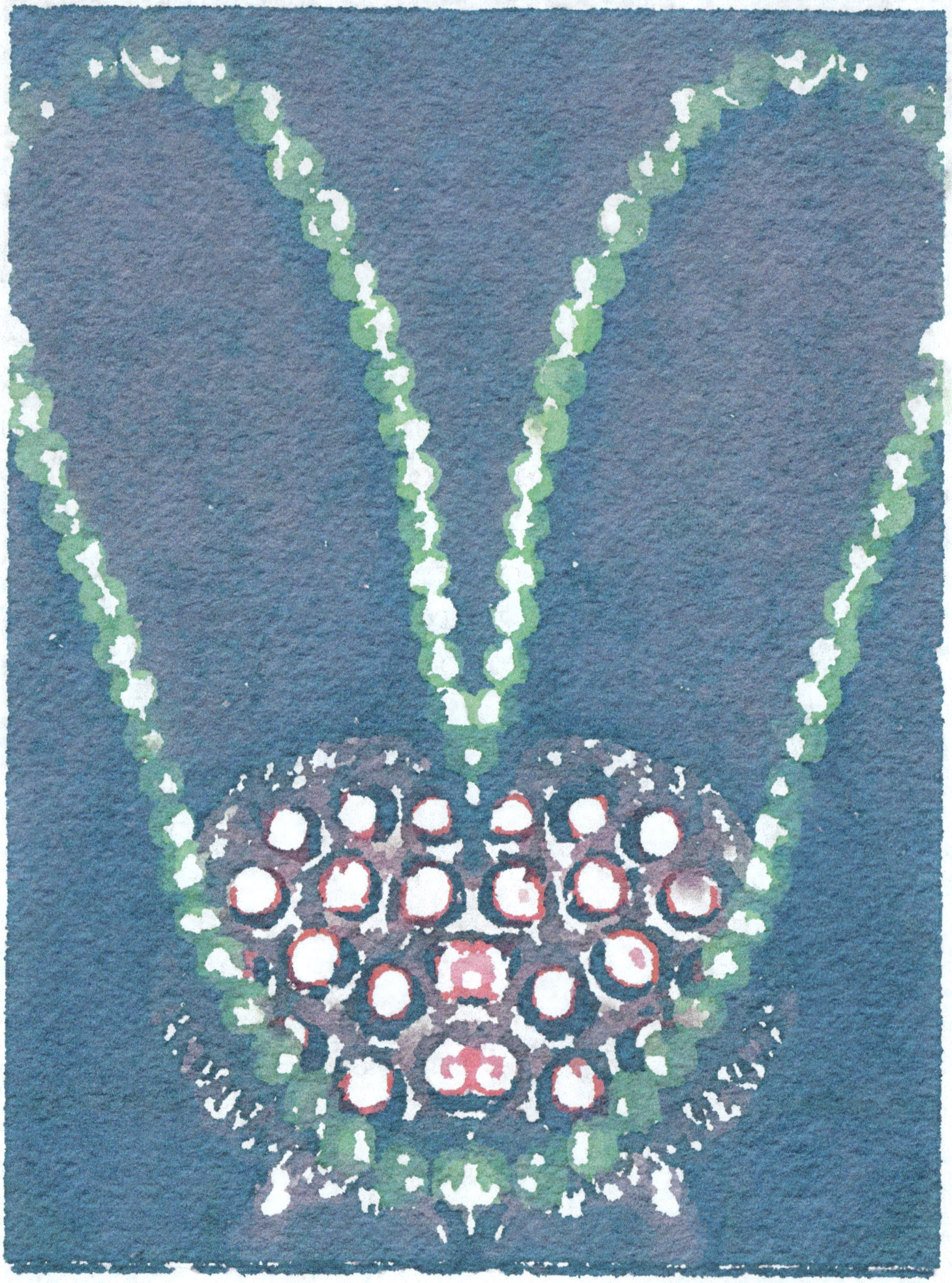

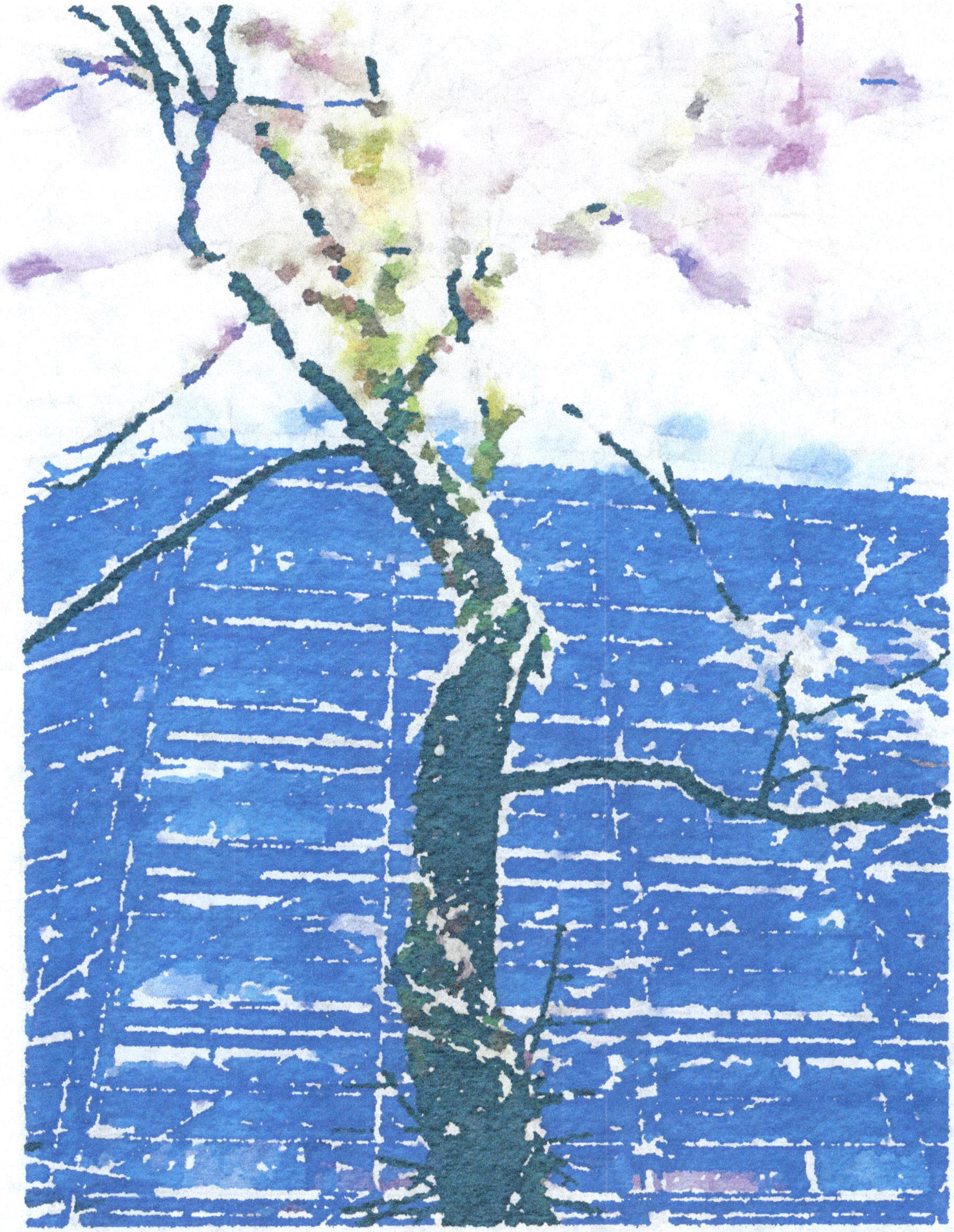

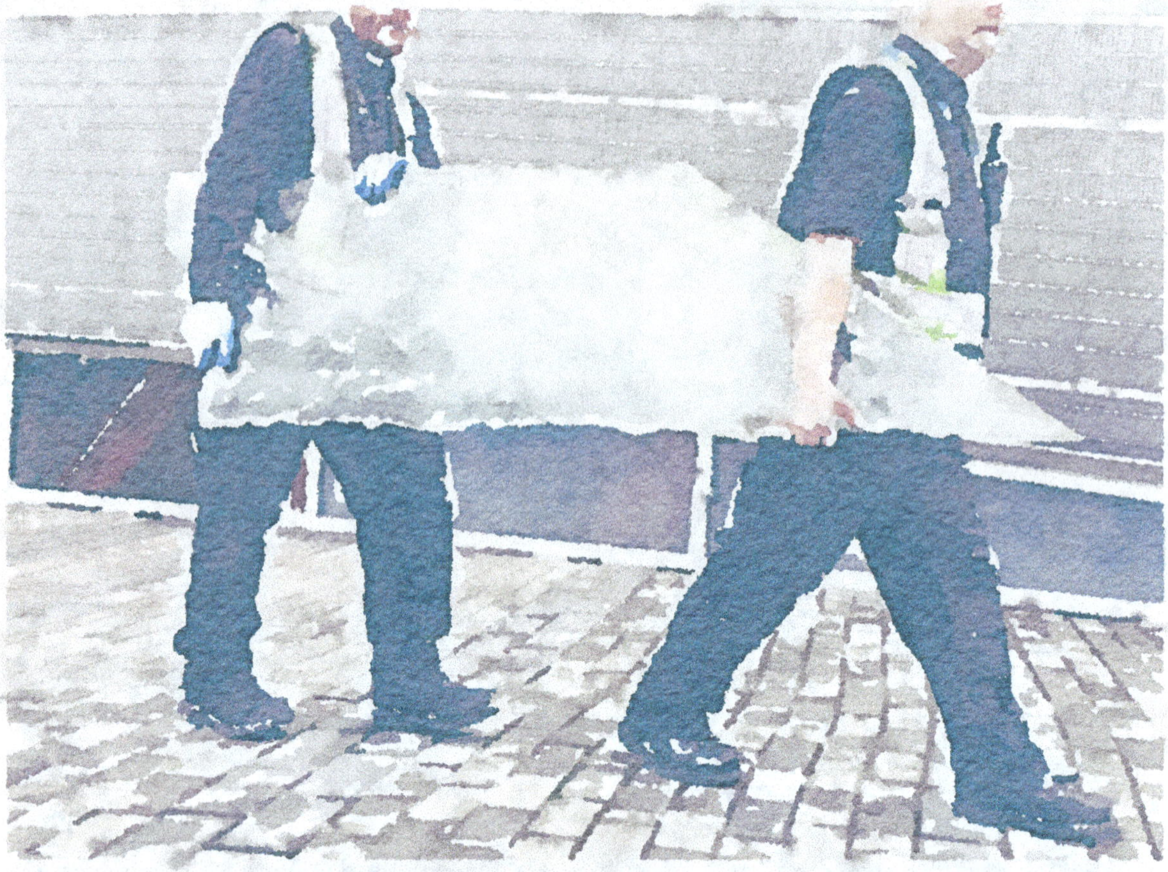

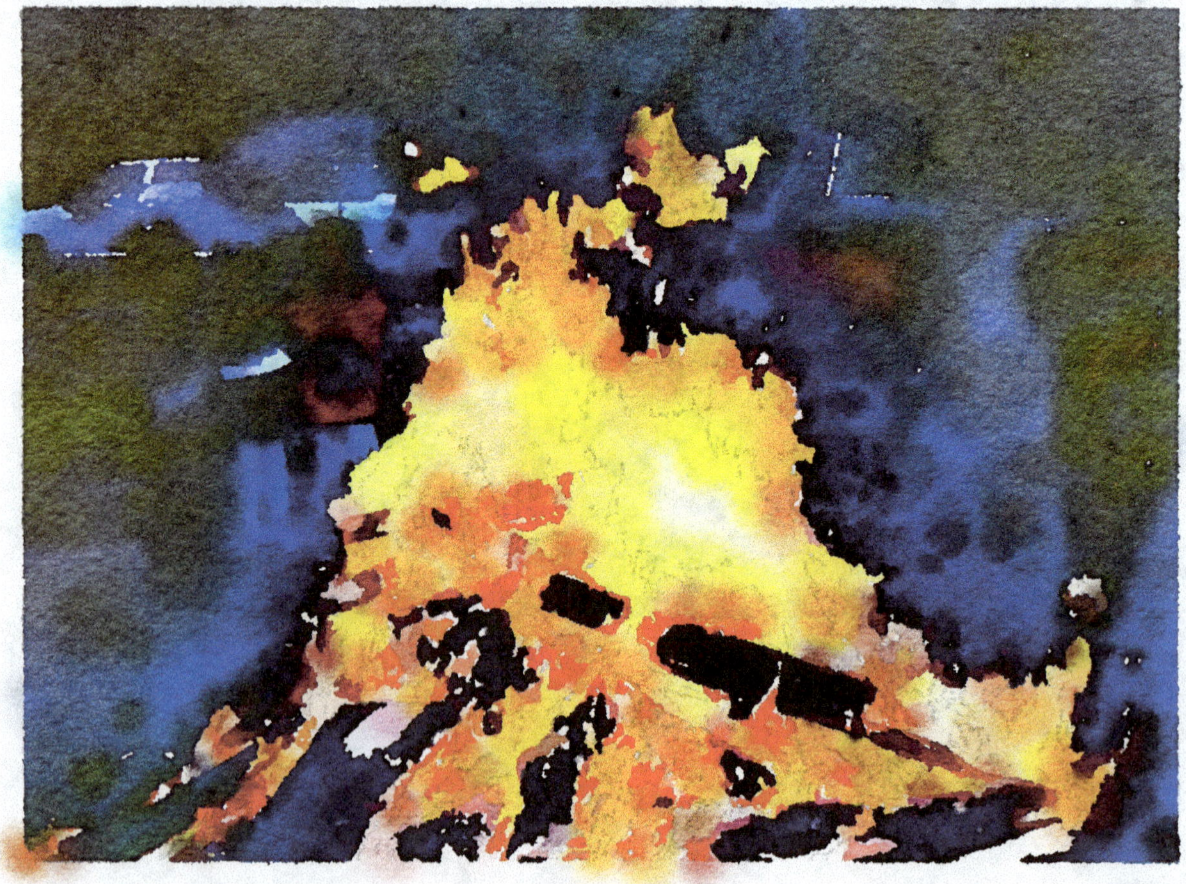

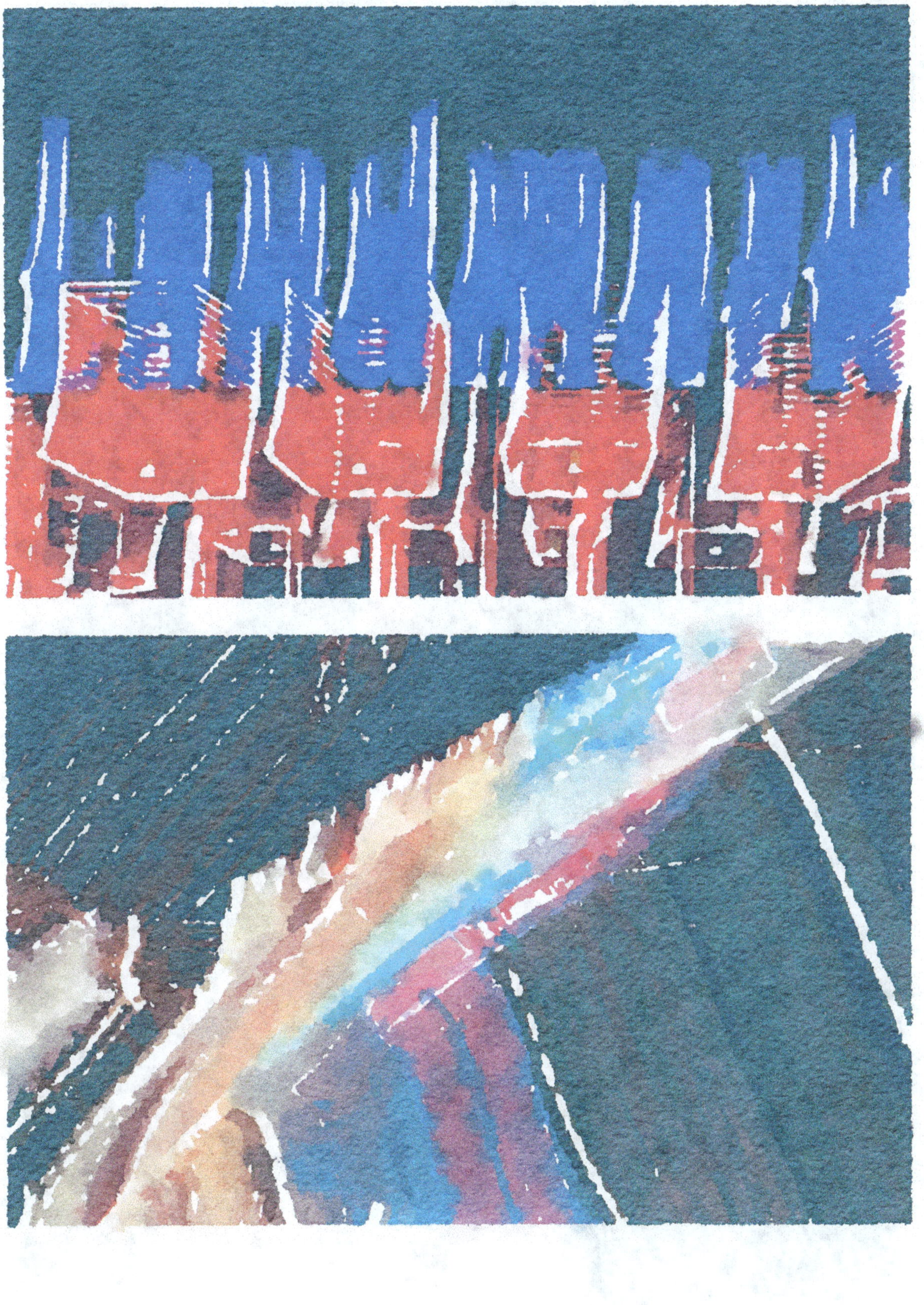

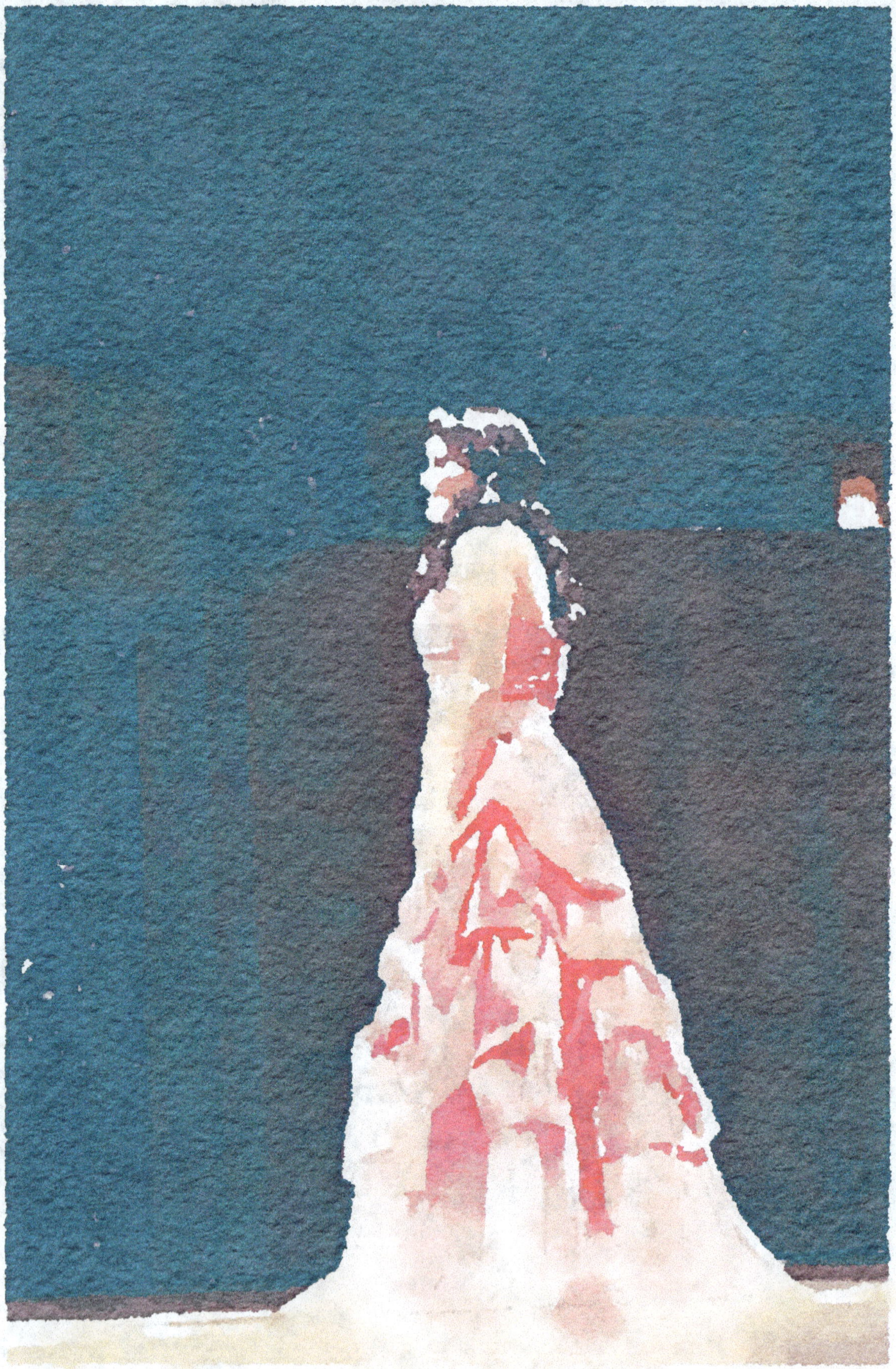

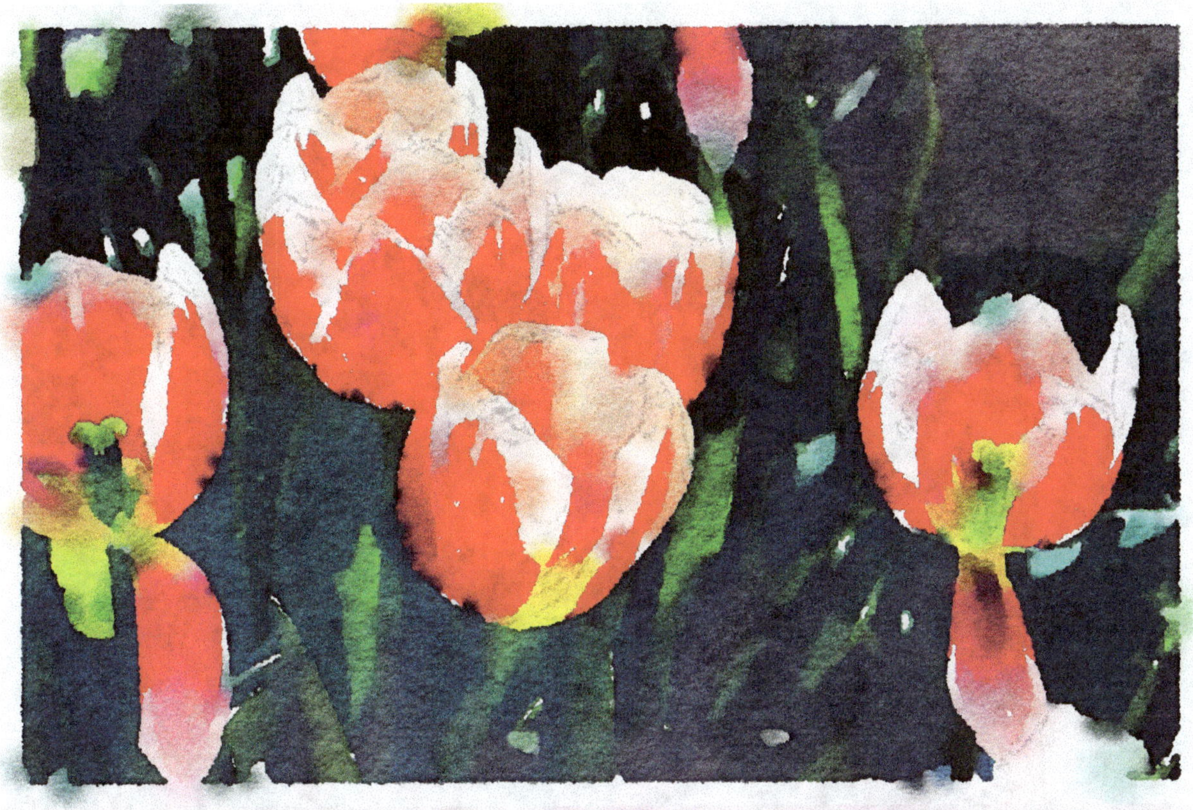

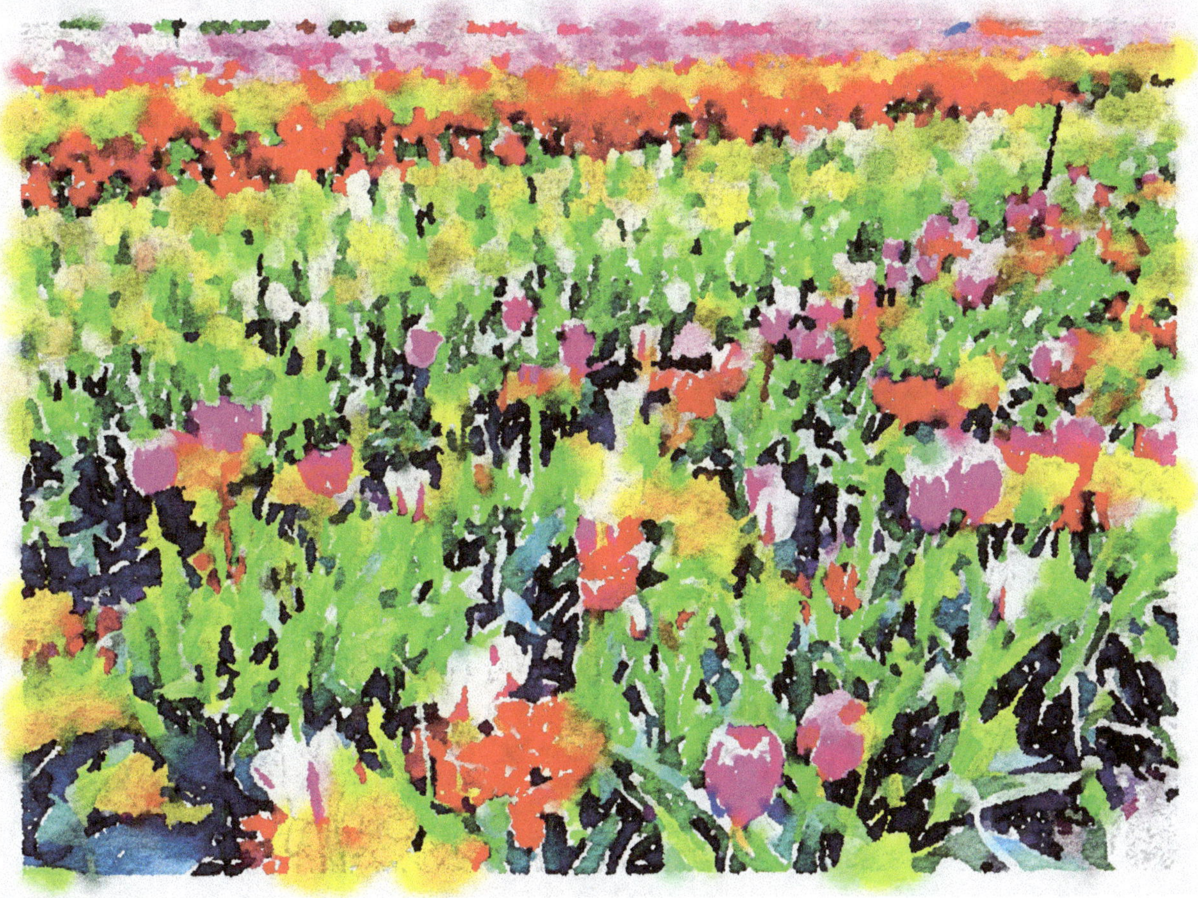

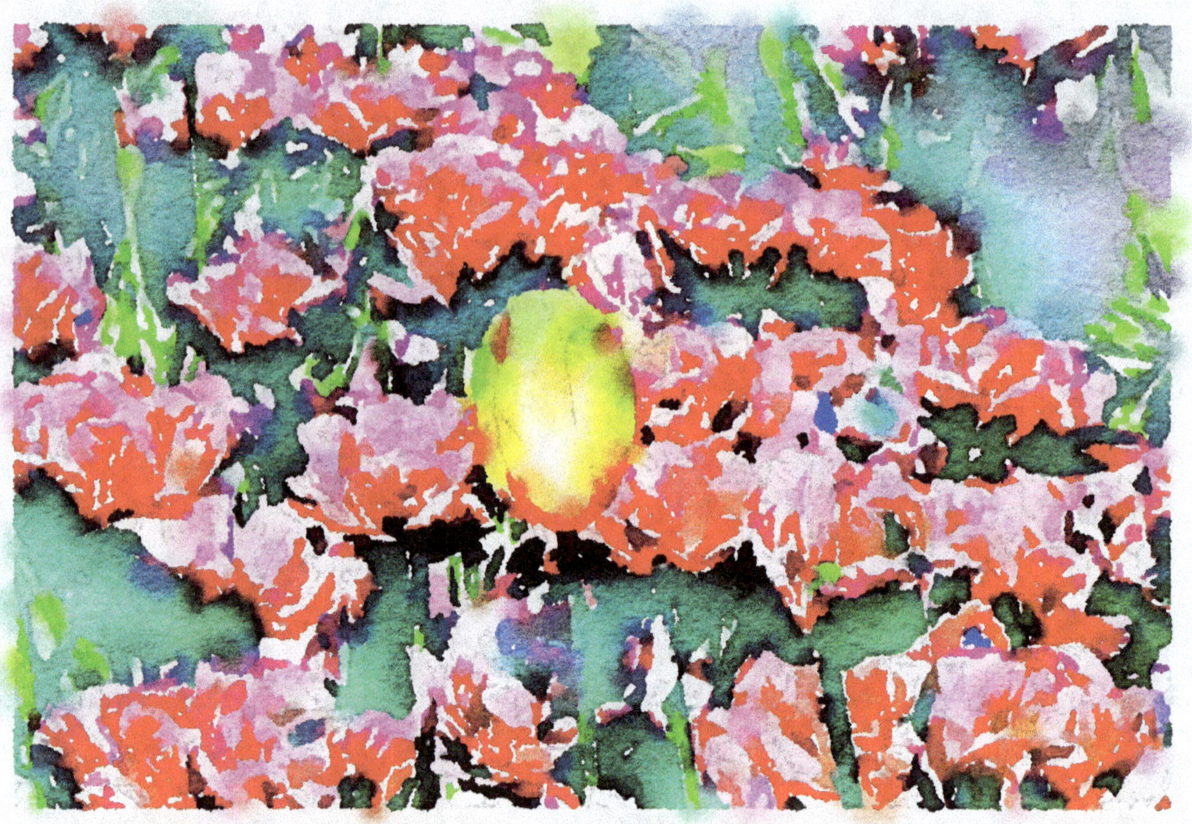

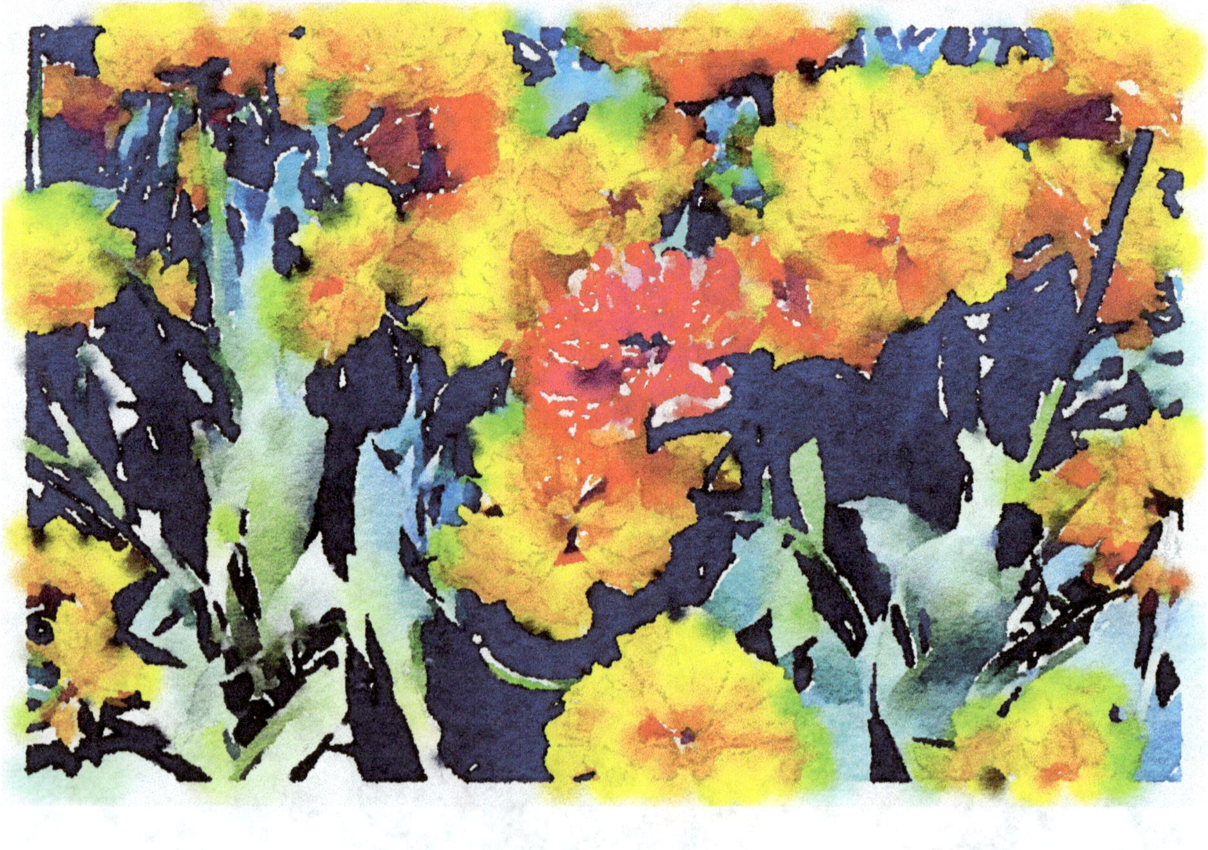

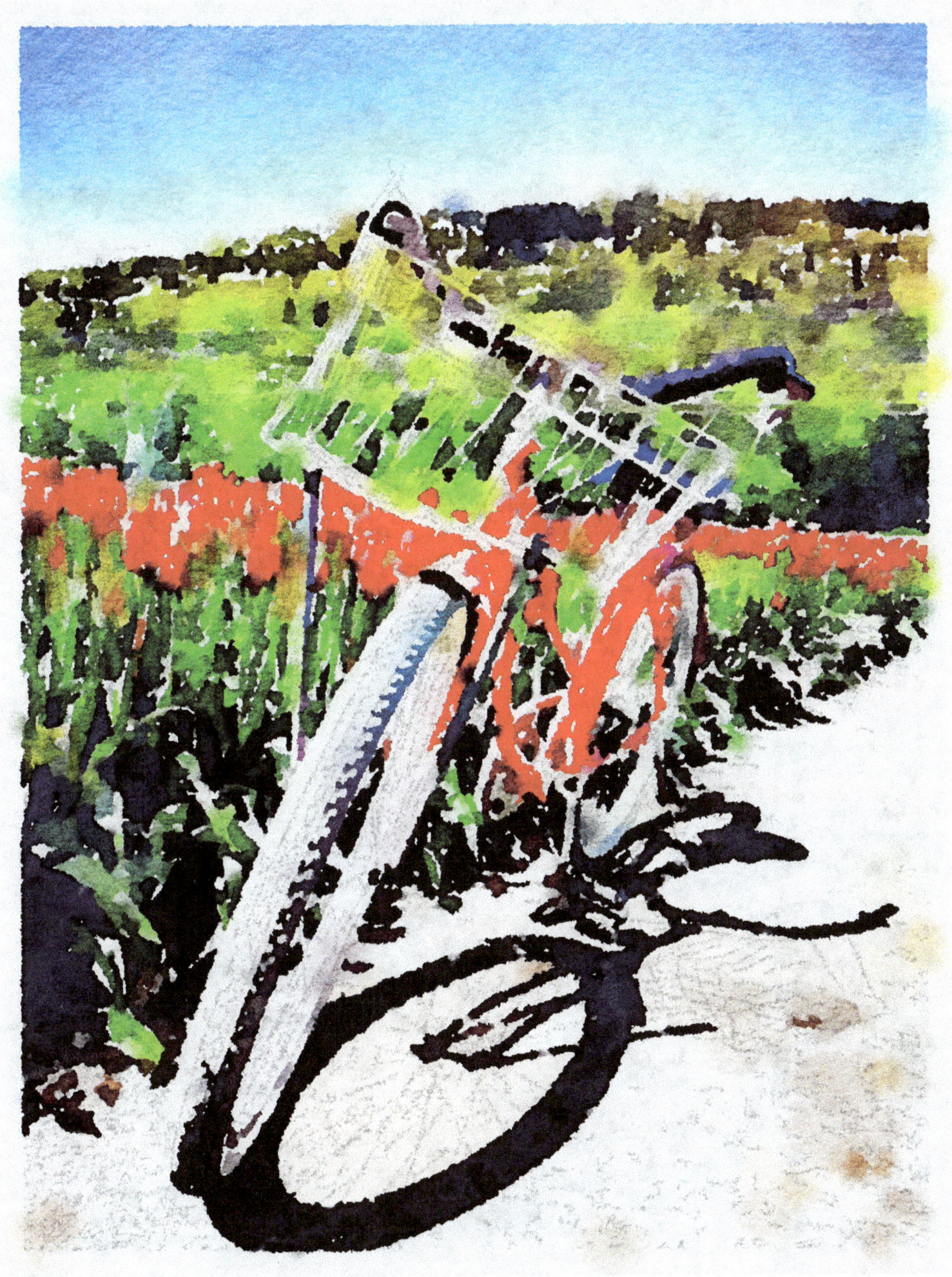

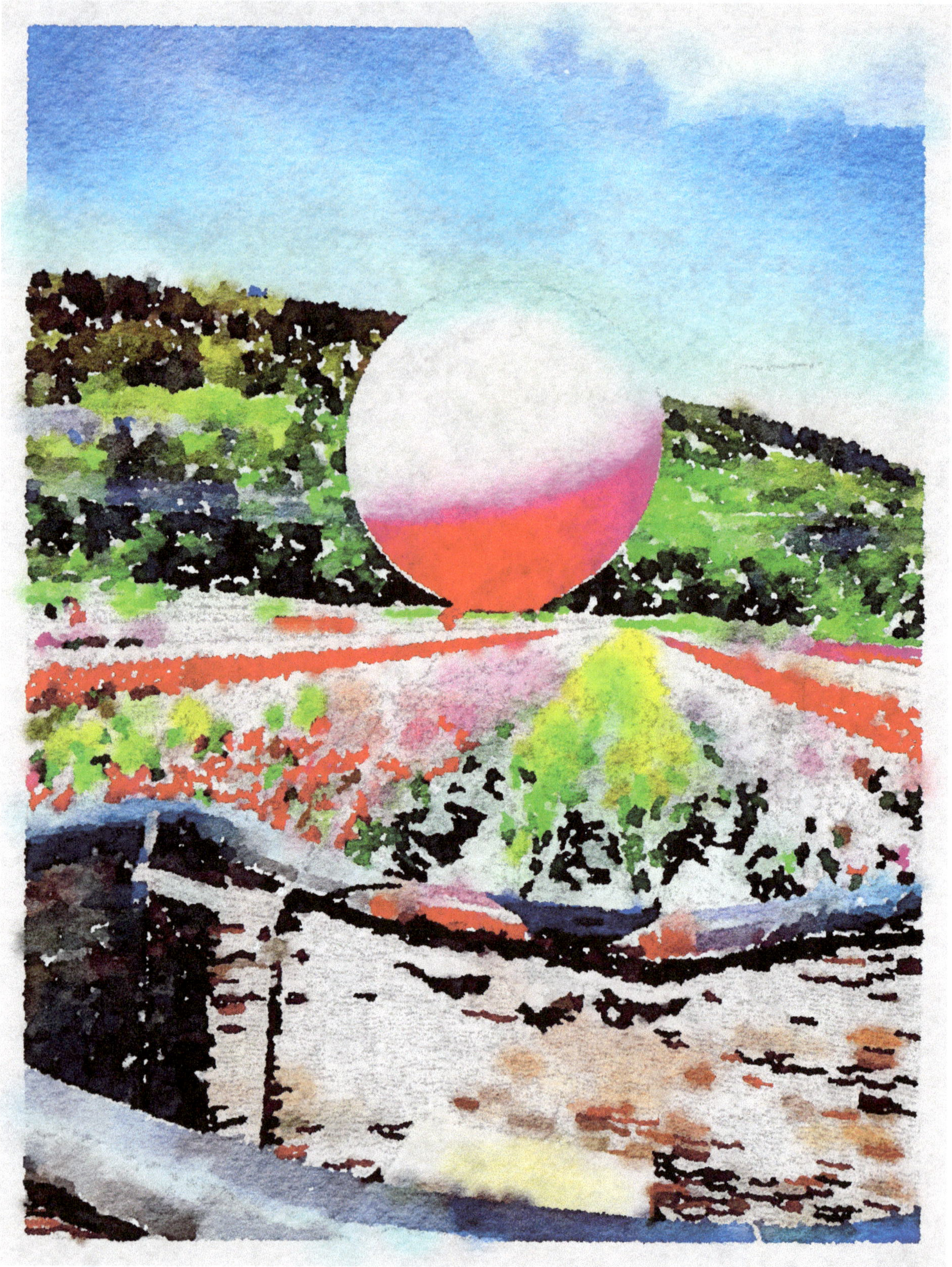

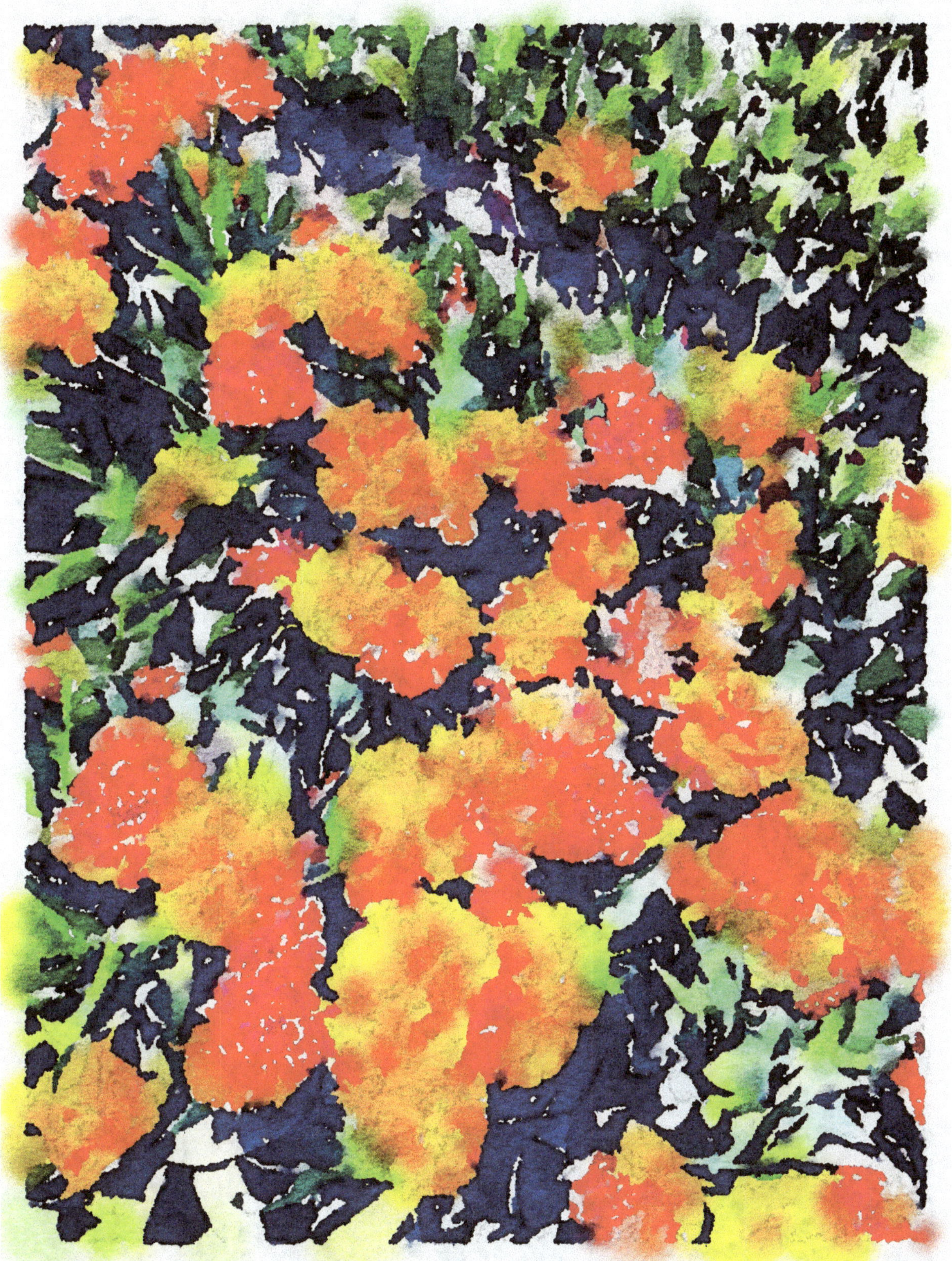

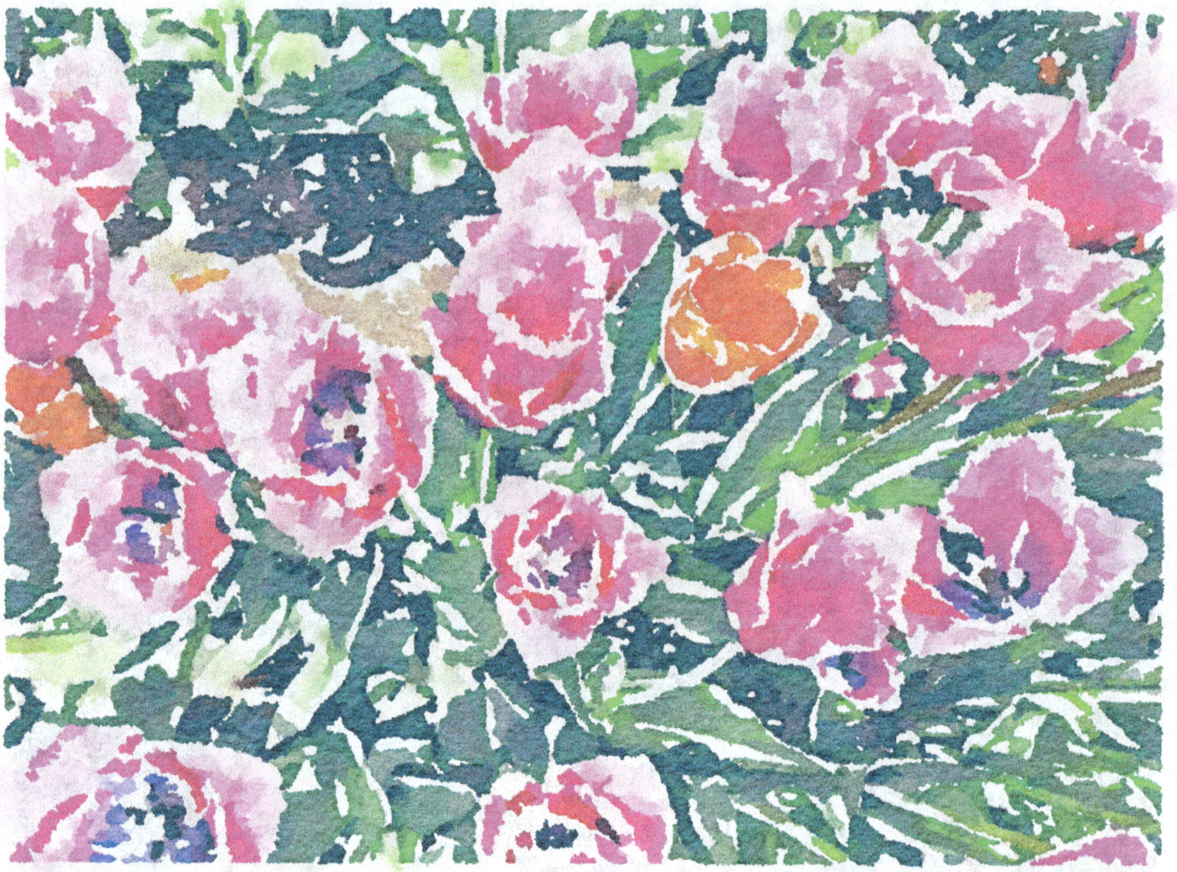

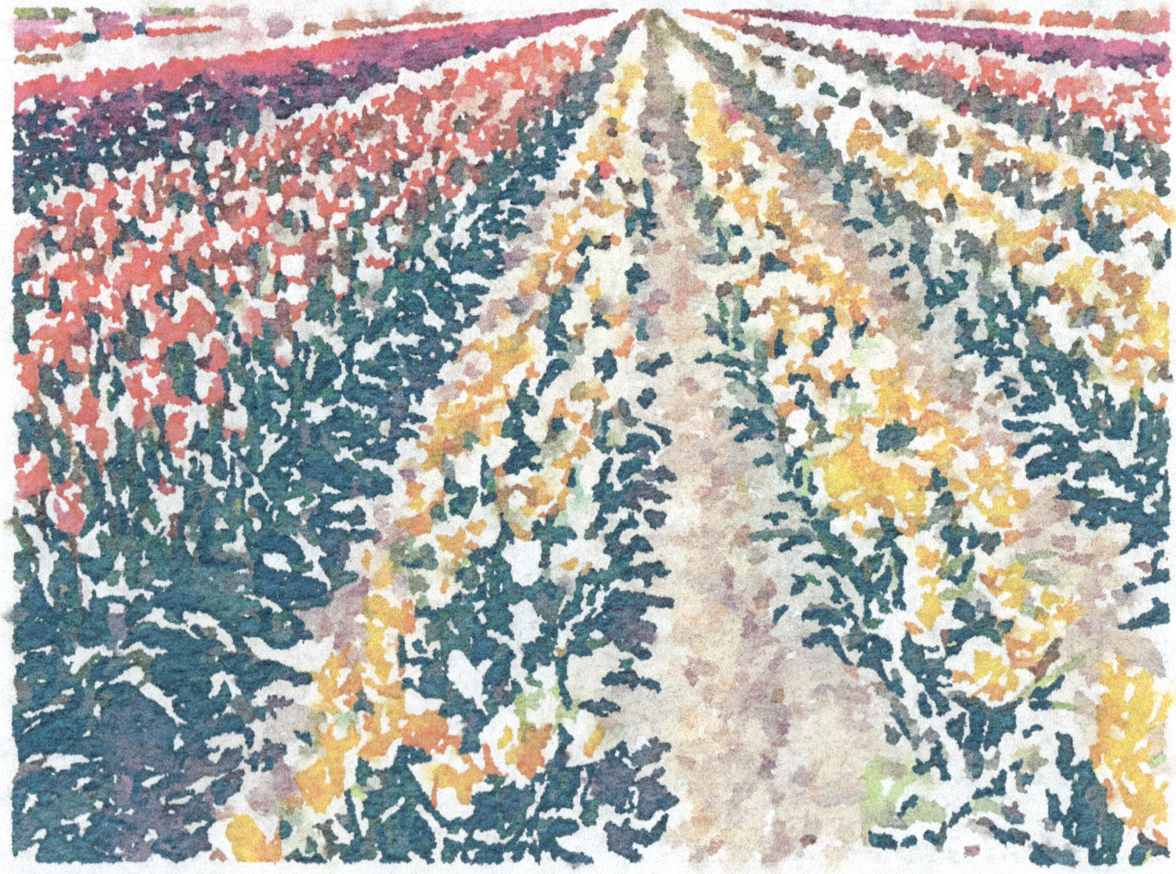

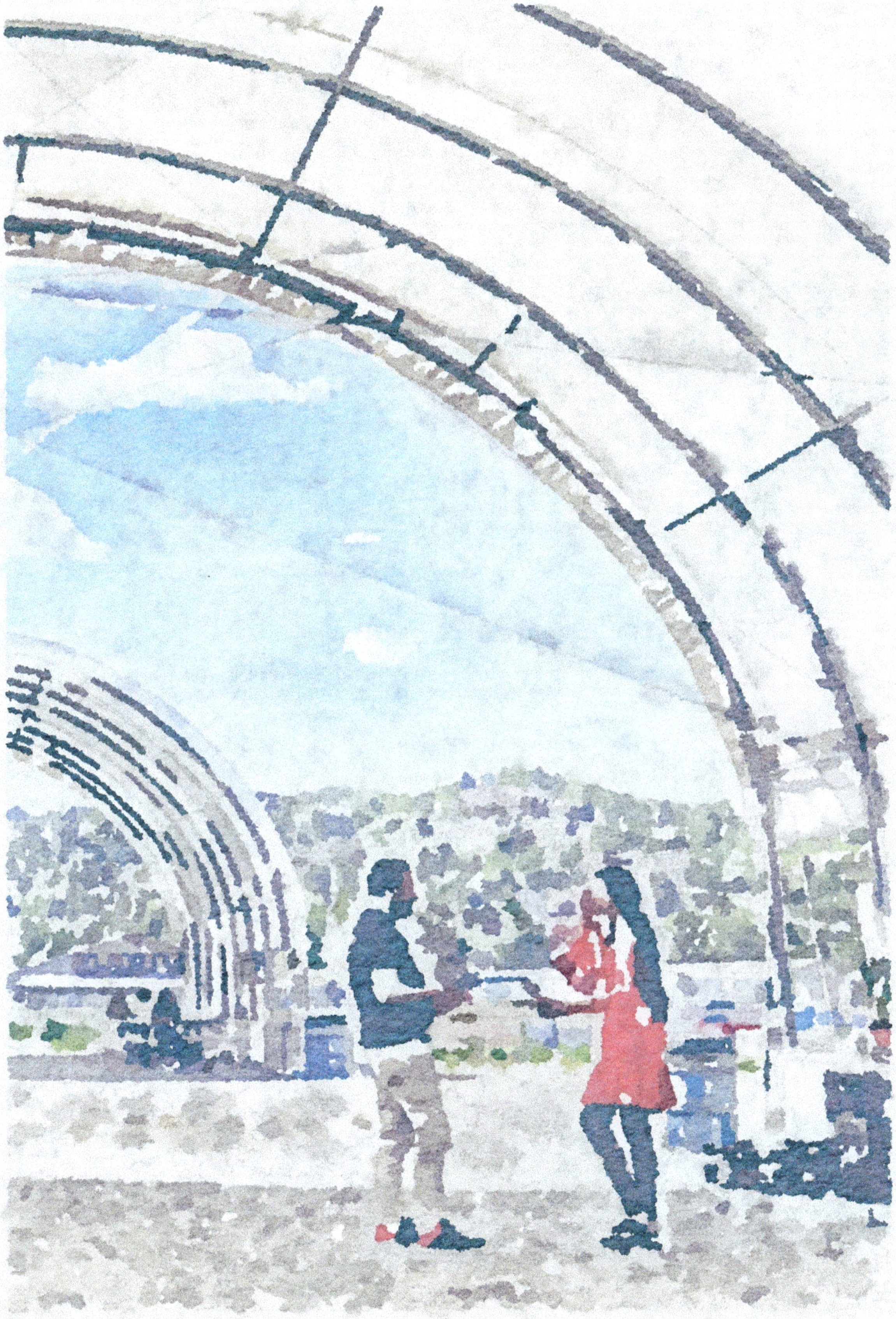

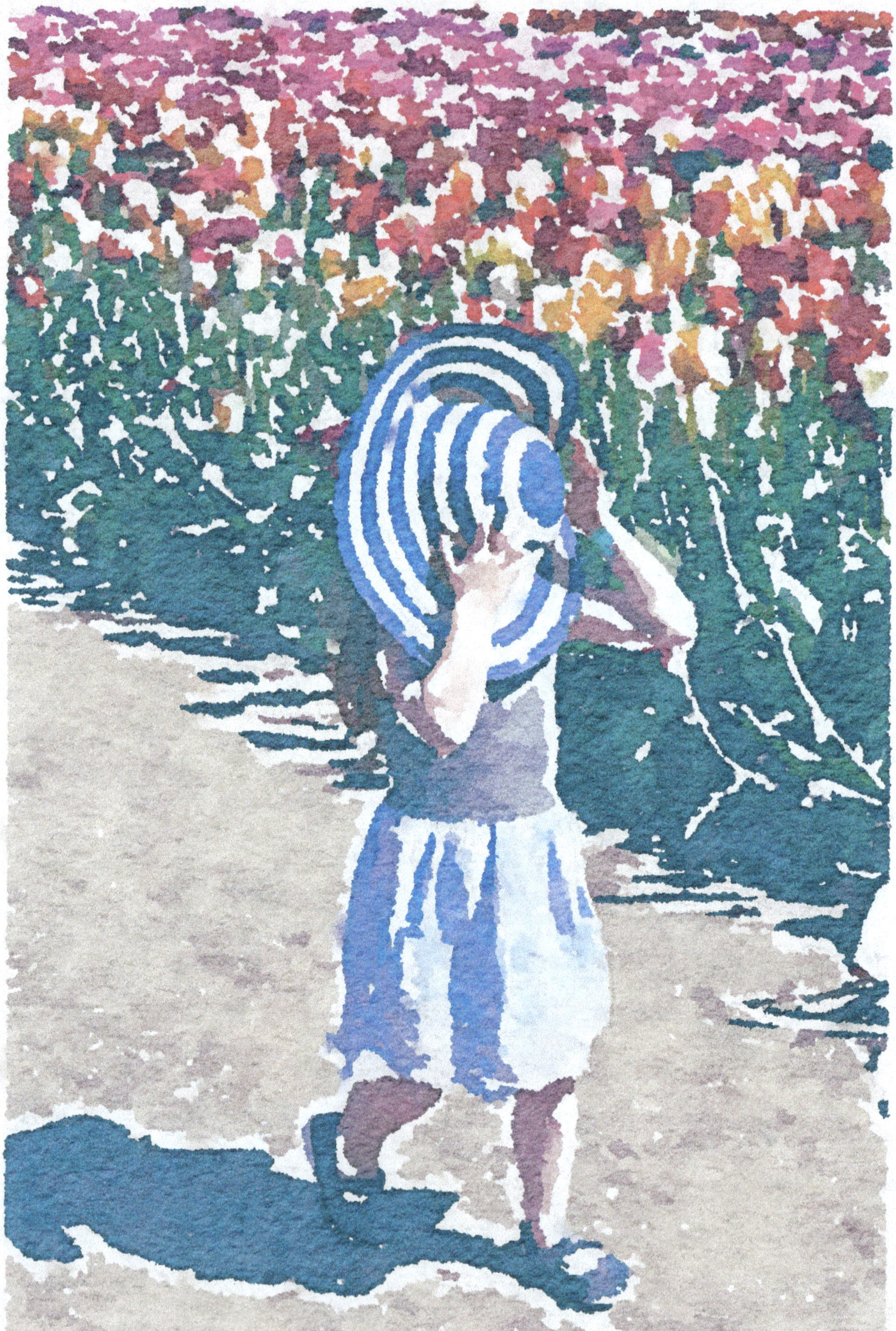

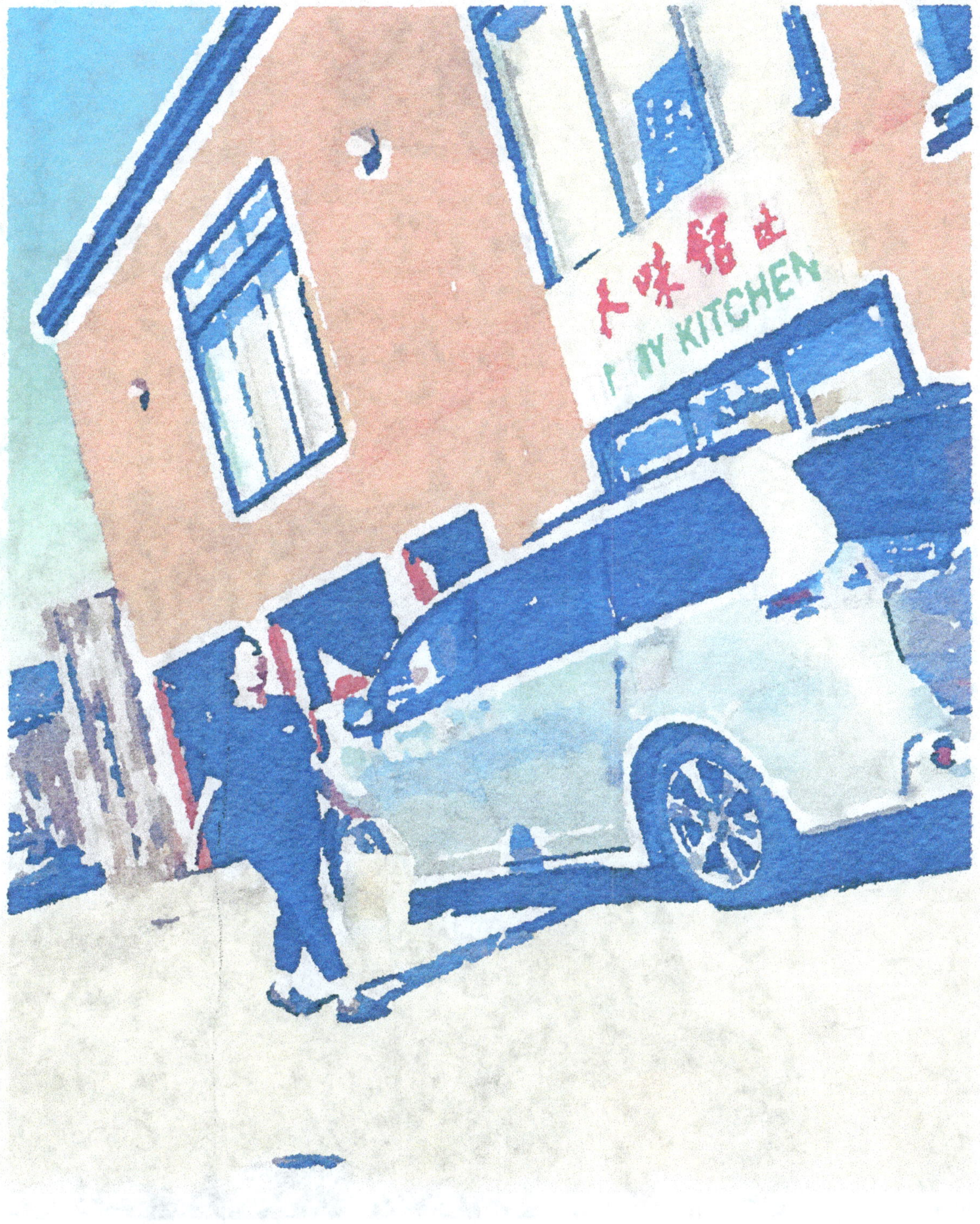
KITCHEN

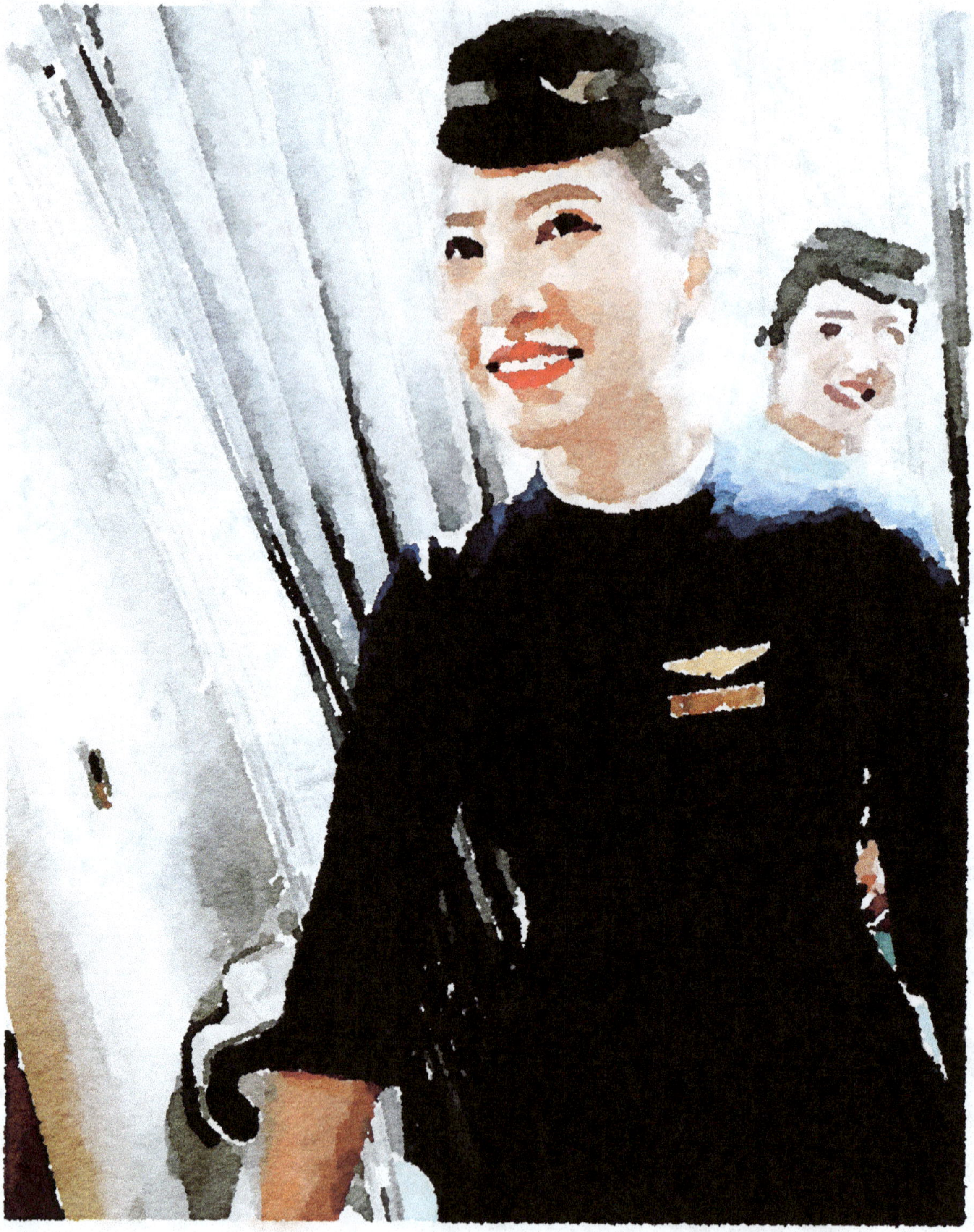

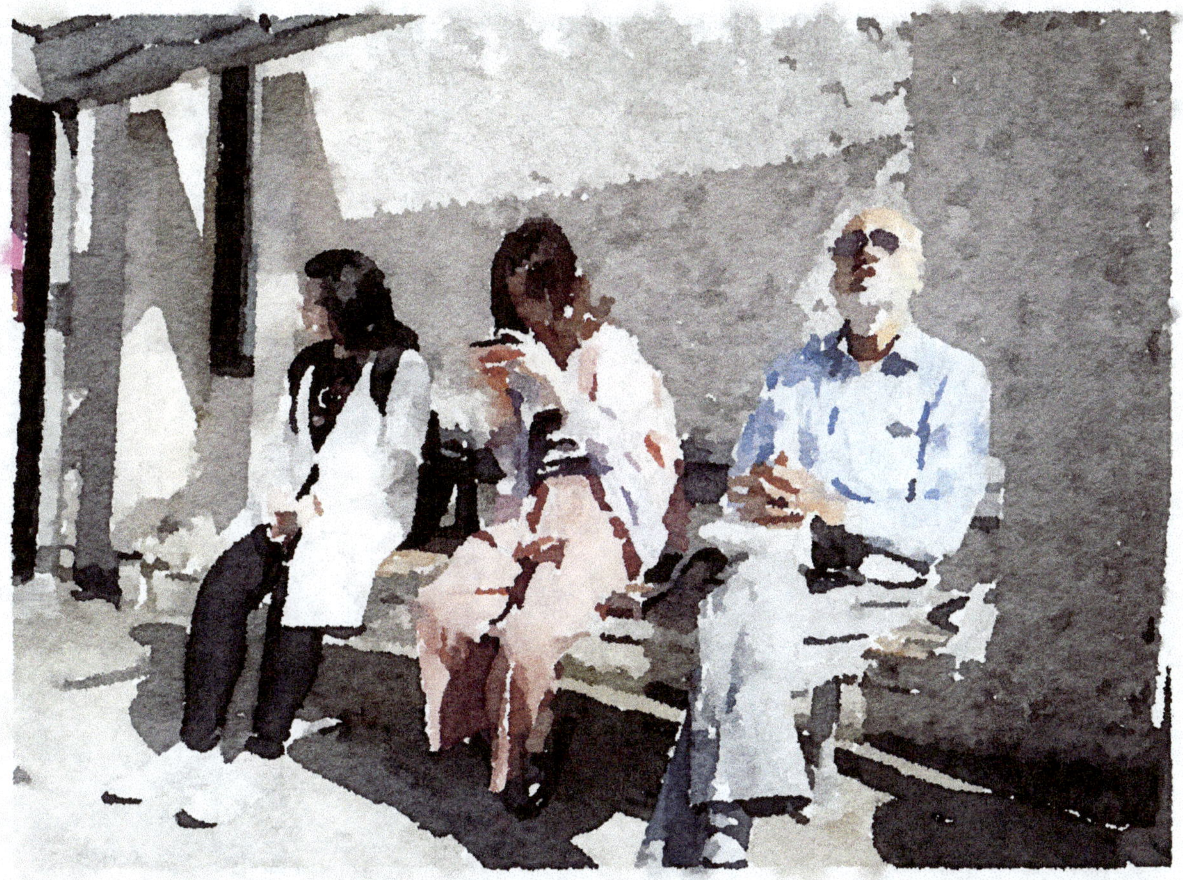

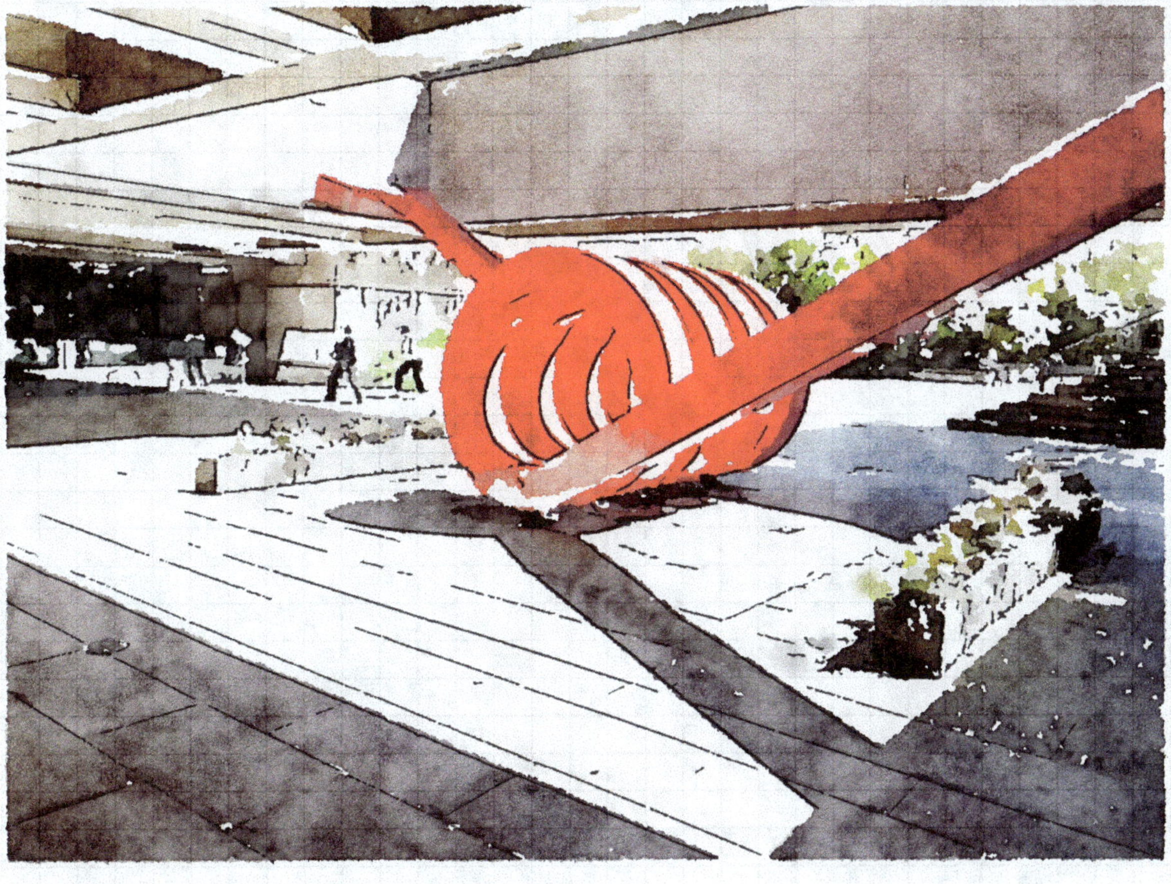

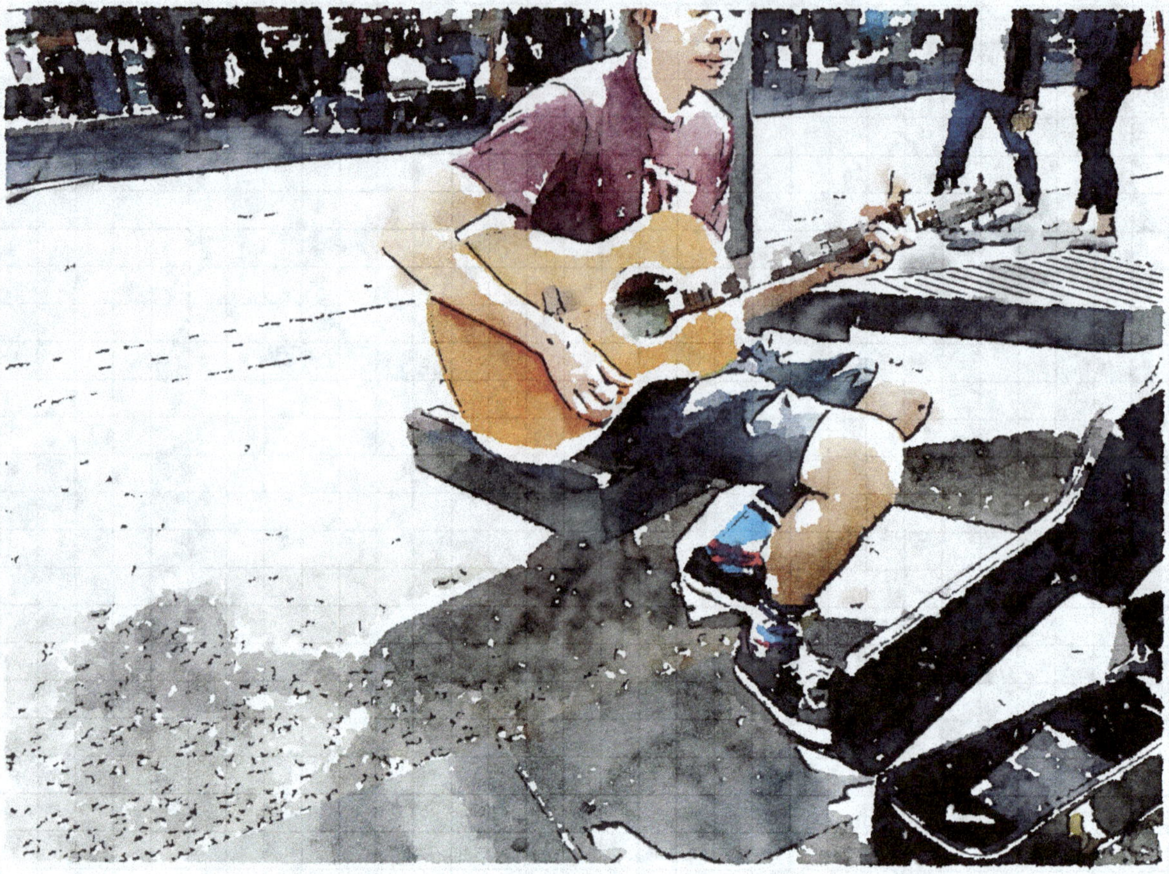

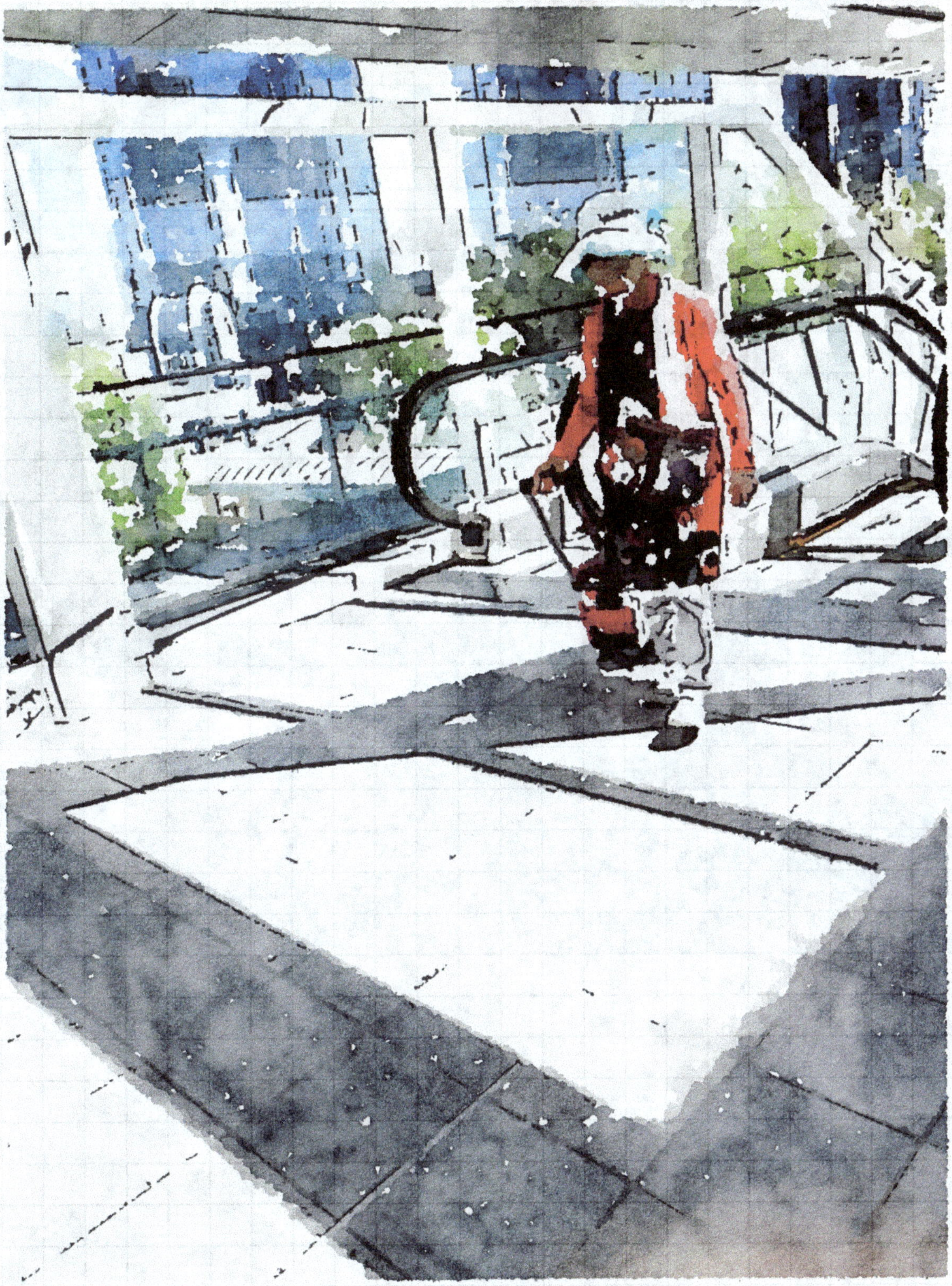

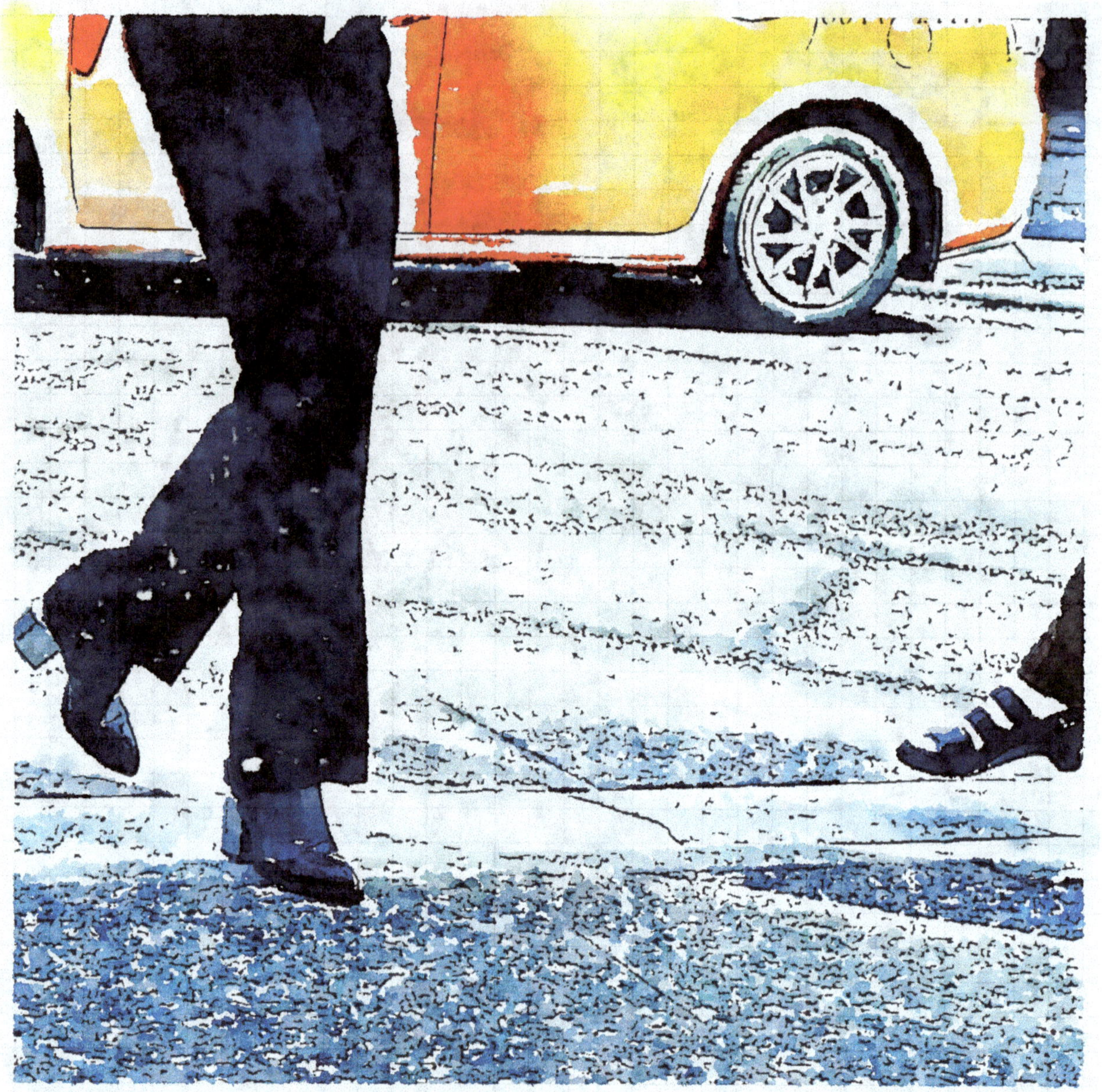

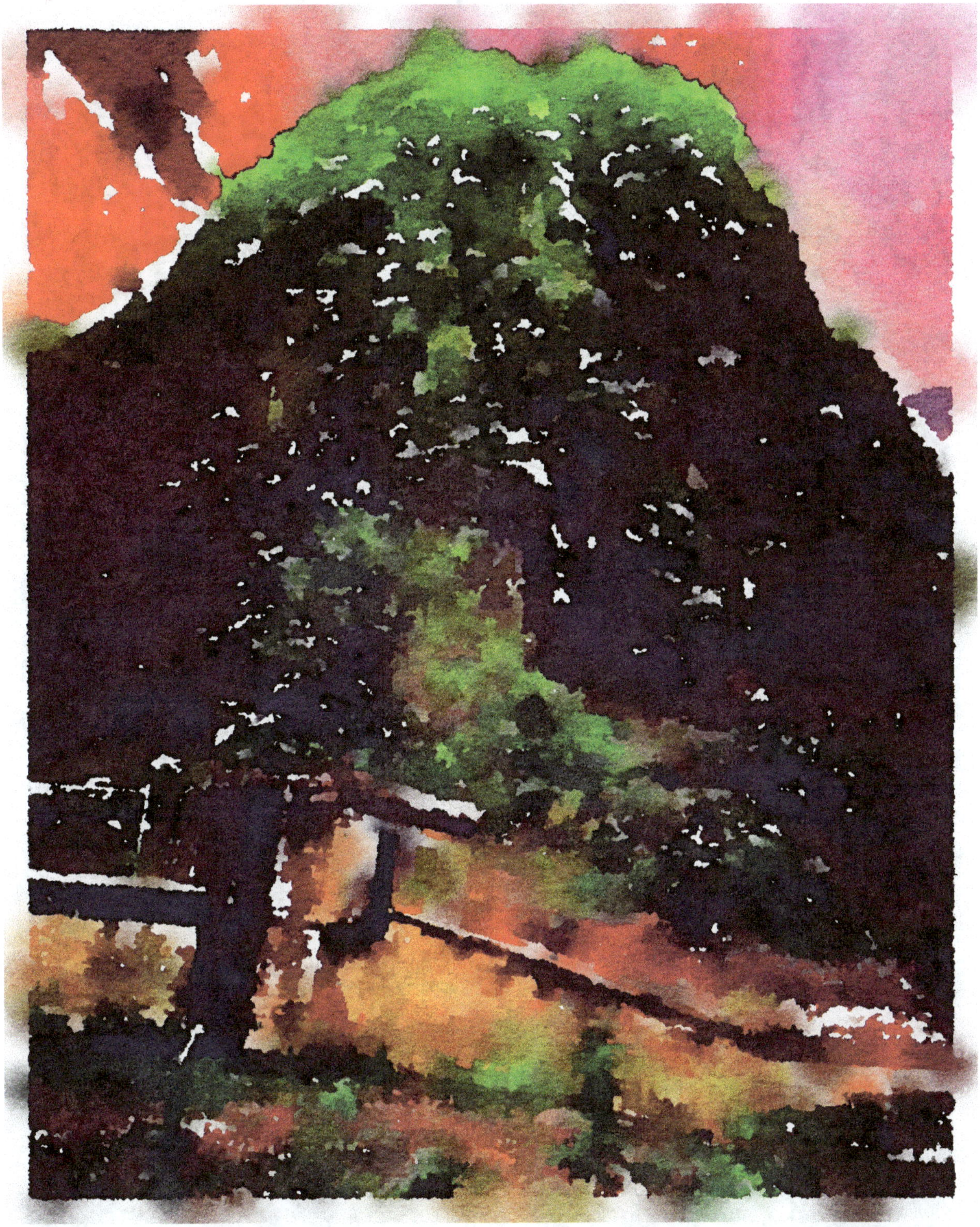

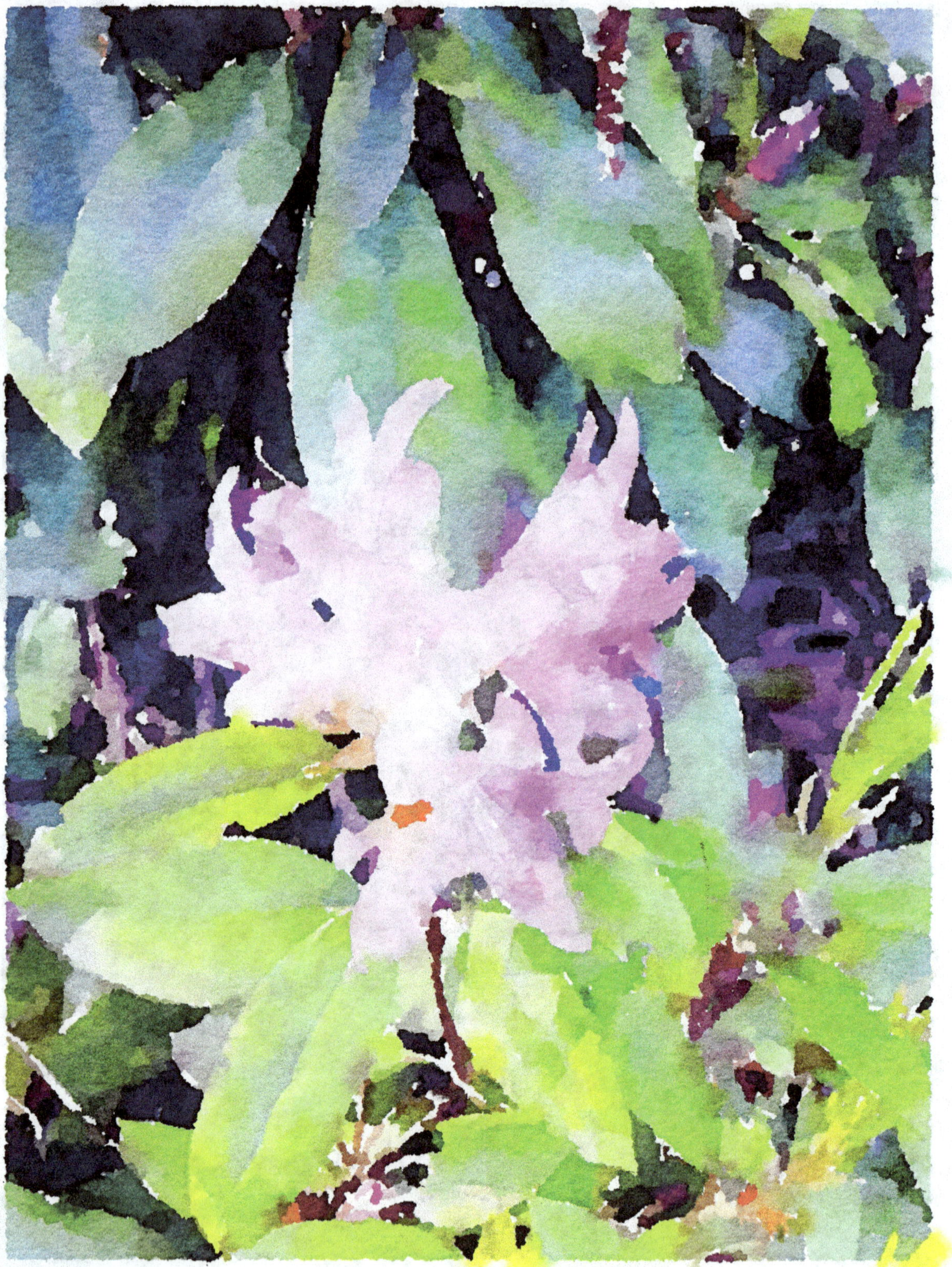

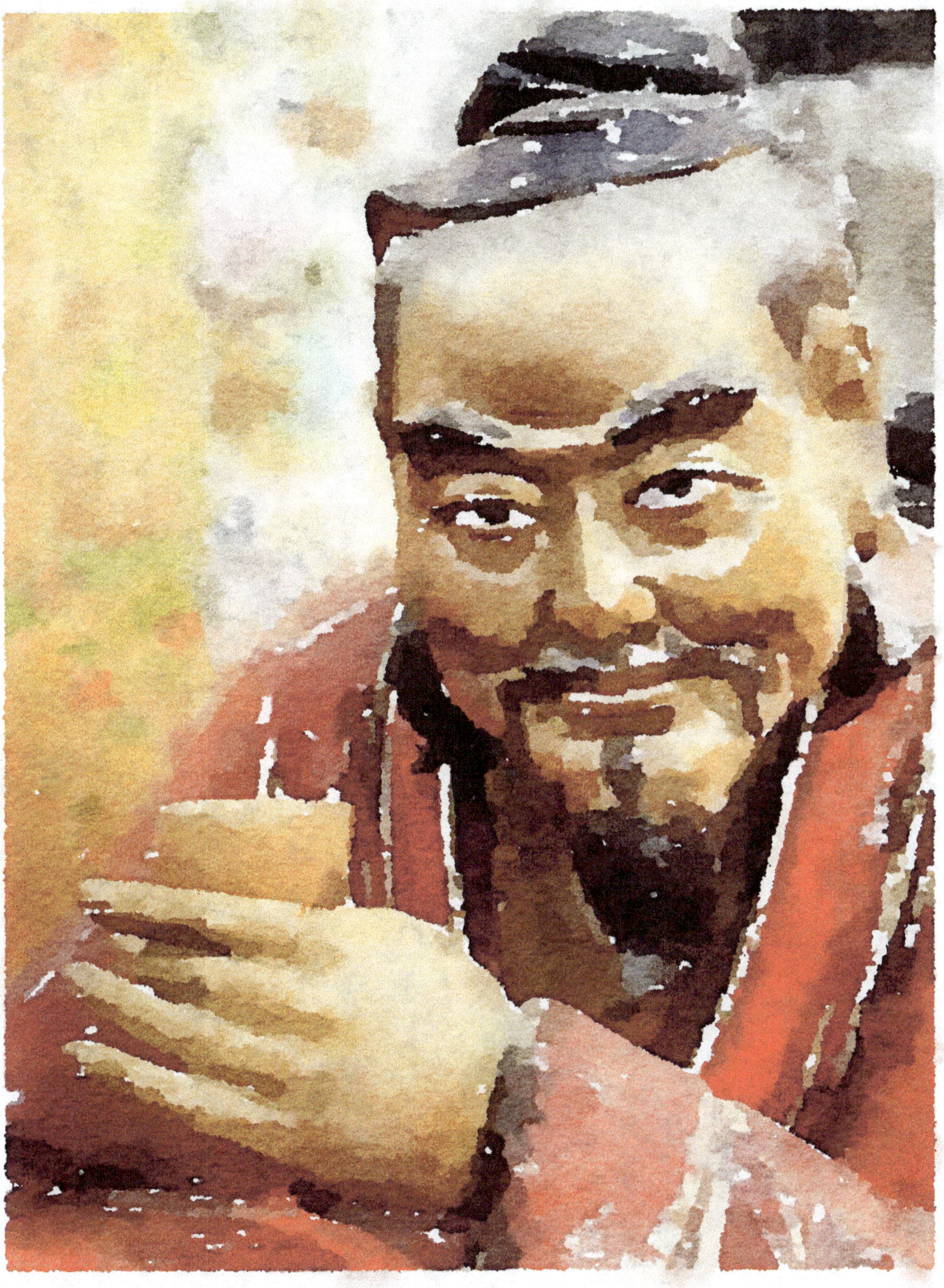

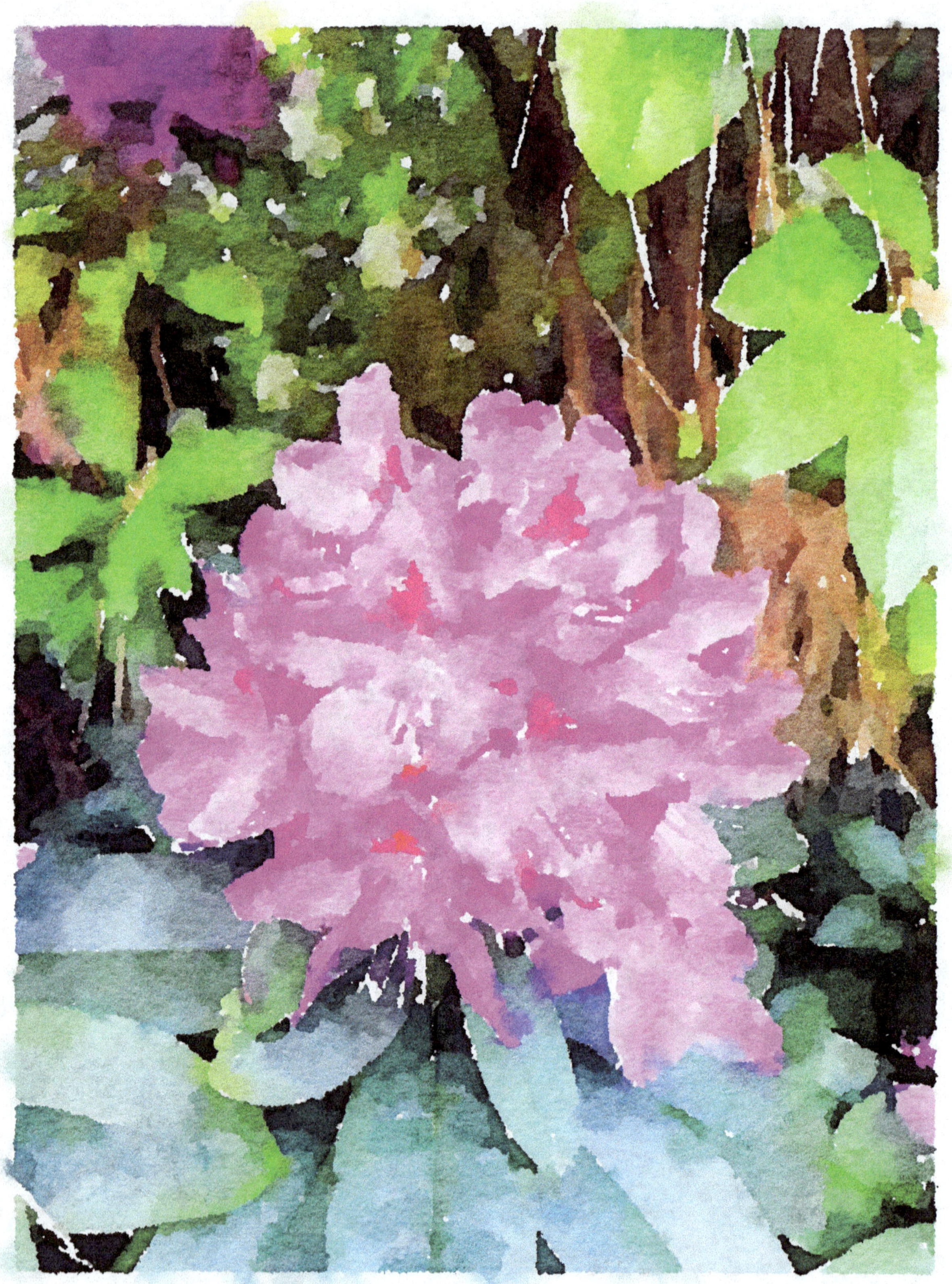

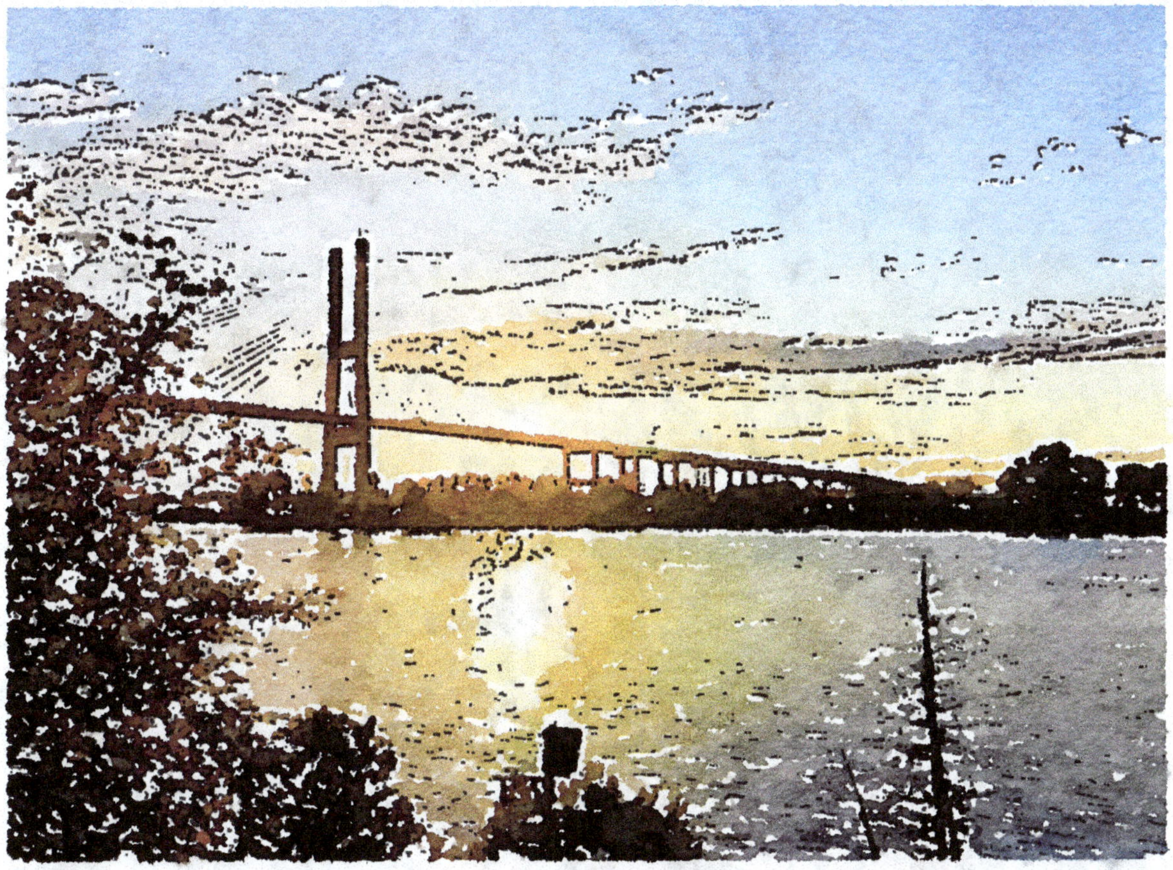

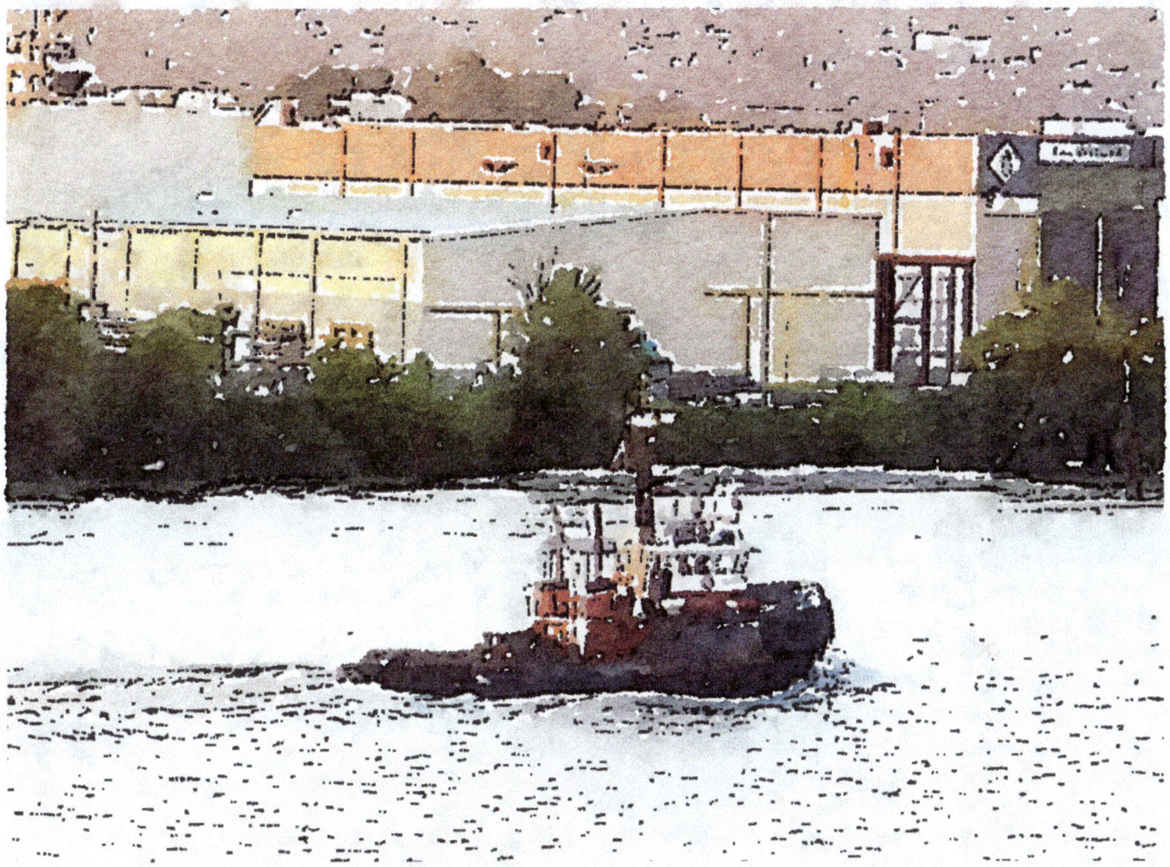

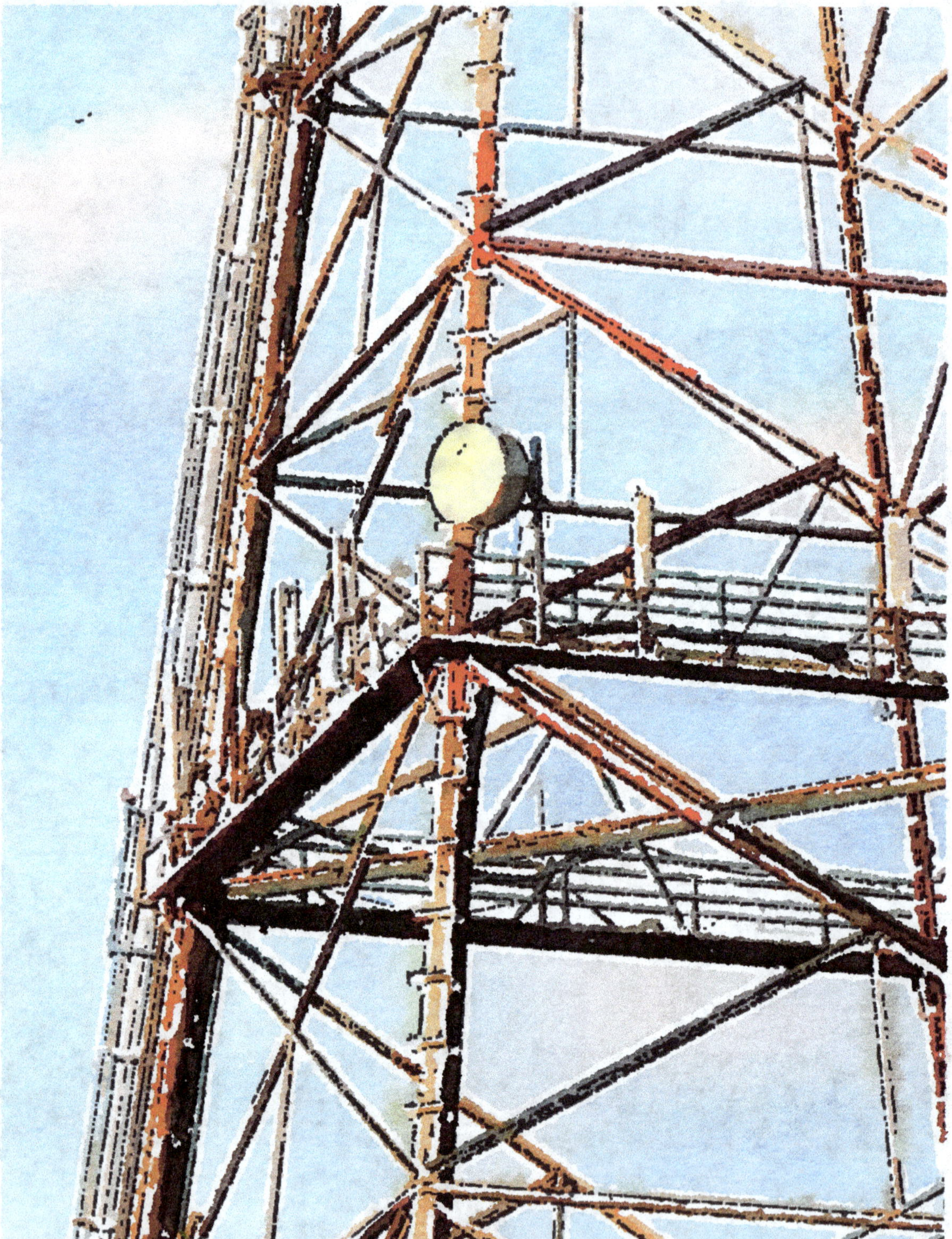

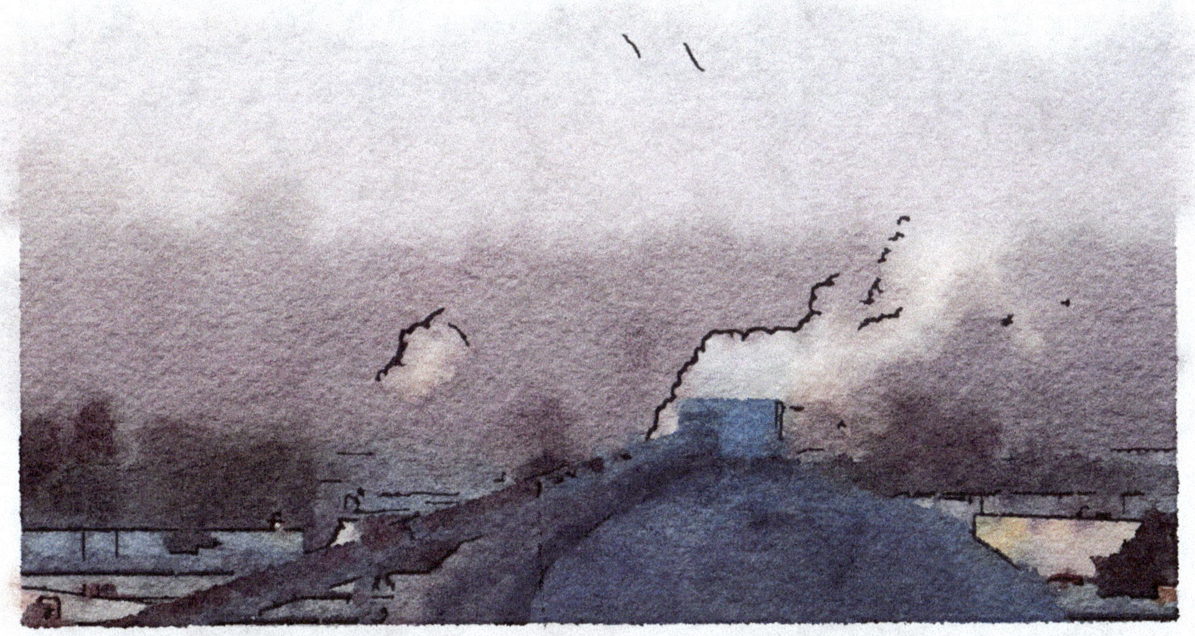

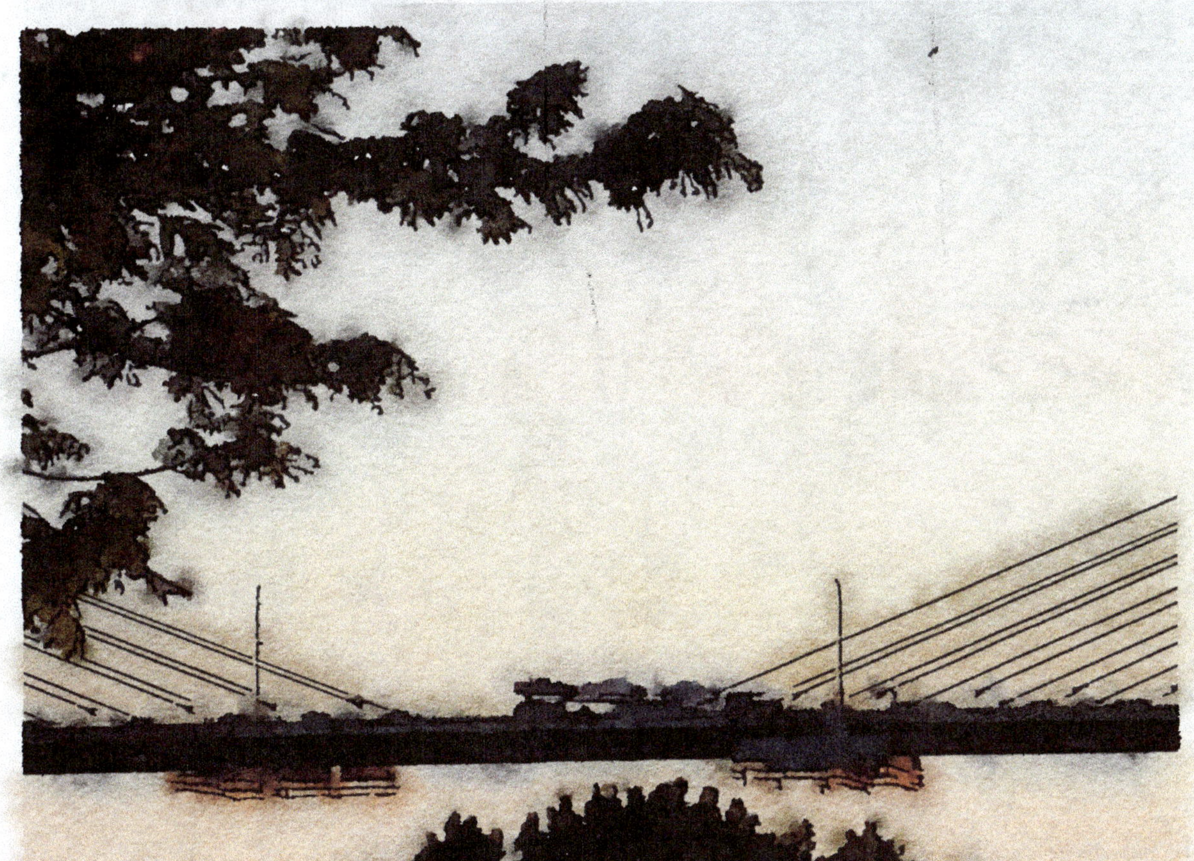

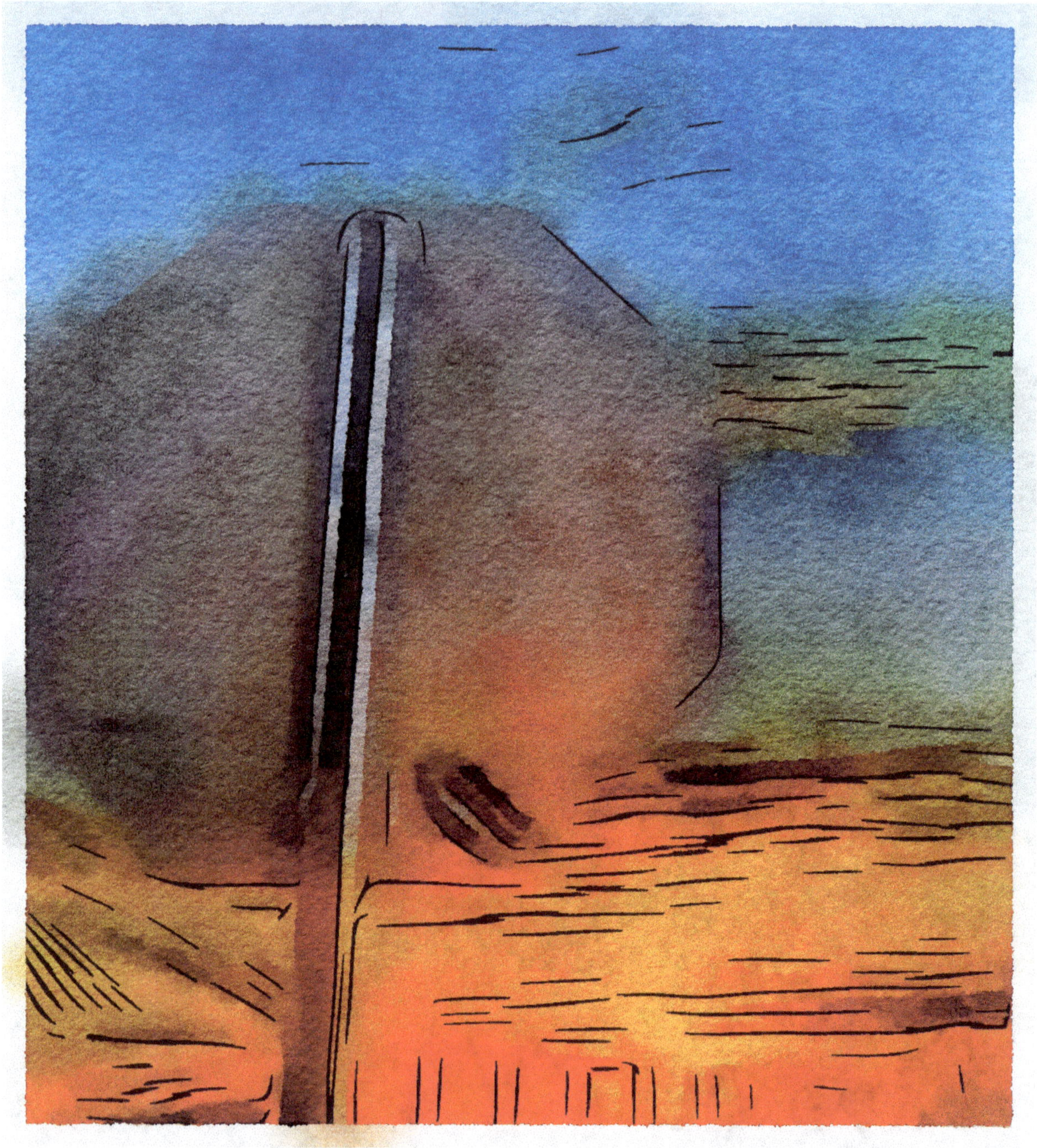

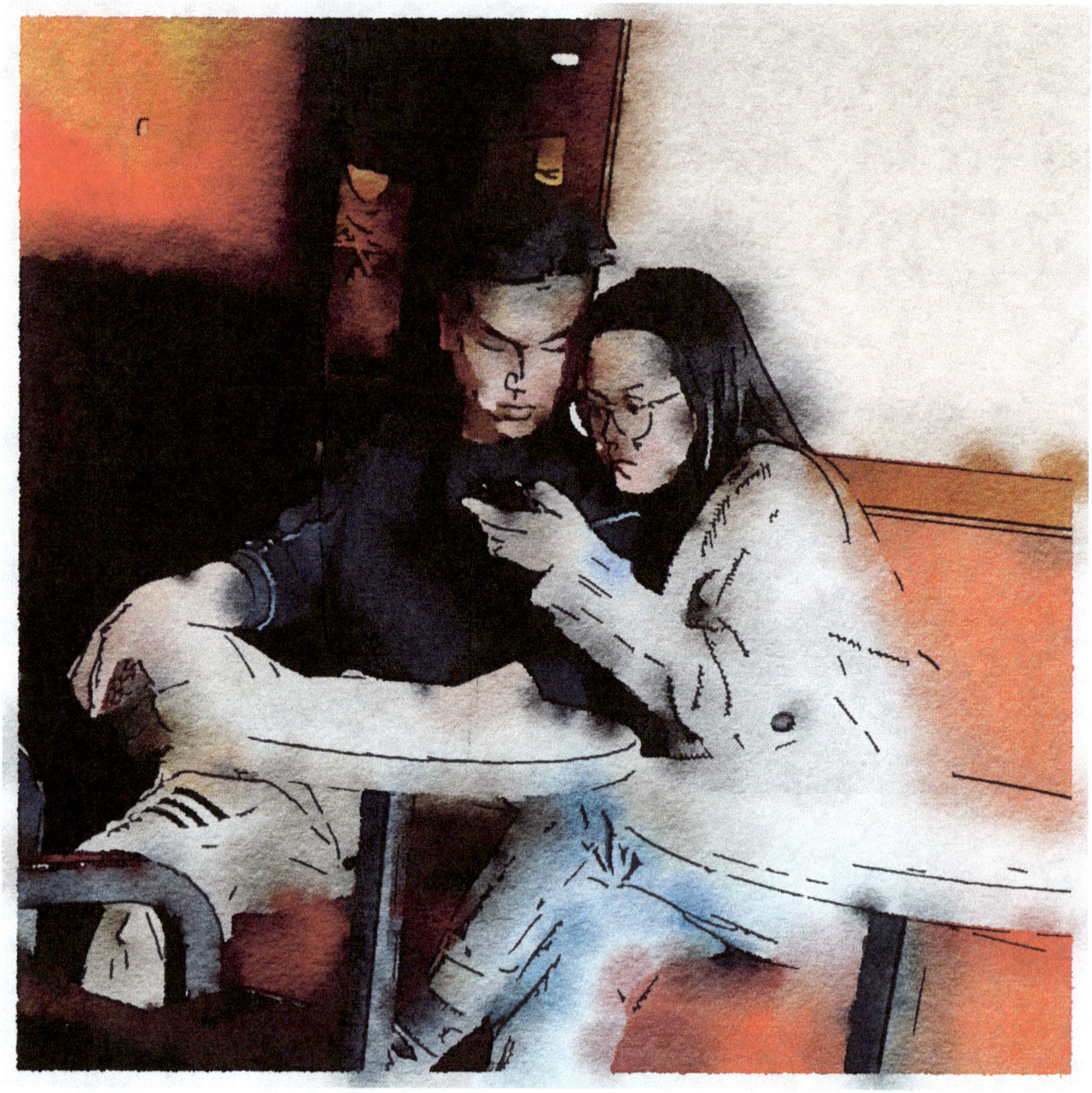

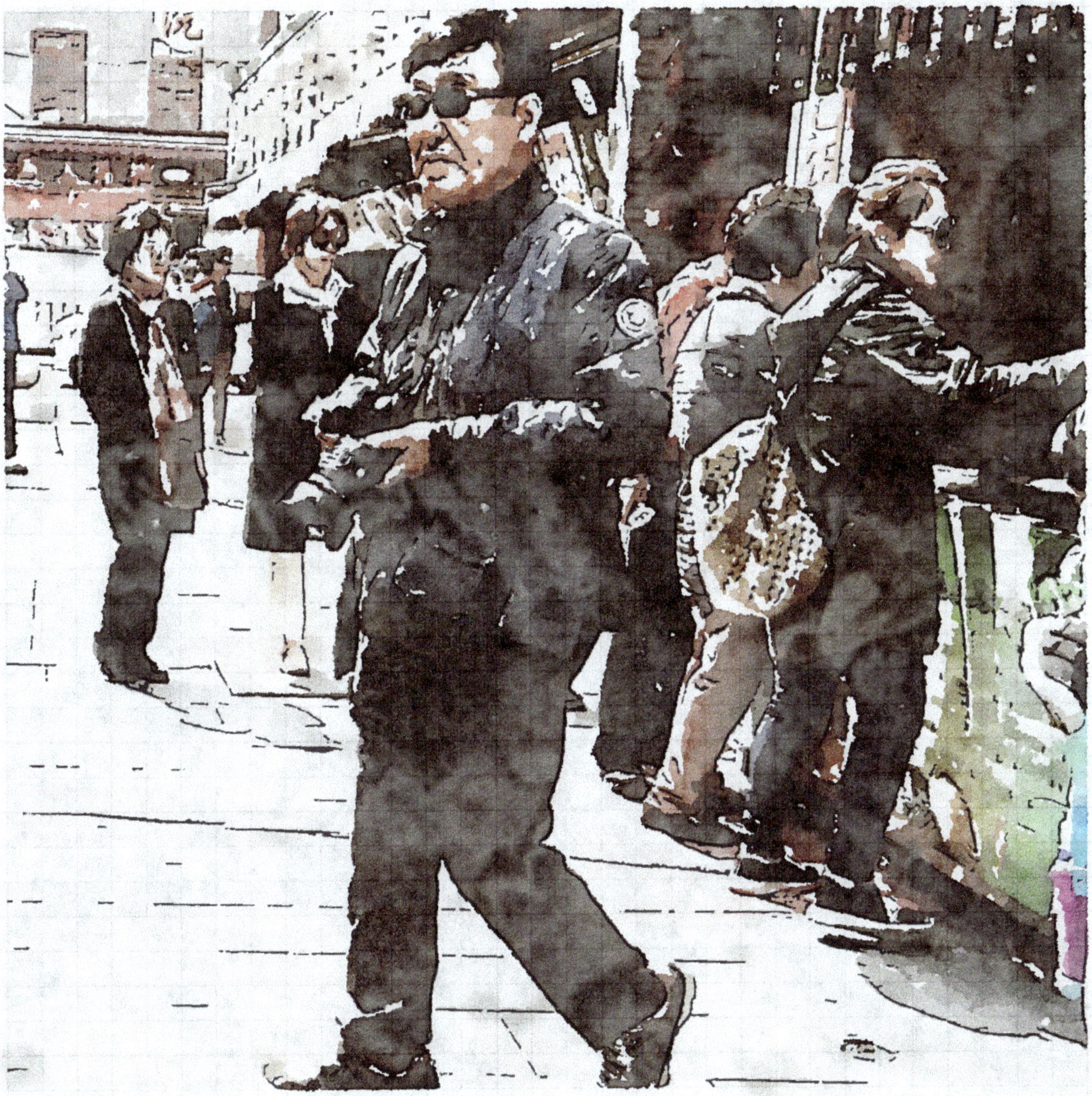

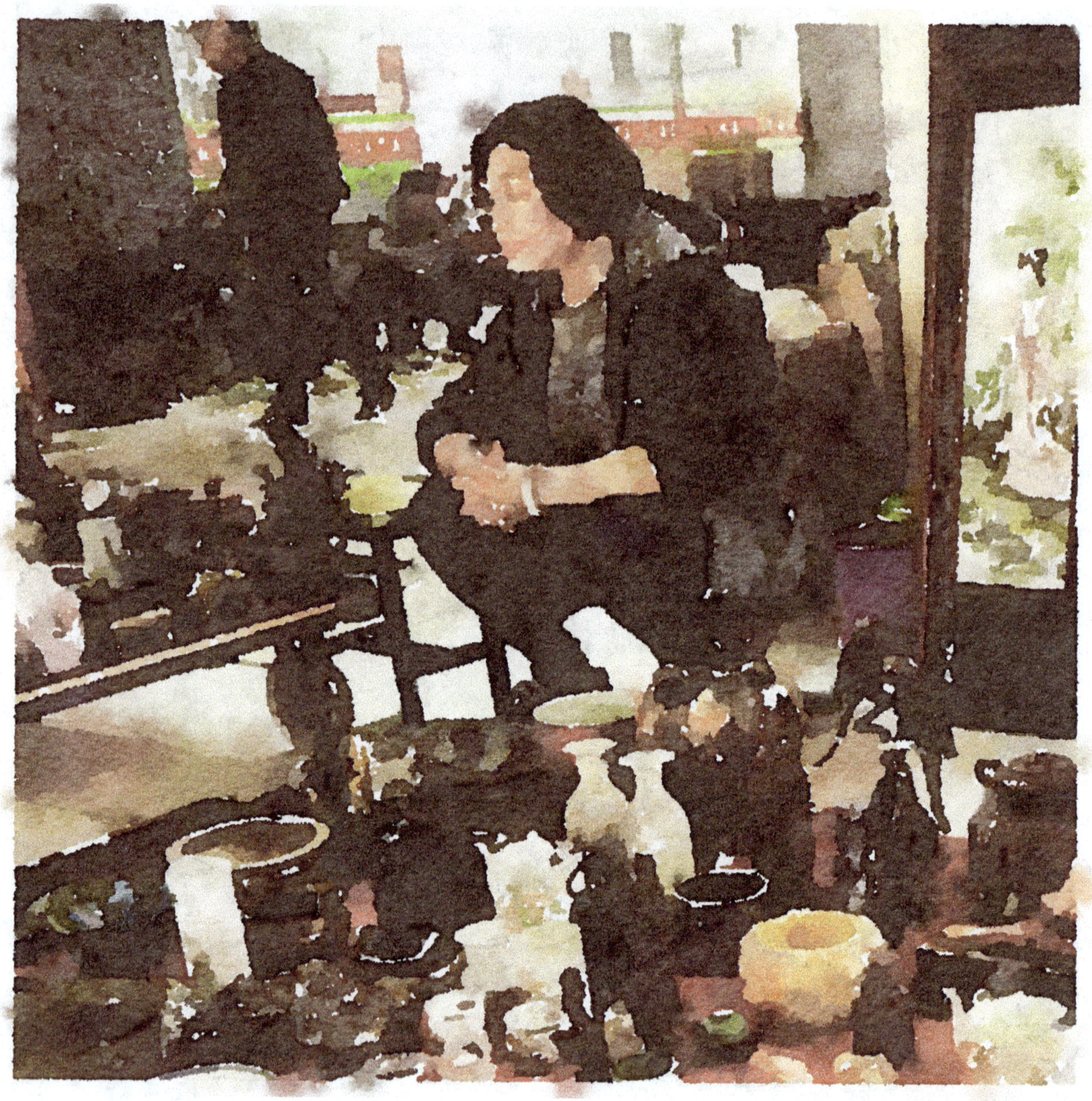

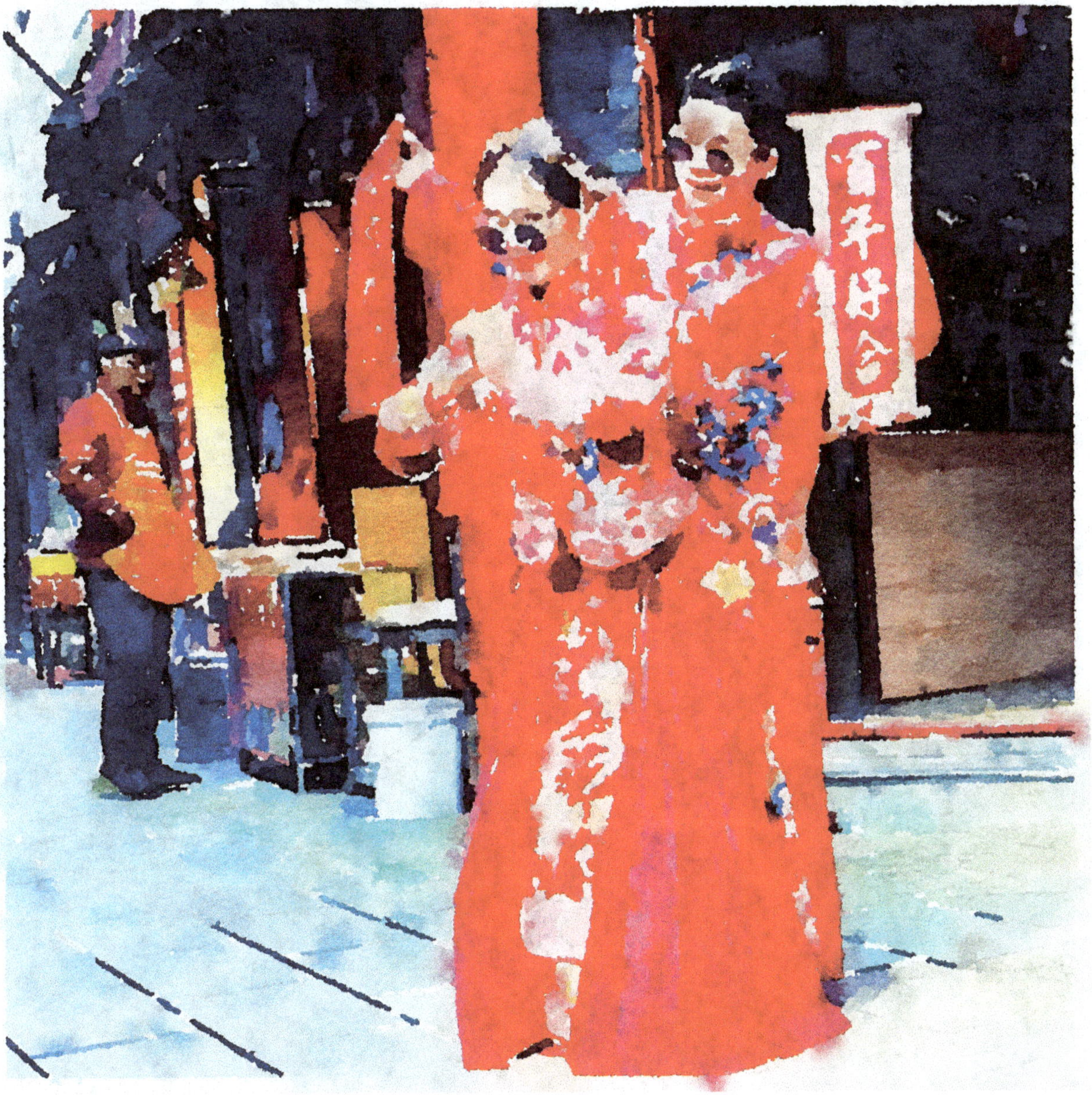

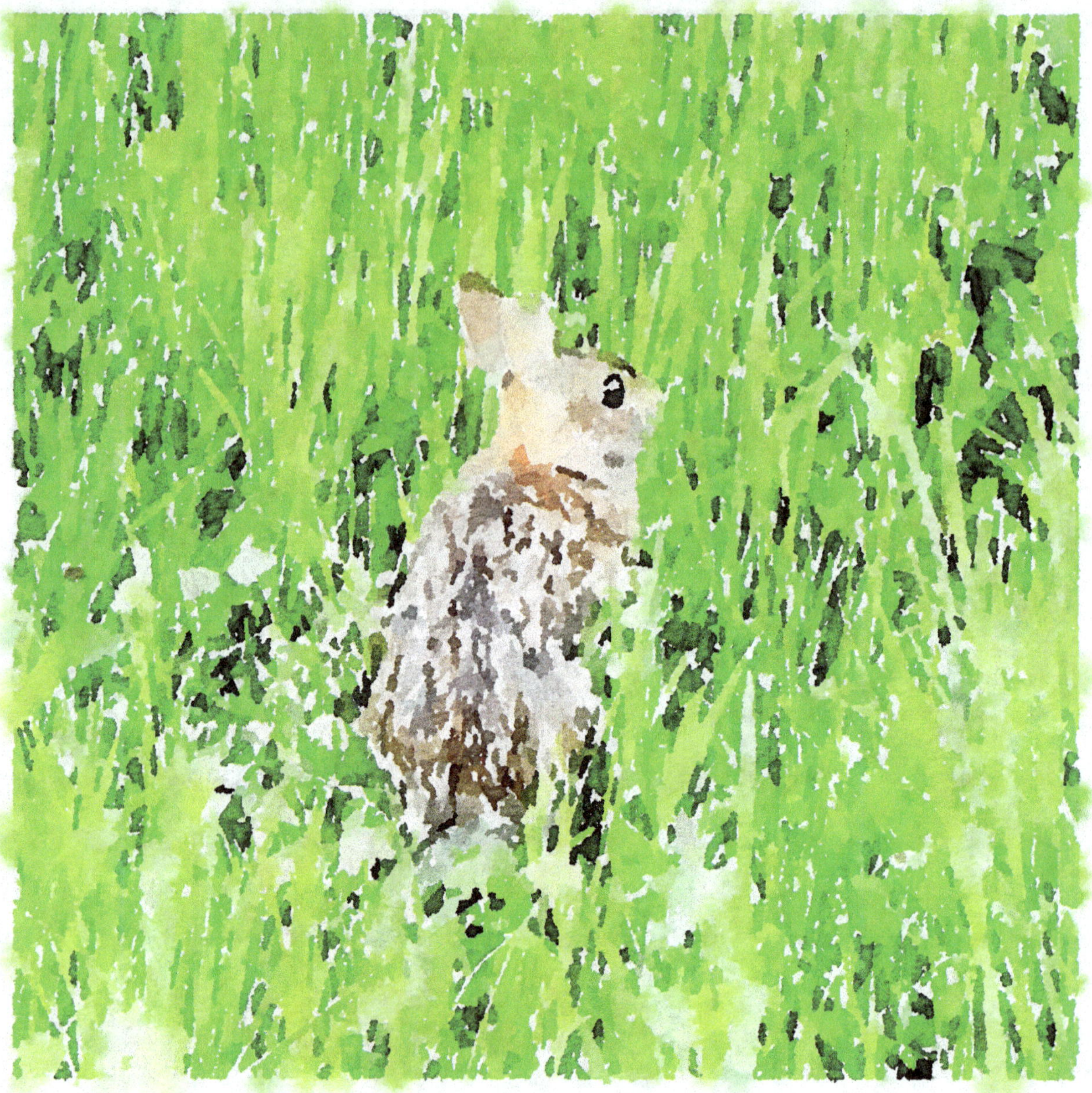

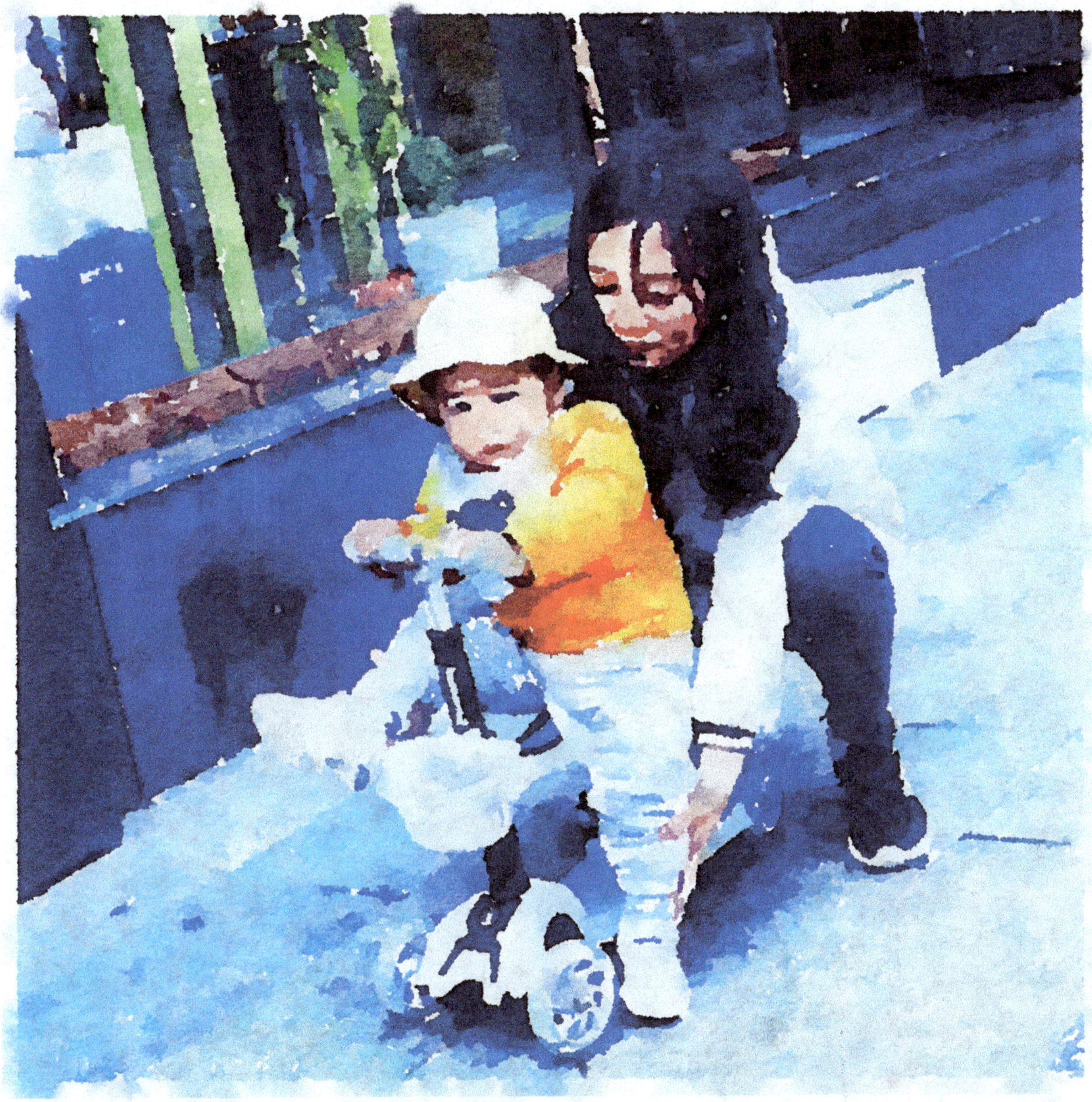

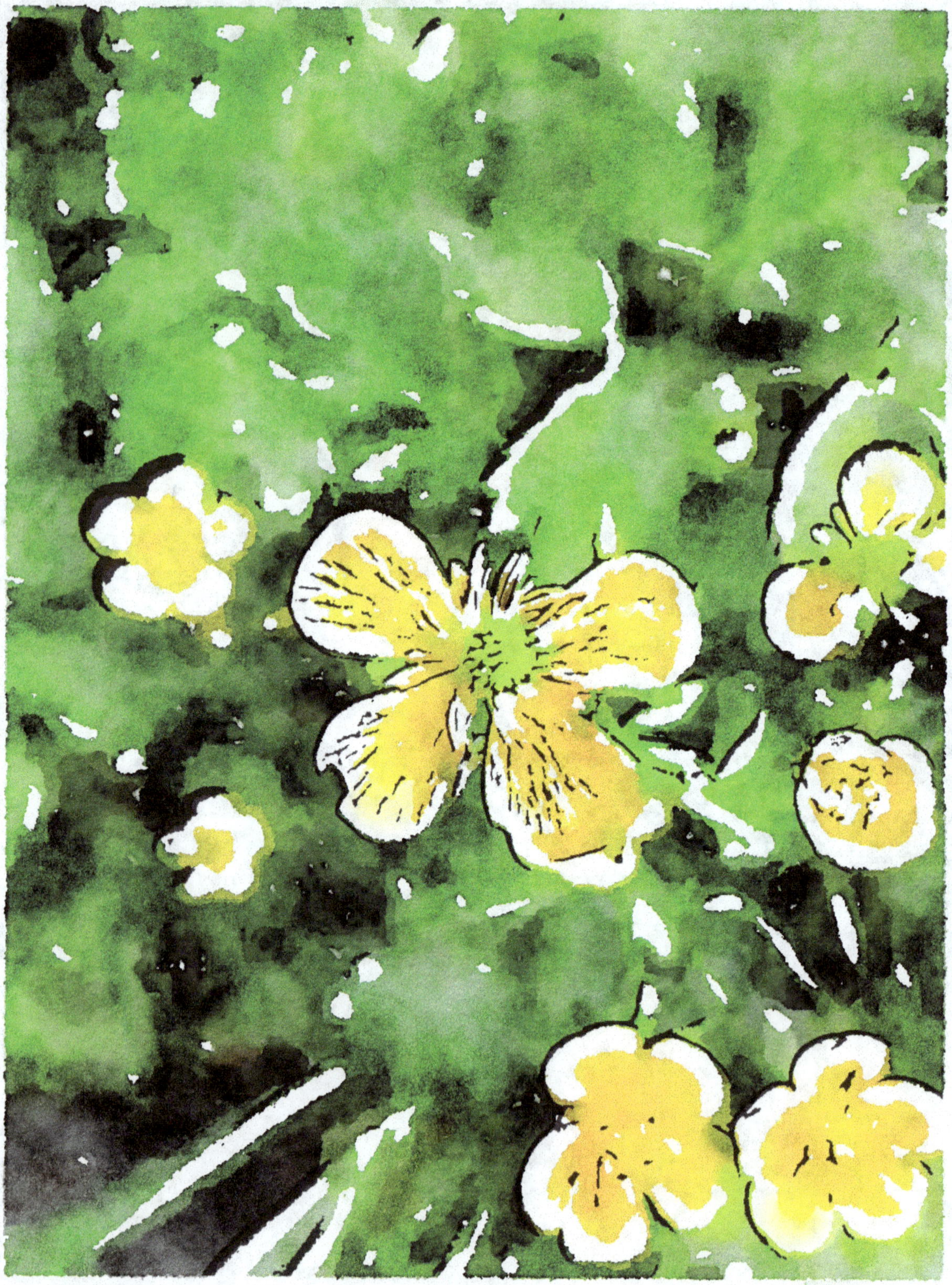

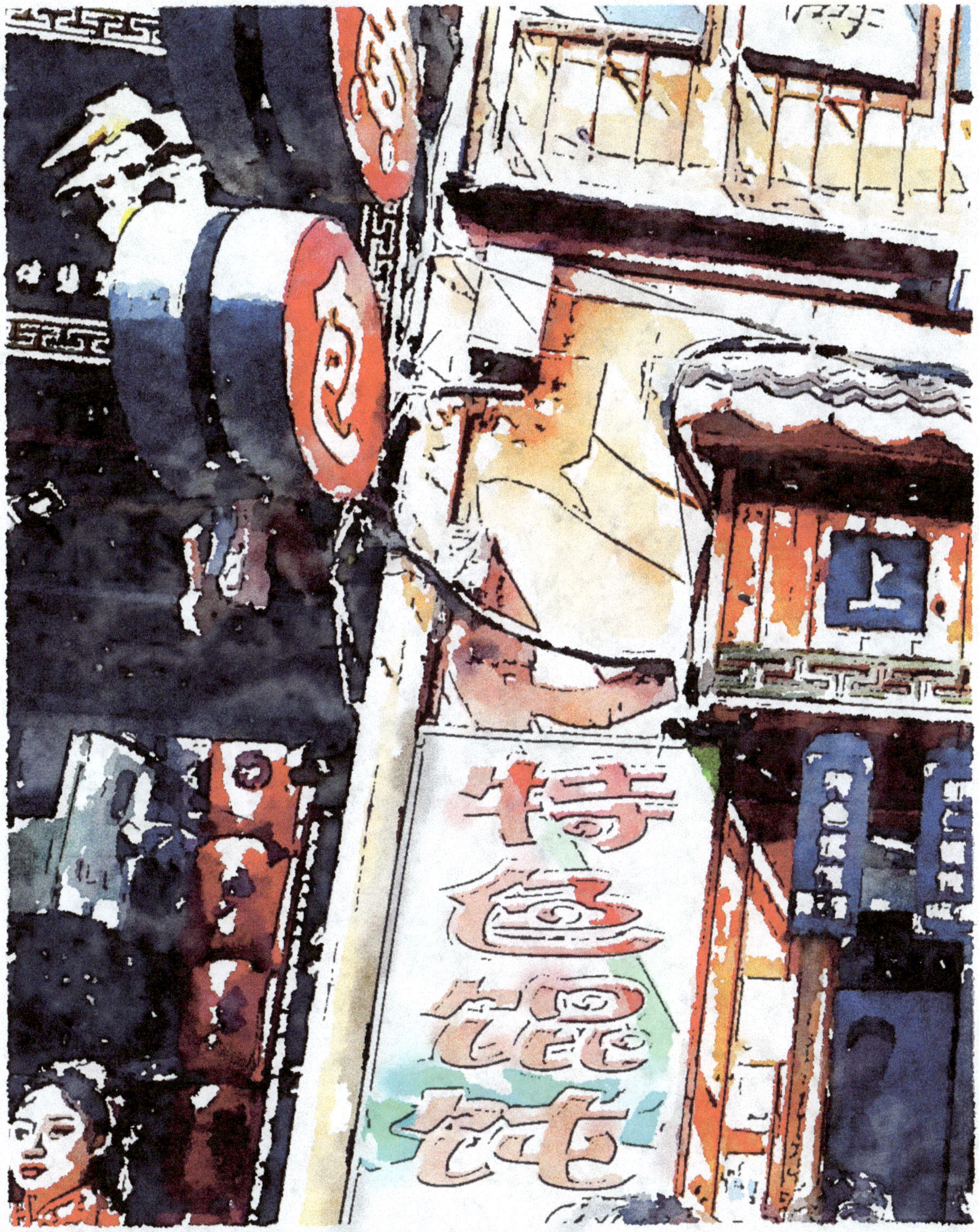

特色馄饨
上

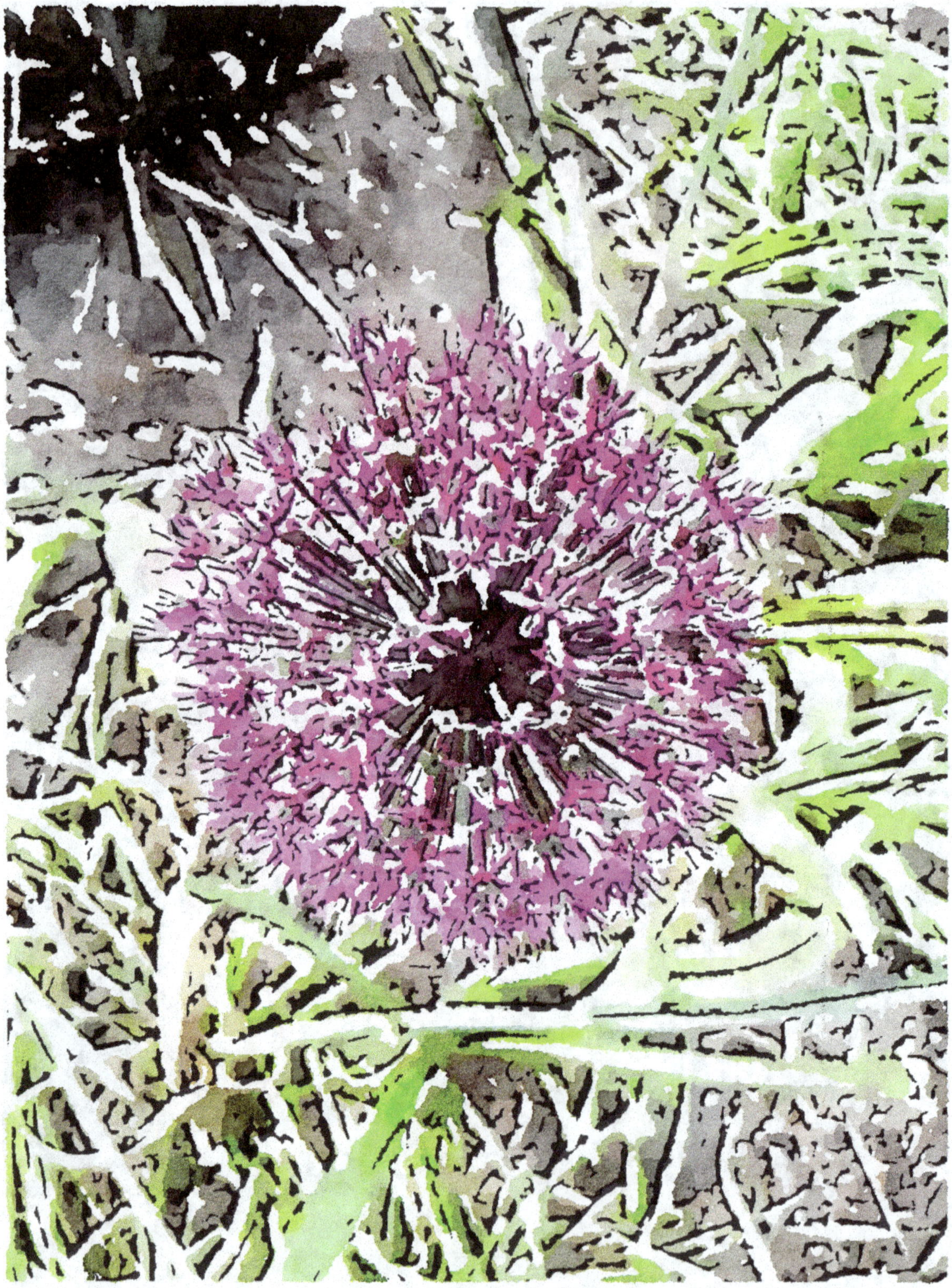

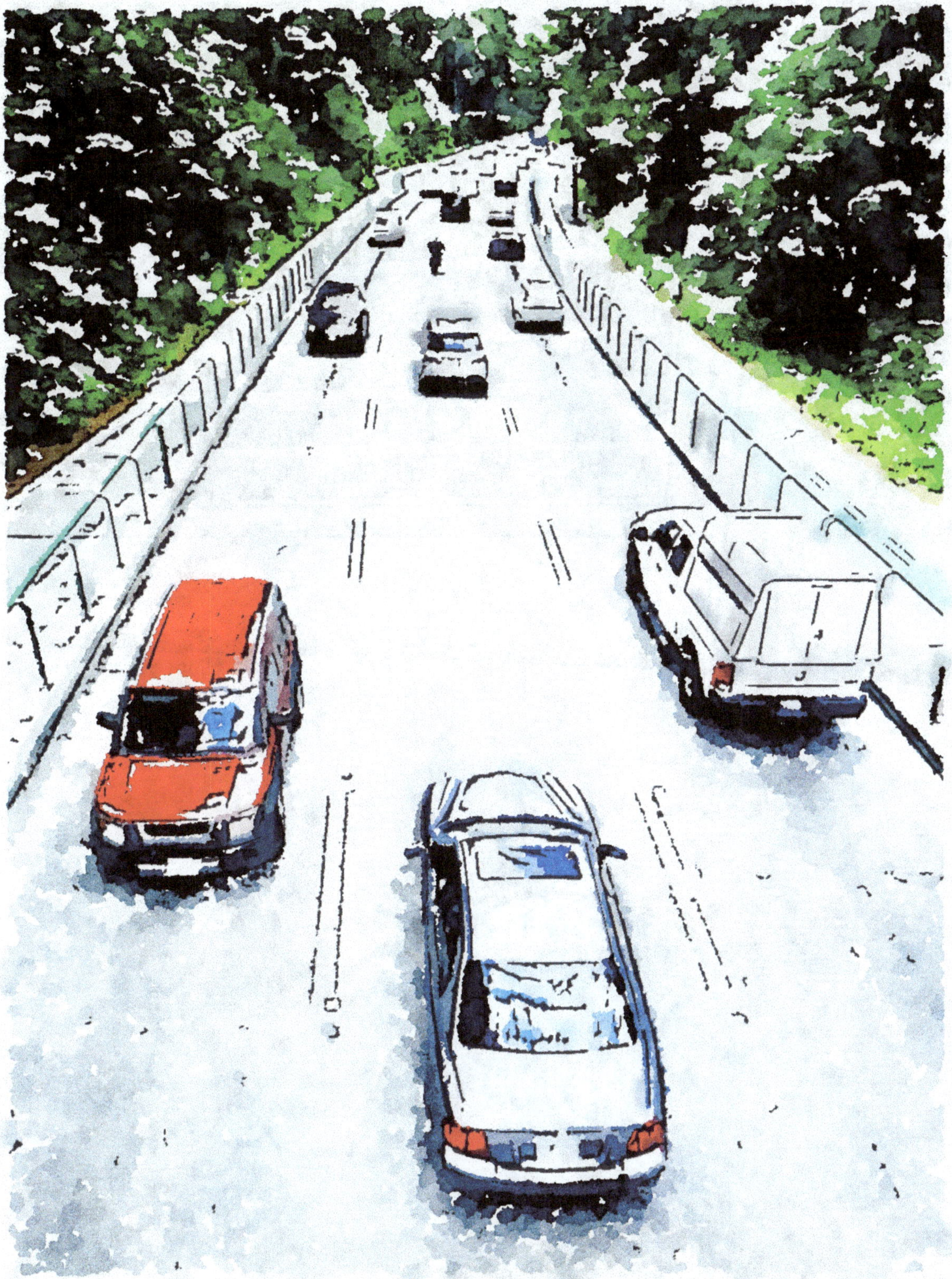

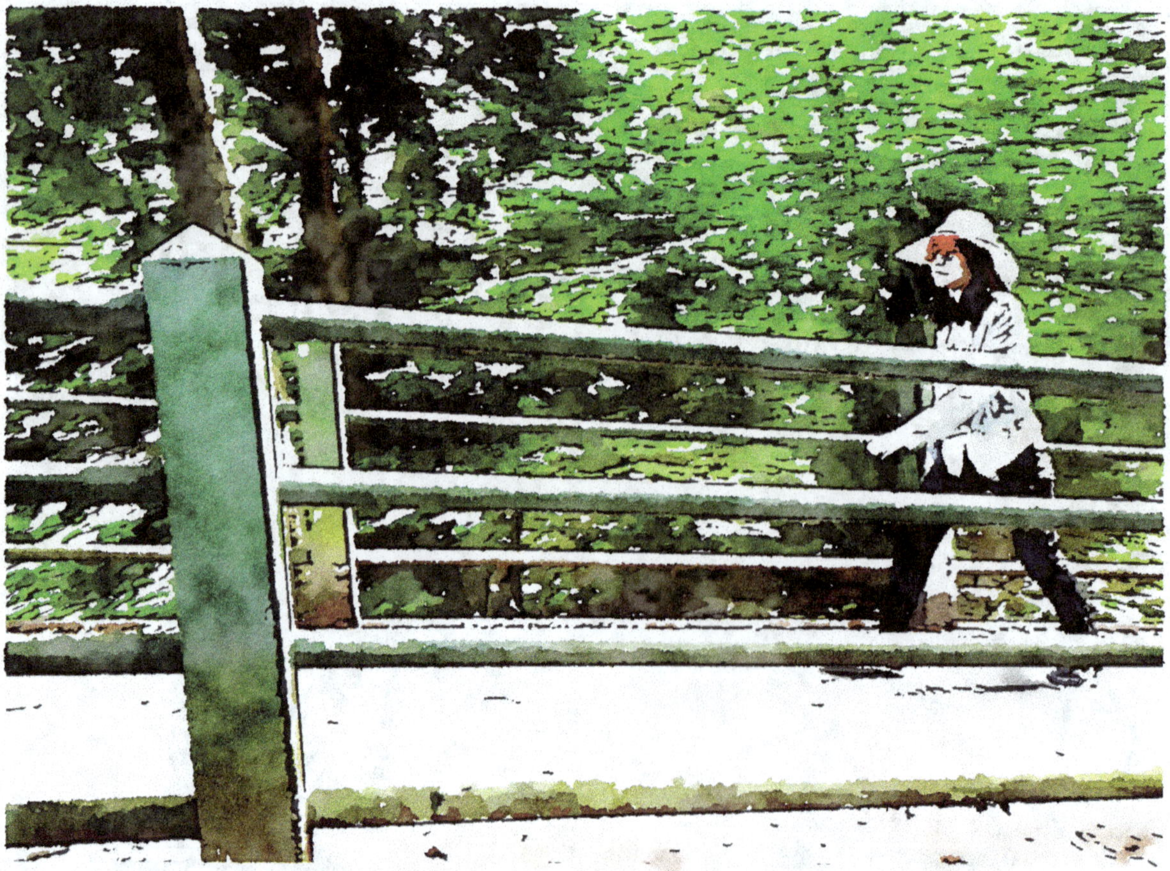

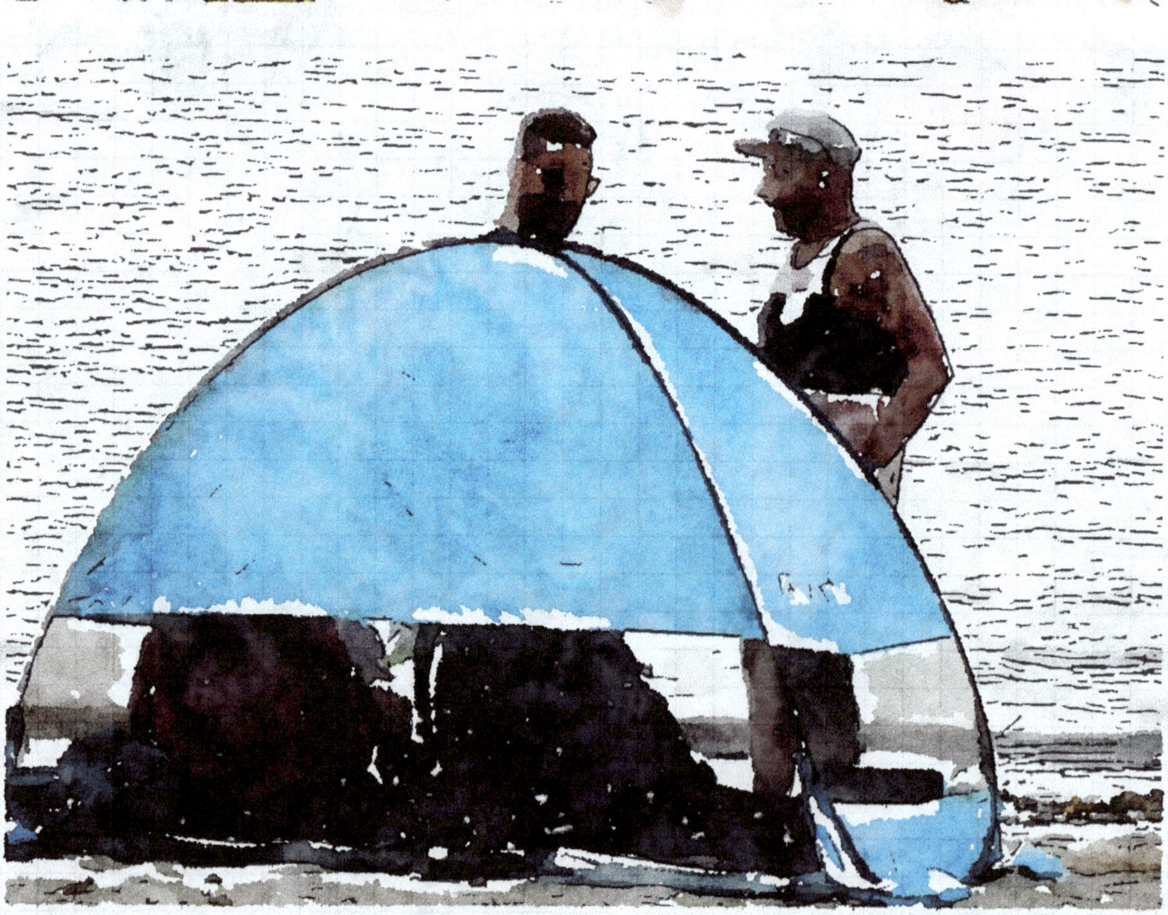

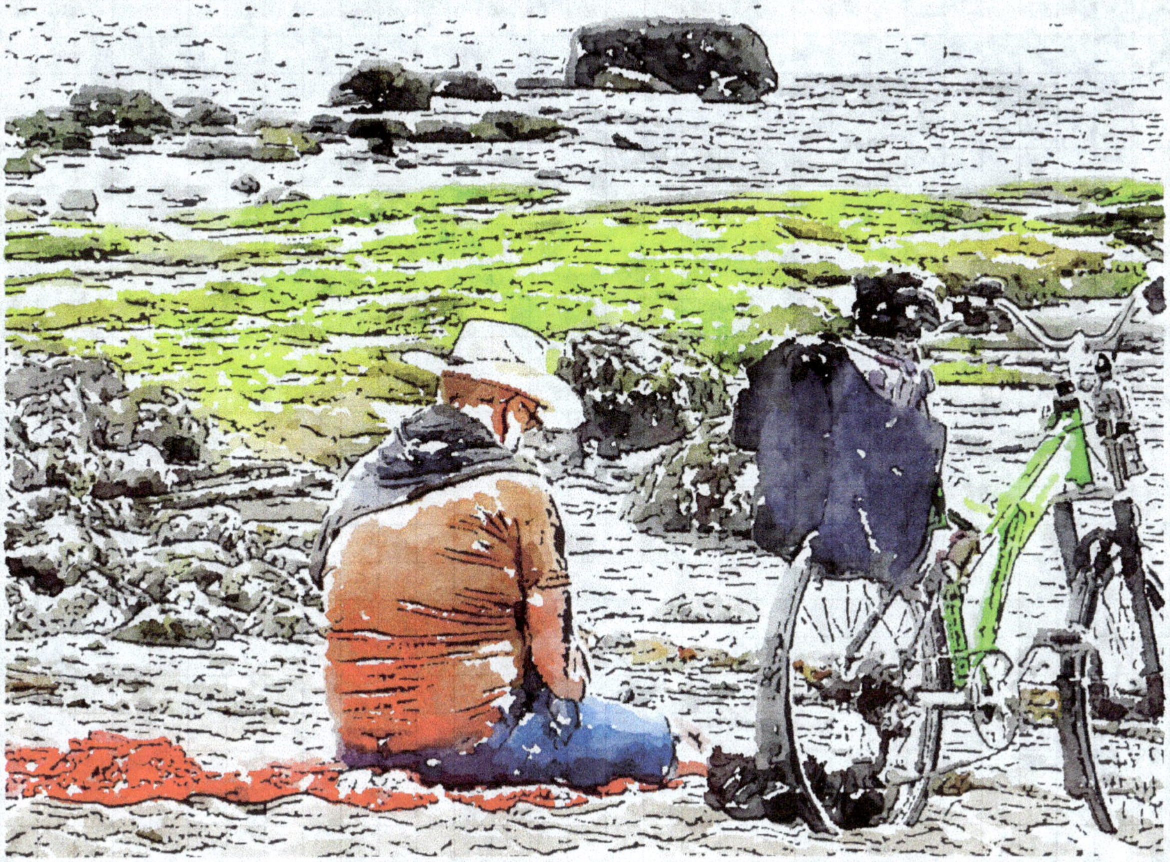

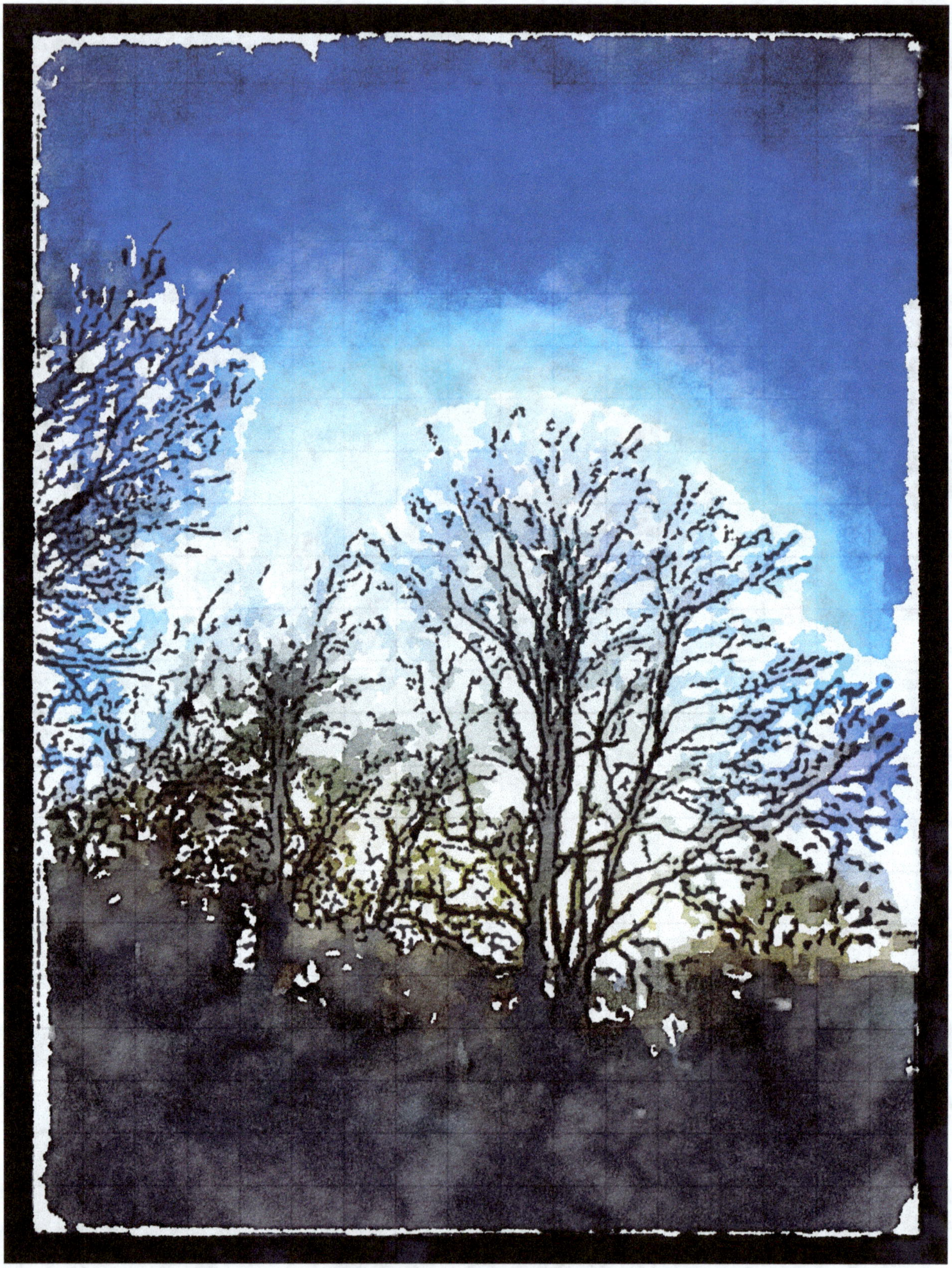

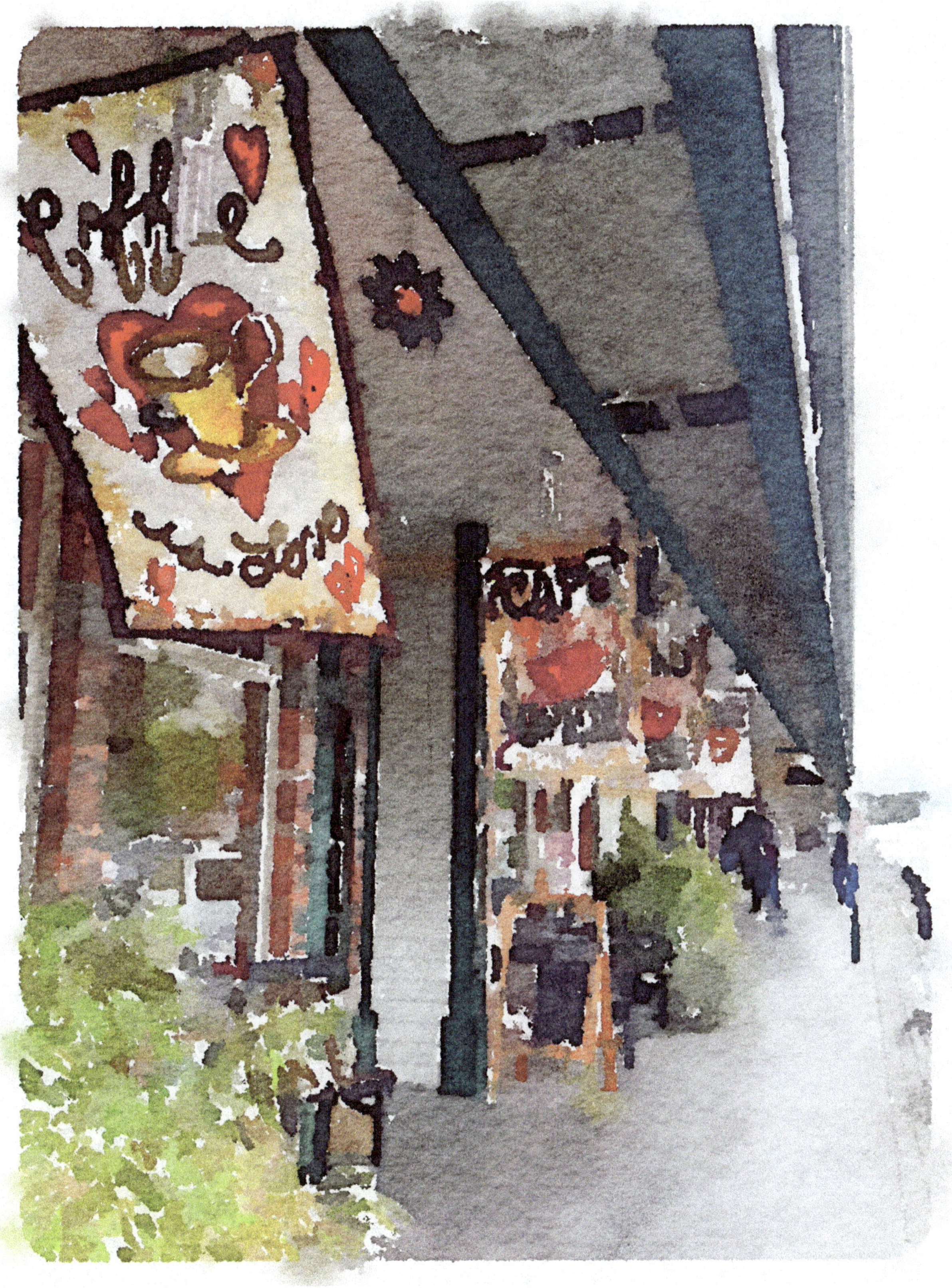

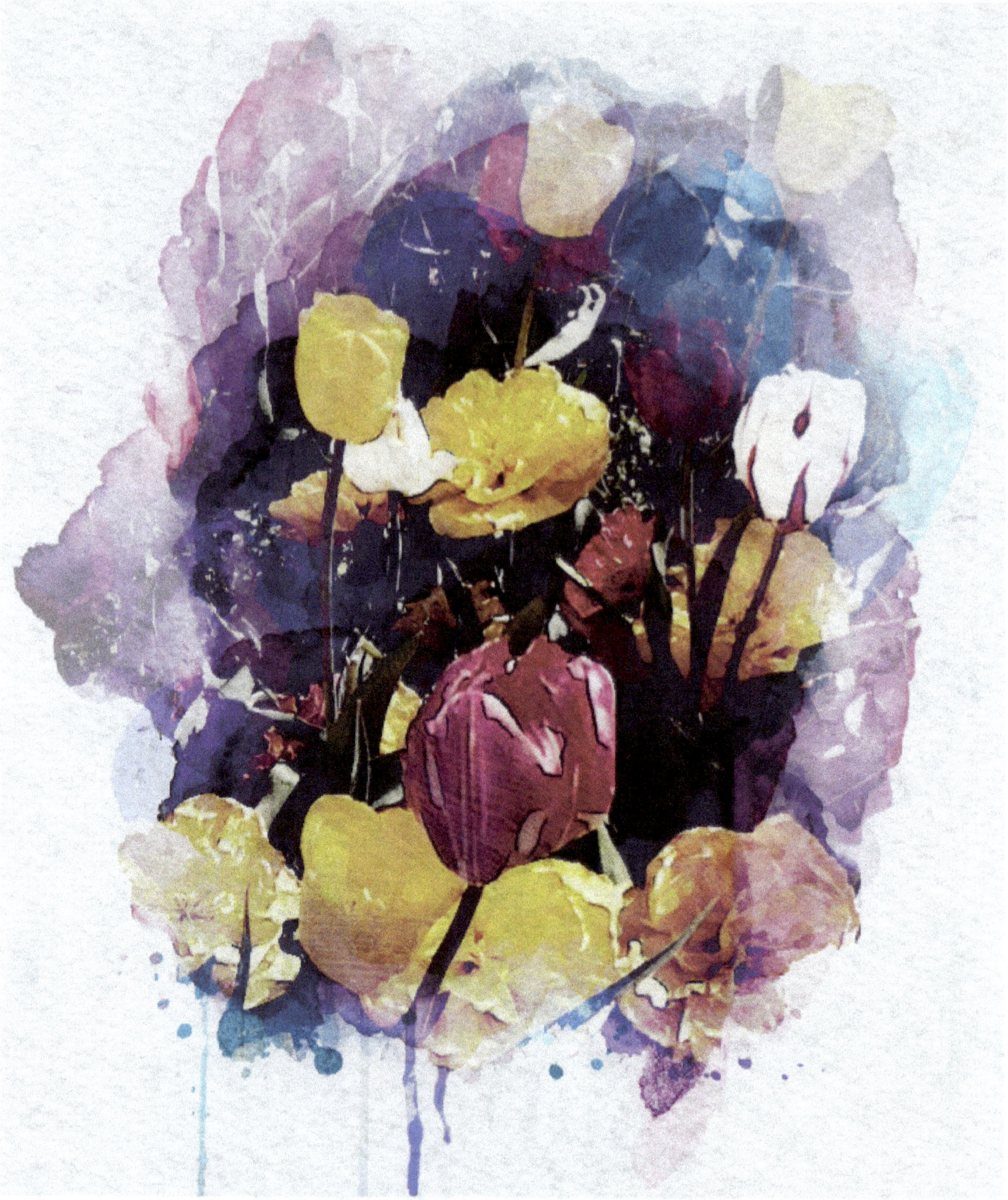

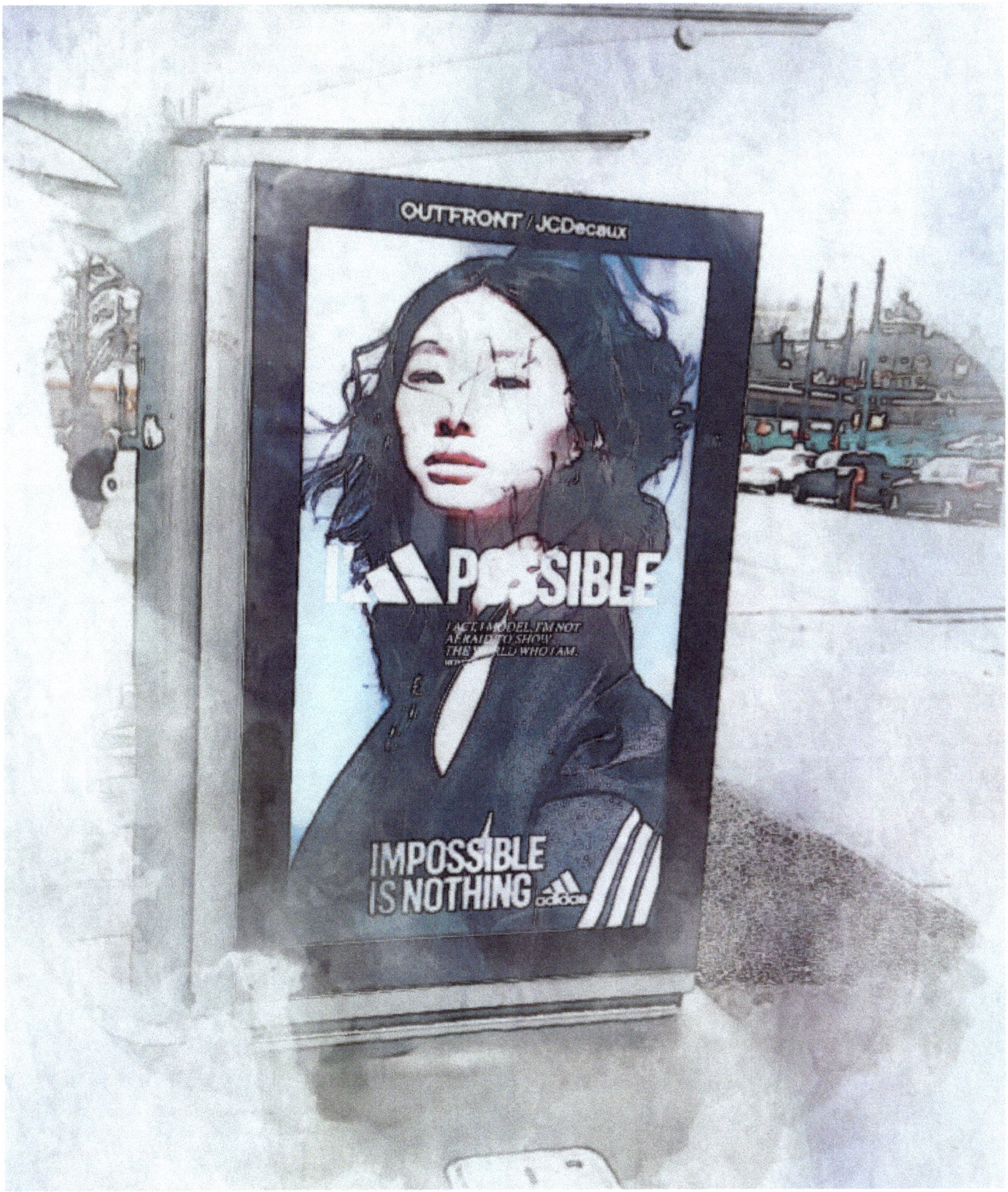
OUTFRONT / JCDecaux
IMPOSSIBLE
IS NOTHING
adidas

www.ingramcontent.com/pod-product-compliance
Lightning Source LLC
Chambersburg PA
CBHW060431220526
45465CB00008B/3093
* 9 7 9 8 8 2 6 3 8 7 9 6 2 *